URTE D

DUKE UNIVERSITY PRESS · SOCIOLOGICAL SERIES
☆ ☆ ☆
Howard E. Jensen and Charles A. Ellwood
Consulting Editors

RELIGION *in the* STRUGGLE *for* POWER

RELIGION

in the

STRUGGLE *for* POWER

A Study in the Sociology of Religion

BY

J. MILTON YINGER

1946
DUKE UNIVERSITY PRESS
DURHAM, NORTH CAROLINA

Carl A. Rudisill Library
LENOIR RHYNE COLLEGE

Copyright, 1946, by the Duke University Press

261
Y i 5r

34067
Sept '56

PRINTED IN THE UNITED STATES OF AMERICA,
BY THE SEEMAN PRINTERY, INC., DURHAM, N. C.

To

E. B. Y.

EDITORIAL NOTE

THIS VOLUME represents an attempt to study religion empirically as a factor in interhuman behavior. It makes no pretense at a comprehensive and definitive treatment of religious phenomena as such. As a treatise in the sociology of religion, it is concerned solely with religion as it emerges in the processes of human interaction and as it is related to other phases of man's collective life. It attempts to analyze the sociological significance of certain institutions and movements, past and present, which are universally regarded as religious. It is concerned with the definition of religion only in so far as it is necessary to identify these phenomena within the societal context, and it claims validity for its generalizations only within that context. In this sense, religion is defined as the totality of man's attempts "to bring the relative, the temporary, the disappointing, the painful things in life into relation with what is conceived to be permanent, absolute, and cosmically optimistic."

The study is, therefore, not concerned with the essence of the religious experience nor with the nature of the religious object. The wider connotations of religion are neither denied nor obscured, but these problems of ultimate origins and basic meanings are left to other specialties. The author does not, as is so often the fashion in this field, cavalierly dismiss such problems as "meaningless." The metaphysical aspects of religion constitute the legitimate fields of philosophy and theology; only its empirical aspects are the proper subject matter for science.

Not the "essence" of religion, then, but the sociological significance of its continuance in terms of the influence it exercises over interhuman behavior and its effectiveness in accomplishing its own stated ends in conflict with other interests, constitutes the central problem of this book.

The attempts of churchmen to bring the powerful nonreligious forces in human society under the influence and control of the Christian ethic have involved the church in a perpetual dilemma. Shall she hold uncompromisingly to her ethical ideal at the price of alienating a majority of her potential constituents motivated by powerful interests in conflict with religious teachings, and thus lose the mass support essential to the realization of her ideal in history? Or shall she so modify her demands in order to broaden the basis of her influence that a large part of that ideal is surrendered? Following the typology of Ernst Troeltsch, the author designates the former tendency as the "sect type," and the latter tendency as the "church type" of reaction. By a factual analysis of religious groups in this "struggle for power" during late medieval and modern times, he discloses the interplay of both types of reaction in the historical development of the churches, notes some of the secular factors that influence the choice of strategy, and demonstrates that the effectiveness of religion in tempering the brutalities of social conflict and in influencing the course of social development is a function of the success of ecclesiastical statesmanship in maintaining a balance between these two types of reaction within the church as a social institution. As Dr. Yinger expresses it, "It seems apparent, in fact, that religion maximizes its power as an agent in social change when the church and sect tendencies are combined by some kind of organizational principle."

The significance of the study, however, is not limited to the field of the sociology of religion, inasmuch as the same types of response are disclosed by nonreligious groups engaged in the struggle for power. As Gunnar Myrdal's recent monumental study, *An American Dilemma,* clearly demonstrates, similar intragroup tensions have been developed within, and a similar strategy has been employed by, the American Negro minority in its organized efforts to secure greater opportunities and improve social status within the framework of our contemporary culture. The struggle for power as represented by feminism, the labor movement, racial and cultural revivals, and other subordinate or minority groups constitutes complexes of social phenomena the future study of which could well profit by the further application of the methods of sociological analysis, to the development of which Dr. Yinger has here made a significant contribution.

Howard E. Jensen

Durham, N. C.
October 27, 1945

PREFACE

SOCIAL SCIENCE is having a difficult time steering the narrow course between the Scylla of uncontrolled theorizing and the Charybdis of raw empiricism. It had no sooner discovered the dangers of the former than it turned sharply toward the equally dangerous rocks of the latter. The significance of Kant's remark, "Percept without concept is blind, concept without percept is empty," is too often missed. Some sociologists have recognized its importance, but have fallen into still another error: in their attempts to avoid methodological subjectivism—the reliance on experience that is available only to the individual—they have disclaimed the validity of subjective data, which is an entirely different matter. They have thus ruled out of the court of science some of the most crucial aspects of human behavior. In this study we shall try to avoid those errors. We shall not refrain from theorizing—far from that, there is a definite attempt here to develop a conceptual scheme that will contribute to the interpretation of our data—but we seek to keep our theory flexible and thoroughly in touch with all available facts. Science is a stairstep process: The researcher stands upon facts, but he must have an hypothesis to lift him to the next level of observation; at the new level "facts" which were not visible before come to light, and they should enable one to formulate a more precise hypothesis, which again will enable one to collect more relevant data. Only if the scientific problem is very small will one or two steps suffice. The problems of the sociology of religion are far from small, and the steps which this volume takes will leave us far from the top. The formulations of the study are flexible, for the data are incomplete. Because the scientific investigation of the phenomena in which we are interested is not far advanced, it is impossible at this point to formulate the concepts and outline the tendencies in precise quantitative terms. We shall not try to obscure the tentative nature of the conclusions by relying heavily on quantification at a stage in which quantification is likely to be inaccurate, incomplete, and therefore misleading. Despite these limitations, however, it is the hope of the writer that the study will sketch the paths of future research and contribute to the scientific understanding of the important phenomena with which it deals.

The scientific questions involved in the sociology of religion are very numerous. No one with any knowledge of the behavior of religious groups will deny that their influence is intricately tied up with the whole problem of the social order and secular power. Beyond that is the question whether or not there is an intrinsic religious power at work in human interaction which cannot be reduced to purely secular considerations. If so, what is its source? How does it operate? What are its effects? How does it relate itself to the obviously secular aspects of "religious" groups? These are among the questions that are raised, either directly or inferentially, in this study.

There are obvious scientific dangers in searching for uniformities of behavior over so wide a field. Historians, particularly, are likely to criticize the scope of a work which brings together for study the data from such widely separated problems. This criticism can be tested only against the validity of the hypotheses that come from the use of these data.

It is a pleasure to acknowledge my indebtedness to the many persons who have contributed to the study. Professor Howard Becker has followed it closely over a period of several years and has made many valuable suggestions and criticisms. Professor Laurence Sears, Professor Guy Sarvis, Professor Hans Gerth, and Mr. Russell Bayliff have read all or parts of the manuscript and given me the benefit of their criticisms. They are in no way responsible, of course, for the errors that remain or for the interpretations. I wish to thank Mrs. Paul Yinger, who gave me valuable stenographic assistance, and Professor Eugene McFarland, who drew the chart found on page 23. My wife has been a constant source of encouragement and help.

J. M. Y.

Delaware, Ohio
September 25, 1945

ACKNOWLEDGMENTS

The author wishes to express his indebtedness to the following publishers and authors for permission to quote from materials on which they hold the copyright:

Ray H. Abrams: *Preachers Present Arms.*

Allen and Unwin: *The Elementary Forms of the Religious Life,* by Emile Durkheim; *The Jews and Modern Capitalism* and *The Quintessence of Capitalism,* by Werner Sombart; and *The Protestant Ethic and the Spirit of Capitalism,* by Max Weber.

America.

Annals of the American Academy of Political and Social Science.

D. Appleton-Century Company: *A History of the Warfare of Science with Theology in Christendom,* by A. D. White.

Association Press: *What Church People Think about Social and Economic Issues,* by N. L. Trott and R. W. Sanderson; and *Our Changing Churches: A Study of Church Leadership,* by Joseph Van Vleck, Jr.

Catholic World.

University of Chicago Press: *American Journal of Sociology* and *Journal of Political Economy.*

Christian Century.

Christianity and Crisis.

John Day Company: *Reason, Social Myths, and Democracy,* by Sidney Hook.

Farrar and Rinehart: *Social Actions,* by Florian Znaniecki.

The Federal Council of Churches of Christ in America: *Federal Council Bulletin,* and *Information Service,* and *A Message from the National Study Conference on the Churches and a Just and Durable Peace.*

Ginn and Company: *Social Causation,* by R. M. MacIver.

Victor Gollancz and David Petegorsky (author): *Left-Wing Democracy in the English Civil War.*

Victor Gollancz and John Lewis (editor): *Christianity and the Social Revolution.*

Greenberg, Publisher: *General Economic History,* by Max Weber.

Harcourt, Brace and Company: *Religion and the Rise of Capitalism,* by R. H. Tawney.

Harper & Brothers: *The Story of Religion in America* (revised edition), by W. W. Sweet.

D. C. Heath and Company: *Social Thought from Lore to Science,* by H. E. Barnes and Howard Becker.

Henry Holt and Company: *The Social Sources of Denominationalism,* by H. R. Niebuhr; and *The Age of the Reformation,* by Preserved Smith.

Little, Brown and Company: *The Religious Background of American Culture,* by T. C. Hall.

Liveright Publishing Corporation: *Primitive Religion,* by R. H. Lowie.

Longmans, Green and Company: *The Town Labourer, 1760-1832,* by J. L. Hammond and Barbara Hammond; and *The Wesleyan Movement in the Industrial Revolution,* by W. J. Warner.

McGraw-Hill Book Company: *Religion Today: A Challenging Enigma,* edited by A. L. Swift, Jr.

The Macmillan Company: *Christianizing the Social Order,* by Walter Rauschenbusch; *Aspects of the Rise of Economic Individualism,* by H. M. Robertson; *The Church and Labor,* edited by John A. Ryan and Joseph Husslein; *Christianity and Eco-*

nomics, by Lord Stamp; *New Frontiers of Religion,* by A. L. Swift, Jr.; and *The Social Teaching of the Christian Churches,* by Ernst Troeltsch.

Methodist Church, Commission on World Peace: *The Methodist Church in a World at War* (pamphlet).

New Republic.

W. W. Norton and Company: *American Faith,* by E. S. Bates; and *Peace or War: The American Struggle, 1636-1936,* by Merle Curti.

Oxford University Press (The Clarendon Press): *Social Ideas of Religious Leaders, 1660-1688,* by R. B. Schlatter.

Random House: *Intelligence in the Modern World,* by John Dewey.

Charles Scribner's Sons: *True Humanism,* by Jacques Maritain; *Protestant Thought before Kant,* by A. C. McGiffert; *Christianity and Power Politics,* and *Moral Man and Immoral Society,* and *Reflections on the End of an Era,* by Reinhold Niebuhr.

Sheed and Ward: *Catholicism, Protestantism, and Capitalism,* by Amintore Fanfani.

Student Christian Movement Press: *The Clue to History,* by John MacMurray.

Time.

The Westminster Press: *Institutes of the Christian Religion.*

John Wiley and Sons and Howard Becker (author): *Systematic Sociology.*

Yale University Press: *The Rise of the Social Gospel in American Protestantism, 1865-1915,* by C. H. Hopkins.

CONTENTS

RELIGION
in the
STRUGGLE *for* POWER

CHAPTER I

INTRODUCTION

THERE is no more important chapter in the history of mankind than the story of man's religions. There may be sharp disagreement with respect to the nature of religious influence and even a great deal of debate over what religion actually is; but few will question the statement that the forces of religion have been of great importance in the relations of men. Many students, aware of the significance of religion in practically all times and places, have attempted to discover its essential characteristics and its sources. We no longer think of religion as a unitary phenomenon, to be sure: the "*varieties* of religious experience" have been given too much attention. Yet the search for a meaningful explanation of the source of religion *in general* has absorbed the energies of many scholars. Such a search assumes, of course, that underlying the variety of expressions there is a basic similarity that can be accounted for.

The problems to be raised in the present study do not require that we join in this attempt to discover the "essence" of religion, the basic factor or factors without which its origin and development cannot be understood. We can take religion as a factor "given" to experience, and need inquire only into its connections with the phenomena we are studying. Sociology's general interest in religion concerns its relation with interhuman behavior patterns. It is far from a complete appraisal of the meaning of religion. The "sociology of religion" seeks to discover how much of the origin and development of religion can be attributed to the processes of sociation (that is, can be explained sociologically), and how religion in turn is involved as a factor in interhuman behavior.

Yet we cannot wholly avoid the problem of definition; we need at least a minimum designation. Because of the many varieties of religion, this task of definition is very difficult. Not only is there disagreement concerning what is *the* precisely religious element, but there are many different motives for the various definitions. Is it an expression of numen, an irreducible, a priori category of mind, as Otto holds? Or, similarly, can one define it, with Troeltsch, as a fundamental trait of man's original nature? Or should one accept Durkheim's explanation that religion is the expression of group solidarity and crowd mentality? Nietzsche has interpreted religion as the "slave in revolt" attempting to obtain some control over his master. Many theologians, on the other hand, define religion as the revelation to man of the reality and majesty of God. Arnold called it "morality touched by emotion."

Faced with these differences, and even contradictions, in the interpretation of the nature of religion, one sees how far students of religion are from agreement concerning the essential element in the phenomena with which they are dealing. To achieve even a minimum definition, one must somehow isolate, from the many complex patterns of behavior in which religion may be found, the *essentially* religious element, that general quality which is characteristic of all faiths despite their apparent differences. The problem of denotation (which, however, is not interpretation) is not difficult in the first steps. As Lowie says, working back from a particular branch of Christianity, we are able to recognize some kinship between our faith and other monotheistic creeds. But what is to be said when we come to Buddhism, with its theoretical atheism? Is this still "religion"? William James said yes, for it evokes a response "in fact indistinguishable from, and in many respects identical with, the best Christian appeal and response." Although this statement may be false, the test is valid: "... *if* Buddhism satisfies that part of the Buddhist's nature which corresponds to the devout Christian's longing for acceptance by the deity, then it is a veritable religion. . . . What we should determine is wherein such satisfaction essentially lies."[1]

Even this test, however, would not satisfy everybody as being the necessary or only test for discovering what is, what is not, religion; moreover, the test itself is very difficult to apply. In face of such problems, it may seem fruitless to write an essay on a phenomenon which cannot be precisely defined. Yet that is not the case. Electricity cannot be defined in terms acceptable to all, or even many, physicists; but they can study it and analyze its interactions. Until definition comes, electricity is taken as a "given." No explanation concerning it is complete, to be sure, but it can be scientifically useful.

For our purposes, any definition we need give of religion can be very general. We are concerned with the specific problem of analyzing the sociological significance of certain past and present institutions and movements. That they are universally regarded to be religious institutions and movements is sufficient warrant to label this essay a study in the sociology of religion. There is no need to prove by rigorous definition that the phenomena with which we are dealing are "really" religious, for generalizations *within the societal context* can be valid whatever the data are labeled. Rigorous definition and classification are necessary only when we seek to extend the generalizations to other (presumably comparable) data. This statement may be taken as an effort to avoid a scientific task. That is precisely what it is. We need not wait for a universally accepted definition of religion before undertaking the investigation of religious phenomena. Precise definition, after all, is not the first step in research. There is no attempt here to forge all the links in the chain of causation. Driven back upon the concept of religion, we take it as a given, offering only this brief and very general definition: Religion is the attempt to bring the relative, the temporary, the disappointing, the painful things in life into relation with what is conceived to be permanent, absolute, and cosmically optimistic.[2]

Thus we leave to more capable hands the search for the origin and basic meaning of religion, and therefore its classification and definition.[3]

The Question of the Significance of Religion

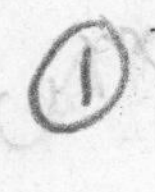

There are two introductory questions, however, that we must discuss briefly. The first concerns the significance of religion for the modern world. Is it gradually disappearing? Is religion—the "explanation of the unknown," as some define it—retreating before the advance of science? Although this question has no logical connection with our study, it is very important for the significance of the conclusions that are drawn, for if religion is rapidly being relegated to the past, it is not likely to be a subject of crucial contemporary interest. Few would deny that an attempt to give a conclusive statement regarding the future of religion would be foolhardy indeed; there are too many different opinions, too much controversial evidence, for a definitive statement. One consideration, however, may throw some light on the problem. Nothing stands out more clearly in the study of religious phenomena than the extreme variability and adaptability of religion on the one hand, accompanied, on the other, by a basic similarity which underlies the various expressions. Witnessing this fact, we can certainly agree with John Dewey that "there is a difference between religion, *a* religion, and the religious. . ."[4] This is a crucial distinction, for if, in the attempt to discover the significance of religion for the modern world and for the future, one does not distinguish between traditional religion and what may be called "intrinsic" religion, he will fall into one of two opposite errors. Either he will contend that the change or collapse of some traditional expression of religion is the end of religion; or, fearing that that would be the case, he will oppose to any necessary extreme all modifications of doctrine or adjustments to new factors in society. Both of these errors underlie the many struggles between men of science and men of religion (see below). They rest on a basic difficulty of language: Should a word be dropped when its referent undergoes important changes? If the word continues in use, the changes are not sufficiently recognized; if a different term is adopted, the continuity is disregarded. There is clearly only one solution to this problem: classify further; refer not only to genus but to species. To the question, Will religion be significant in the future development of mankind? we can answer only equivocally, yes-and-no. But with regard to the significance of a particular traditional element of religion, we can trace out lines of evolution, measure its harmony or lack of harmony with other important systems of thought and centers of power in society, and thus approach an unequivocal answer.

A distinction between traditional and intrinsic religion does not, of course, solve any problems of itself: it simply raises the investigation to a more meaningful level by eliminating terminological disputes. The crucial question, What is traditional, what intrinsic? remains. There are few today to claim that the medieval cosmology was an essential part of Christian doctrine; but executions and excommunications and decades of bitter controversy are evidence that it once was considered vital. Most Americans accept, if they do not understand, the theory of evolution; but thirty years ago a William Jennings Bryan could see in it an attack on all true religion. There are many today who contend that supernaturalism is not an intrinsic part of religion, but a traditional survival, reminiscent of the mode of thought that prevailed when our religions took their rise.[5] Most people, however, hold this to be rank heresy and an attack upon the very heart of religion. Which view is correct, we need not attempt to say here; we only suggest that a recognition of the complexity of the phenomenon we call religion, particularly by an effort to discover what is traditional and what is intrinsic, will help us to avoid many errors. Many of the writers to whom we have referred have been seeking precisely to discover that which is fundamental to religion. Their main method of approach, whether they have dealt with the problem from a theological, a psychological, or a sociological point of view, has been to try to discover the origins of religion. This is an invaluable study, provided only that they recognize that a human phenomenon can develop far beyond its origins. In other words, the psychosociological meaning of its *continuance* (or its continuing origination, to use a clumsy phrase) must also be explained before one can predict the future of religion. Those who have gone most deeply into this problem—although they differ widely in their judgments concerning what is merely traditional—are in rather general agreement that religion will continue to be a powerful force during the foreseeable future.[6] There would be a great many to agree with Durkheim's statement that "there is something eternal in religion which is destined to survive all the particular symbols in which religious thought has successively enveloped itself."[7]

We are not unaware that there is also strong opposition to this statement. Among the early "naturalists," illustrated best perhaps by Spencer, there was the implication that "religion" (insufficiently classified) was a primitive trait, and therefore a survival, destined to pass slowly out of the picture. This point of view was due, at least partly, to the immersion in primitive data and the accurate observation that *primitive* religion was gradually disappearing. There seems to be less tendency today to equate any particular manifestations of religion with "the religious."

There is a more vehement protest against the statement that intrinsic religion is likely to have a long life. This comes from Marxian socialism. In a strange paradox of history, however, the Marxians are partly proving, in the very act of denial, the continuing importance of religion. It is a matter of frequent observation that they have not only borrowed many of their central doctrines from Christianity and Judaism, but also share many aspects of the general religious point of view. Von Hugel was perhaps the first to note the great similarity between the apocalyptic and the Marxist interpretation of the movement of history, their similar faith in a "citadel of hope built on the edge of despair." This is not a chance relationship, for there is a direct historical connection between the Marxist pattern of thought and Christianity. John MacMurray writes:

Hegel maintained that he had embodied in his philosophy the full content of Christian doctrine. After his death the Hegelian school divided on the question whether their philosophical position was compatible with theism. The left wing of the school decided, in my opinion rightly, that it was not. Consequently they rejected the belief in God, and became materialists. They were thus committed to the task of disentangling the essential content of Christianity from its religious form. In particular, it led Feuerbach to call his chief philosophical work *The Essence of Christianity*. Its aim was to restate the content of Christianity in purely humanistic terms. This work was a turning-point in the development of Karl Marx, who went so far as to say that no one could reach the true Communist position without being baptised in the Fire-brook. Against Feuerbach, Marx maintained that he had failed to carry the process to completion. His philosophy still remained tainted with sentimental idealism and imperfectly realistic because it was not rooted in the recognition of labour—of actual, physical work—as the determining factor in human experience. It was left to Marx to complete the process of restating the sentimental religious idealism of Christianity in the form of a practical materialistic humanism.[8]

Other writers not only have emphasized the historical connection between Marxism and Christianity, but have declared that Marxism has genuine religious elements. Reinhold Niebuhr observes: "In some of its aspects the Marxian mythology of history is a profoundly religious one. For it, life is not a simple harmony but a chaos which has the possibilities of harmony within it."[9] Jacques Maritain puts the matter even more strongly:

. . . considered in its essence and its principles, communism as it exists,—above all the communism of the Soviet republics,—is a complete system of doctrine and life which claims to reveal to man the meaning of his existence, to answer all the fundamental questions which are set by life, and which manifests an unequalled power of totalitarian inclusiveness. It is a religion, and one of the most imperious quality: certain that it is called to replace all other religions; a religion of atheism, for which dialectic materialism supplies the dogma, and of which communism as a rule of life is the social and ethical expression.[10]

One could quote at length from writers of many different points of view, to show how widely this idea is held.[11] It is obvious that no definitive statement could be made on the subject without an equally definitive description of what religion is. Since we have largely avoided this difficult problem, we can say only that the frequently stated opinion that Marxism has a strong religious element is supporting evidence, both of the necessity for distinguishing the traditional from the intrinsic in religion, and of the continuing importance of religion.

Much of the controversy regarding the significance of religion is concerned with its relation to science. That Christianity is becoming more and more acclimated to a world of science is evidence of its flexibility. Whether one thinks that in making this adjustment Christianity is forced to surrender its essential quality depends again on his conception of the essence of religion. If the essence is held to be a particular body of belief and dogma, then Christianity and science are often in direct contradiction; and one who holds such a view must inevitably be opposed either to science or to religion. If, on the other hand, the essence of religion is held to be the contribution which it attempts to make to man's adjustment to life (particularly to the frustrating experiences, to the pessimism, as Niebuhr says, that arises from the failure to control most of the "imperialistic" impulses), then there need be no conflict between science and religion. One need not agree with the particular opinions of the philosopher-scientists, nor even with their aims, to recognize the importance of their attempts to bring about a *rapprochement* between science and religion. Their work implicitly declares: That part of religion which conflicts with science is traditional, not intrinsic. They are part of a movement which was given a good deal of impetus by the well-known book of Andrew Dickson White, *A History of the Warfare of Science with Theology in Christendom,* where the thesis was vigorously defended that the struggle was not between science and religion but between science and dogmatic theology. White wrote:

In all modern history, interference with science in the supposed interest of religion, no matter how conscientious such interference may have been, has resulted in the direst evils both to religion and to science, and invariably; and, on the other hand, all untrammelled scientific investigation, no matter how dangerous to religion some of its stages may have seemed for the time to be, has invariably resulted in the highest good both of religion and of science.[12]

While this last statement can hardly be said to have been validated, it is expressive of a widely held belief. If the history of religion up until now is not a wholly inadequate guide, we are likely to see the reconciliation of science and religion carried to great lengths, at least in those areas of society where science itself has become crucial. Those who feel that even such a "reformed" religion can only serve to buttress a given power arrangement and/or make inflexible a new traditionalism will see nothing to be gained by the shift. Those who feel, however, that a religion adjusted to the modern world can contribute to the quality of man's response to that world will both welcome and sponsor the reconciliation.

The Economic Interpretation of History

There is another introductory problem to which we must refer before turning to our specific question. That concerns the much debated topic of the "economic interpretation of history." While repeated references to this subject appear throughout this volume, and our position is implicit in the whole treatment, a few direct words in connection with this important problem may forestall misunderstanding. No student of sociology, recognizing the enormous influence of institutions, folkways, and beliefs on behavior, can hold to a narrow economic interpretation of history. Marx certainly did not. The only question concerns the point at which ideas and beliefs enter into the field of interaction: Are they prime movers? Can they arise independently of material conditions and help to create new arrangements; or do they only reinforce, rationalize, and preserve the old? With reference to religion, our question is: Is there a source of religious ideas and energy which cannot be traced back eventually to material conditions, or, slightly more generally, to the struggle for power? Put in this way, it is clearly part of the question of the origin of religion; and no precise answer is possible. Troeltsch declares that "all impartial religious research reveals the fact that, to some extent at least, religious thought is independent; it has its own inner dialectic and its own power of development. . . ."[13] But Engels wrote, echoing Goethe, "Im Anfang war die Tat." Marx, in an oft-quoted passage, elaborated this statement:

> In the social production which men carry on they enter into definite relations that are indispensable and independent of their will; these relations of production correspond to a definite stage of development of their material powers of production. The sum total of these relations of production constitutes the economic structure of society—the real foundation, on which rise legal and political superstructures and to which correspond definite forms of social consciousness. The mode of production in material life determines the general character of the social, political and spiritual processes of life. It is not the consciousness of men that determines their existence, but, on the contrary, their social existence determines their consciousness.[14]

Basic changes in the relations of production do not come as the result of the energy of a new idea, which has somehow arisen independently of the existing structure; but rather, according to Marx, because there has been a shift in the forces of production. This shift makes the existing power arrangement and the superstructure built upon the old forces inappropriate, because it is not equipped to take advantage of the new forces of production. The old elite, which enjoys an advantaged position, will not see their lack of fitness for the new situation, not simply—or not even largely—because they are "selfish," but also because they identify the social order of which they are the apex with the very principle of social order and hence regard any challenge to it as an attack upon eternal verities. The masses of people, being equally bound by tradition and habit, will support the claim of the elite until their incompetence and increasing lack of justice (forced upon them by their attempts to solidify their power position) finally crystallize class divisions. Therein is the revolutionary situation which must lead to the overthrow of the ruling class and the appearance of an elite better able to take advantage of the new productive forces with less injustice. In all of this process, ideas play an important role, according to Marx. They are rooted in the situation, but they react upon the situation. In *The Eighteenth Brumaire of Louis Napoleon* he wrote: "Men make their own history, but they do not do so at will in conditions of their own choosing, but under given conditions, left to them by tradition. The tradition of the dead generations weighs on the brains of the living like a nightmare. . . ." Thus ideas are anchored in history. This is not in such sharp contrast with the statement of Troeltsch, quoted above, as might at first be supposed. Thought has historical derivations, but it also organizes, speeds, or retards the movement of history; and in that sense can be said to have "its own power of development." There is a good deal of insight in Maritain's remark concerning Marx: ". . . just as one can speak of a first 'spiritual' impulse in his thought (i.e., indignation at man's condition oppressed by the things born of his own work and himself degraded to the level of a *thing*) so one may say that, despite certain formulas, he always believed in a reciprocal action between economic and other factors. . . ."[15]

We are not so much interested here, however, in "what Marx really meant," as in gaining a perspective on the economic interpretation in its relation to our problem. It does not yet seem possible to judge whether or not Marx has closed the door too tight in granting no *prime* initiating power to thought. The deeper we go into the subject, however, the more it seems apparent that the search for some ultimate first cause is not a scientific quest in any event, for it does not increase our ability to predict. How far up the stream of causation one needs to traverse depends upon the scientific task he has outlined, but the search for prime movers is scarcely ever involved in science. It may often prove necessary in some scientific problem to accept an idea-system as an autonomous causal system, not because in some ultimate sense it is the starting point of a series of events, but because one is interested precisely in predicting events when that idea-system is a given. This point is illustrated by a quotation from Znaniecki (which was made, however, in another connection):

> . . . if we treat the multiform empirical variety of data in any field as having evolved gradually from some original uniformity, we must also treat this evolution as progressing by stages, every stage being characterized by the appearance of something essentially *new* and *not reducible* to what was before.
>
> In this progressive differentiation a certain similarity naturally remains and binds the earlier with the later stages. But in a long and complex evolutionary process the thread of similarity between the earliest stage and later stages may become so slender as no longer to justify scientifically any conclusions drawn from the nature of the former about the nature of the latter. How much similarity there must be between the original stage and the final stages to make the study of their genetic connection scientifically useful, how far back we ought to go in any given field to trace the origin of a present variety of empirical data, it is for the student of these data to decide; for only he can tell, from what he knows by direct study about the character of present reality, at what stage in the past reality of this kind began to exist.[16]

We strongly suspect that historical materialism is often guilty of the reductionism which is of no scientific value.[17] For the requirements of any particular investigation, it may be necessary to take an idea-system as a given, without making any attempt to trace its own derivations. Even if one were to start from the assumption that ideas eventually reach back to material conditions—and this can be scarcely more than an assumption—he must also understand that *within any manageable field of interaction* ideas are often "independent" causal factors: the search for their ultimate "genetic connections" is not scientifically useful. That is not to deny that there is a great deal of truth in "the economic interpretation of history" (nor to accept its position in an extreme form), but simply to point out its irrelevance for certain scientific problems. After one has said that material considerations are extremely important in most situations and for most problems, he has said as much as science can say; for when materialism becomes a search for the uncaused cause, science withdraws and speculation and polemics take over.

Having thus located our problem in a general scientific field, we turn to our specific investigation—a study of typical responses of religious groups to changes in their environment. We start from the assumption that there is a religious "interest"—to use Weber's term—which is often in conflict with other interests.[18] We are attempting to study part of the dynamic process which results from this conflict. There will be two questions involved throughout this volume: What positions do churchmen and religious groups take on the subjects we are studying—do they tend to be conservative or liberal? Secondly, what effect does this position have on the actual course of events? With regard to this latter question, one must distinguish (a) an ability to retard the appearance of a new situation, and (b) an ability to cause or speed up the appearance of a new situation. Failure to distinguish between these questions can lead to a great deal of confusion.

In the last analysis this is a study in power. It raises the question: How much influence does religion exercise over the behavior of men? How much, in the competition with other powers, is it able to control behavior *in accordance with its own standards?* Clearly a great deal that appears to be religious power, because it is carried on under the auspices of nominally religious persons, groups, or institutions, may be some other power which is employing religious symbols or garb. Our judgment concerning the effectiveness of religion must be based squarely on this criterion: How well does it succeed in accomplishing *its own stated ends?* We are primarily interested, moreover, in the moral judgments of religion; we raise the question, that is, of the power of religion to control the relations of men to each other according to its precepts.

Chapter II

A TYPOLOGY OF RELIGIOUS GROUPS

Our task in this chapter is to develop a theory of religious group behavior that will serve as a useful conceptual scheme for the interpretation of the action patterns of religious bodies. The theoretical formulations in this chapter are not intended, however, to be a complete sociology of religion, for the data used and the problems raised set definite limits to the investigation. There are two general limitations to the applicability of the concepts developed here: they are developed only with relation to Christian organizations, and therefore may have only very limited usefulness with regard to other religions, although the researches of Max Weber would seem to show a relative similarity in the purely secular meanings of the various religions.[1] Secondly, they are concerned with religious groups only as human institutions, and with their relations to secular activities, particularly economic. More specific limitations of time and place will be made during the application of the concepts to concrete instances.

The first step in our development of a theory of religious group behavior will be the construction of analytic types of religious groups. It is not necessary here to undertake an analysis of the ideal or constructed type as a methodological tool,[2] more than to say that it is an attempt to devise a unit of measure by means of which the data in a given field can be compared. If a given phenomenon compares rather closely with the pattern of the constructed type, one is enabled to trace out the "expected" course of action, and thus predict its behavior. In terms of our problem: having constructed typical action patterns of religious groups—by means of careful analysis of the histories of various groups, focused by some hypothesis—one can gain some predictive power with regard to other organizations which correspond somewhat closely to one of the types; or, in terms of historical data, one can interpret their behavior meaningfully.

While the description of the typology used here comes in the early part of the paper, it is obvious that for any kind of validity, the types must have grown out of a careful study of historical data. They then, in turn, inform the study of comparable data. In later chapters the typology will be applied primarily to three problems; early Protestantism, in order to investigate the religious response to the emergence of the modern world; the economic ethics of contemporary American churchmen; and the relation of religious groups to war. The first problem is in part a matter of what Howard Becker has called "retrospective prediction,"[3] and in part simply an interpretive essay; the latter two questions involve elements of both interpretation and prediction.

We have noted in Chapter I that mankind has a manifest "interest" in religion, however that interest may be explained. For the purposes of the following discussion, there is no logical necessity for taking a position regarding the meaning of that interest. The interpretation of a Marx or a Nietzsche, an ethical formulation, or a purely transcendental explanation of the meaning of religion can each be made to harmonize, at least in part, with this essay. That is not to say that the "true" meaning of religion is an insignficant question, but rather that the answer to it is beyond the scope of this volume and in part, at least, beyond the scope of science. Since we are not interested in a total causal explanation of religious behavior, but in prediction on only one level, we can leave open other equally important and interesting questions.

We may start, then, with the assumption of a religious interest which in one of its aspects takes the form of a desire to mold one's own behavior, and that of others, after a pattern that is prescribed by religious doctrine. These rules of behavior often attempt to put restrictions on the more purely egocentric tendencies in human conduct—the world of "sin" or of "nature." The strength of these egocentric tendencies no one can deny. They force upon religious groups and religious individuals (and we share with Weber the assertion that interest in religious matters varies greatly from person to person) a sharp dilemma: If the religious group demands too much allegiance to the religious ideal, particularly in spheres which require sacrifices of things held dear in a particular society, it comes into conflict with secular powers and is either persecuted or neglected. On the other hand, of course, if it does not make demands on behavior, in terms of its norms, it is also without influence. The dilemma is to keep in a position of power without sacrificing the goals for which the power was originally desired.[4]

As one would expect, there are many different ways of attempting to resolve this dilemma. These attempts vary according to many factors: the strength of religious symbolism of the time; the quality and temperament of the leadership; the tradition of the group involved; and, above all, as we shall see, with the secular interests and the class position of the persons to whom the religious movement appeals or attempts to appeal.[5] In the following paragraphs we shall formulate certain ideal-type reactions to the religious dilemma. These will not correspond necessarily to any empirical reality, nor are they likely to be of great value for problems other than those involved here.[6] They are heuristic devices, and should be judged with reference to their ability to aid in the interpretation and prediction of religious group behavior.

The primary division is simply twofold, classifying the religious groups into what Troeltsch has called churches and sects. The church as a type is a religious body which recognizes the strength of the secular world, and rather than either deserting the attempt to influence it or losing its position by contradicting the secular powers directly, accepts the main elements in the existing balance of power and thus attempts to remain in a position where it can get a hearing. It is built therefore on compromise;[7] it is mobile and adaptive; it claims universality; "it dominates the world and is therefore dominated by the world" (Troeltsch). An individual is born into the church, which tends to become synonymous with society. The doctrine is conservative; the existing powers are supported in peace and war. A church tries to organize the forces of society on whatever level they are found and to control them for its own stated ends—which have been, for the most part, individual salvation.

The sect, on the other hand, stresses acceptance of literal obedience to the Synoptic Gospels; it tends to be radical, with a small, voluntary membership that lacks continuity; it is usually associated with the lower classes. The sect stresses individual perfection and asceticism; it is either hostile or indifferent to the state, and opposes the ecclesiastical order. It rejects compromise with the world of "nature" and the church's concept of "relative natural law" (which is discussed later). The sect is lay religion, free from worldly authority, able therefore on one hand to forget the world in asceticism, or on the other to fight it in radicalism. It "prefers isolation to compromise." Troeltsch thus lists its traits:

> . . . lay Christianity, personal achievement in ethics and in religion, the radical fellowship of love, religious equality and brotherly love, indifference toward the authority of the State and the ruling classes, dislike of technical law and of the oath, the separation of the religious life from the economic struggle by means of the ideal of poverty and frugality . . . , the directness of the personal religious relationship, criticism of official spiritual guides and theologians, the appeal to the New Testament and the Primitive Church.[8]

Thus "on the one hand, there is development and compromise, on the other literal obedience and radicalism."[9] It should be remembered, however, that church and sect flow one into the other. The sect grows out of certain aspects of the teachings of the church and, if it is to survive in the historical current, must grow again into a church.[10] Moreover, both types are an expression, as we shall see later, of the original Christian doctrine, which included in its first formulation the dilemma which necessitates a twofold reaction. From one point of view the history of the church can be read as a struggle between these two tendencies to deal with the dilemma. The church type usually dominates the historical current, but there is a continual resurgence of the sect type whenever and wherever the conditions are favorable.[11] Swift expresses well the conflict between, and yet the relatedness of, these two type reactions when he writes that the prophet, although he is soon forced from the church and though he challenges the social order of which the church is a vital part, is, at the same time, a "product of the best in the tradition and belief of the church that drives him out." The major prophets came out of an organized religion, but it is a mistake to emphasize the withdrawal and to forget the tradition from which they came. New religions and sects "are the products of, as well as the protest against institutionalized religion."[12]

While church and sect are the two chief sociological types that we shall use in this study, a further subdivision is necessary in order to achieve analytic precision.[13] This subdivision will indicate that in truth the types are heuristic devices, not concrete illustrations; and therefore empirical examples will seldom, if ever, correspond precisely to the pattern. With regard to the church-type, the chief distinction that needs to be made concerns the relative achievement of the quality of "universalism," which we have listed as a church characteristic. In this connection there are two modal types. On the one hand is a group which is relatively successful in achieving a unity of society, a universalism, under its direction. This type is best illustrated by the Catholic Church of the thirteenth century. It is fairly close to what Becker has called the ecclesia:

> The social structure known as the ecclesia is a predominantly conservative body, not in open conflict with the secular aspects of social life, and professedly universal in its aims. . . . The fully developed ecclesia attempts to amalgamate itself with the state and the dominant

classes, and strives to exercise control over every person in the population. Members are *born into* the ecclesia; they do not have to *join* it. It is therefore a social structure somewhat akin to the nation or the state, and is in no sense elective. . . . The ecclesia naturally attaches a high importance to the means of grace which it administers, to the system of doctrine which it has formulated, and to the official administration of sacraments and teaching by official clergy. . . . The ecclesia as an inclusive social structure is closely allied with national and economic interests; as a plurality pattern its very nature commits it to adjustment of its ethics to the ethics of the secular world; it must represent the morality of the respectable majority.[14]

The chief difference between our first modal type of church, which we shall call the universal church, and the ecclesia described above concerns the success with which the group we are typifying encloses the sect elements in a systematic and effective way. The church of the thirteenth century was relatively successful in finding a place (the monasteries) for the expression of the radical-individualizing tendencies of Christianity. This union between the two tendencies was in part only institutional, but in part also integral—as it demonstrated by the flexibility and influence of the church.

The other modal church type is less successful in achieving universality. It is still a church, in our meaning of the term, because it accepts the legitimacy of the prevailing societal structure. The failure to achieve universality is due to geographical and class boundaries, and the failure to incorporate sect elements. Lutheranism is perhaps closest to this modal type. The Church of England is somewhat nearer the universal type (still, however, on a national scale); and Methodism approaches nearer universalism by the inclusion of some sect tendencies. None of these, however, is anywhere near the medieval church, and each must be classified separately from it. Of modern churches, only early Calvinism can begin to rival the universality of Thomism.[15] In general this second modal type of church is thoroughly conventional and "respectable"; it has gone rather far along the road of compromise. This is partly due to the fact that in a society of religious divisions, in contrast with the unity of the Middle Ages, the sect elements in Christianity form their own institutions, instead of being incorporated into a universal church. There remains some sectarianism, however, in the most static of churches (for instance, the Greek Orthodox in Russia), which forces periodic "reforms," or breaks away from the main body.

A similar gradient can be worked out for our general sect-type religious group. On the farthest extreme is the purely personal, noninstitutionalized religious experience of a group of people tied together only by common religious emotions and needs. By the very nature of the case this arrangement is very unstable, for either the group disintegrates when the members die, or it has been molded into an institution with techniques for admitting new members and preserving their common interests. In its original form, this group is similar to what Becker has called the cult. If it is more highly organized and self-conscious, even in its early years, it is the modal type of what we have described above as the sect. In the second and third generations, however, both sect and cult undergo a transformation in which they gradually take on some of the characteristics of the church. They become more fully adjusted to the societal situation in which they find themselves; there is a tendency for their otherworldliness to be modified. The direction of this selective adaptation depends, in general, upon the original reason for the sect movement. If it has strong political undercurrents (as, for instance, Lutheranism), the sect will move back rapidly toward the religious type of the mother church when the political end is achieved. (This is assuming that no other factors are involved.) If, in fact, it represents—or is captured by—any emerging power group, it will move rapidly toward the church type. If, however, it represents a rather stable religious and social division, it will develop into what we shall call an established sect. A religious group of this type shares many of the traits of a church of the "lowest power." It is more accurately classed as a sect, however, because it is still seen as a group apart. It remains of rather limited membership generally and, most important, tends to dominate a large part of the life of its members.[16] In this it is approached only by the universal church, of which there is no contemporary representative (although the modern Catholic Church, as we shall show, is nearer to it than any other). A fairly accurate way, in fact, to discover whether or not a religious body is a sect, as we are using that term, is to find if membership in the group is put at the top of a list of characteristics of the communicants. In most cases one would not say: "Oh, yes, I know him; he is a Presbyterian." But it would be far from unusual for a noncommunicant to say: "Oh, yes, I know him; he is a Quaker." Quakerism is near the modal type of the established sect.

The following chart gives a schematic picture of our typology.

A TYPOLOGY OF RELIGIOUS GROUPS

THE THEORETICAL POINT OF GREATEST POWER IN ACHIEVING THE PURELY RELIGIOUS ENDS

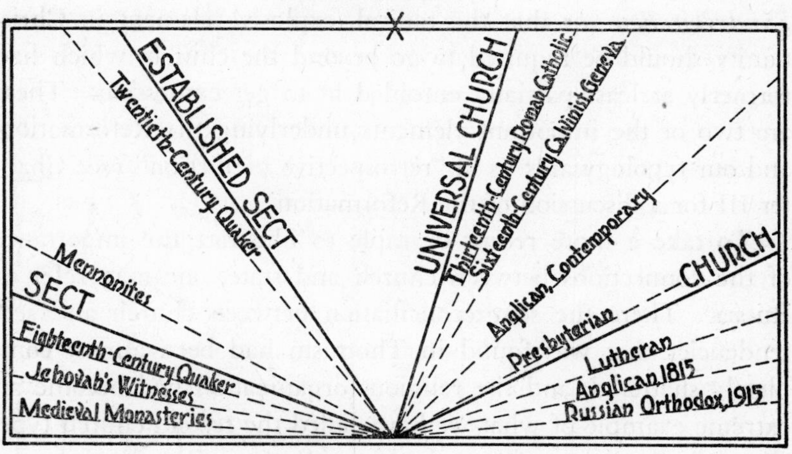

THEORETICALLY COMPLETE WITHDRAWAL FROM THE WORLD — THEORETICALLY COMPLETE ACCEPTANCE OF THE WORLD

Note that this chart concerns religion only in its ethical dimension—that is, its effects on the relations of man to man. For other religious factors, this typology may be quite inadequate.

Point X, at which church and sect tendencies are in balance, is the point where the ability of religion to control the behavior of individuals, according to its established norms, is at a maximum. Even this maximum, however, when compared with other powers, may not be great.

The location of the various religious groups on this chart is only a rough estimate, for purposes of illustration, and should not be taken as objectively established measurements, which are not possible at this stage of the study.

During the discussion the criteria which help one to determine the type of religious group will be shown. Size is by no means the only criterion, although it is one rough measure. Wealth, insufficient by itself to determine religious type, also aids in the classification. There is a good deal of sociological truth in the statement, "For where thy treasure is, there shall thy heart be also." The nature of the relation between churchmen and rulers and the class origin of the clergy are very valuable measures of religious type. Thus in the fifteenth century, after the breakdown of the universalism of the church and the appearance of independent secular powers, the higher clergy in Italy, and to some extent in France, were in closest association with secular rulers, from whom indeed a great many of them came.[17] Under the circumstances it is not surprising either that the nobility of other countries should seek their own religious justification—the *Landeskirchen*—or that the radical, explosive element in Christianity should be required to go beyond the church, which had formerly at least partially enfolded it, to get expression. These are two of the important elements underlying the Reformation, and our typology aids us in "retrospective prediction" (see Chapter III for a discussion of the Reformation).

To take a more recent example to illustrate the importance of the connections between church and state, one may refer to Russia. There the semireconciliation between church and sect tendencies that was found in Thomism had been almost completely shattered, and the religious organization had become an extreme example of what we have called the second church type. The Czar had to profess orthodoxy; the Over-Procurator was a member of the senate—the highest court in the land; each bishop could appoint a clergyman to the provincial lay councils; the state police were an invaluable aid in forcibly suppressing nonorthodox groups and sects; the church hierarchy, with some few exceptions, was thoroughly conservative. Under such circumstances it is not surprising either that sect protests were frequent, or that they were vigorously persecuted. Even the Old Believers, whose membership reached into the millions, were faced with almost continual persecution. The result of all this, of course, as one would expect, was that the great majority of the church hierarchy clung to the Empire to the end, and fell with it.[18] It is not altogether fanciful to say that some of the "religious" energy of communism in Russia is the sectarian tendency in Christianity, suppressed, persecuted, and driven from the church. Thus the political connections of a church are a valuable clue in predicting its behavior in face of a new situation.[19]

The Dilemma of the Churches

It is not difficult thus to describe the various ways in which religious groups are related to the social organization. This becomes meaningful, however, only when we ask what is behind the choice of one response or the other. The sources of this variation in response made by religious groups to the social situation are revealed by a discussion of the dilemma of the churches. As we have already pointed out, there is a serious conflict between the demands of the religious ideal and the claims of secular interests. The achievement of the values of a religion demands some kind of power over often recalcitrant human beings, and thus the religious expression seeks embodiment in organization. This organization may, however, defeat its original purpose by adopting methods used by secular institutions—"discipline, fear-governed obedience, and early indoctrination"[20]—made necessary by the relative lack of a strong religious interest in most individuals. Not only is the religious group forced to adopt secular methods, but it is also invaded by secular interests, so that its ostensibly religious functions become, at least in part, another weapon in purely mundane conflict. The institutional embodiment of religion manifests two contradictory sets of values, one clustering about the religious idea, the other centering in the secular power of the institution. The more inclusive the scope of the institution, the more nonreligious interests it is likely to enclose. Faced with these powers which it cannot simply dismiss or overcome, the religious group has to make some adjustment. Either it has to accept their legitimacy and therefore to compromise its own demands when they are in conflict with the prevailing secular claims, or it must be ready to accept a limited sphere of influence. The former is in a sense an optimistic reaction. It is likely to be the adjustment of persons and groups who fare relatively well in the distribution of goods and power in their society and therefore think that the compromises are in any event not crucial, since they naturally believe that there is nothing *basically* evil about a society which has treated them so well. The latter adjustment is the result of a pessimistic view of the world, a conviction that there are basic evils with which one must not compromise. It is not surprising that this is frequently the reaction of the least privileged groups in a society. An arrangement that treats them so poorly is clearly not one with which their most exalted aims can compromise; consequently, they withdraw from "the world." They hold that the religious idea can be maintained only in freedom from the impact of the secular powers; they therefore form themselves into a purely religious body. In so far as the sectarian impulse was entirely religious, the withdrawal may be relatively effective in achieving its goal; in so far, however, as it also contained a moral element of more than personal scope—the desire to improve, according to some standard, the relations of man to man—obviously the withdrawal can be effective only in indirect ways.

Thus both horns of the dilemma are sharp. The church must compromise to maintain its position. The sect, by refusing to compromise, puts itself into opposition with some of the most powerful secular beliefs and groups. John Wesley, in asking himself why Christianity had done so little good in the world, wondered whether its ineffectiveness was due to a tendency for Christianity to undermine itself:

For, wherever true Christianity spreads, it must cause diligence and frugality, which, in the natural course of things, must beget riches. And riches naturally beget pride, love of the world, and every temper that is destructive of Christianity. Now, if there be no way to prevent this, Christianity is inconsistent with itself, and of consequence cannot continue long among any people; since, wherever it generally prevails, it saps its own foundation.[21]

The observation is sound, although perhaps not the explanation (see Chapter IV); Christianity formed into a church tends to succumb to egocentric secular powers; its institutional expression becomes formalized. The kernel of explosive in its original doctrine remains, however, and reappears, in schism and sect, when social conditions permit. Sects often recall the church, at least temporarily, to its original intention. The weakness of the church adjustment to the dilemma is revealed by the very fact that sects do arise. Their appearance represents a protest against the failure of the churches to control the social conditions which tend to fashion them into caste organizations that are incapable of making a *basic* challenge to the existing society, with its injustices. There is a tendency, as H. R. Niebuhr says, to sacrifice their religious loyalties "to standards and institutions only remotely relevant if not contrary to the Christian ideal," a failure "to resist the temptation of making their own self-preservation and extension the primary object of their endeavor."[22] We must not forget, however, that simply to give up the task of organization and the search for power because they are dangerous is no road to the goal which religion is trying to achieve—to establish "a working synthesis between the seemingly opposed qualities of individual anarchy and social harmony."[23] For the sect, too, faces the dilemma. It may compromise less, but it maintains a relatively purer ethic at the expense of breadth of influence.

This dilemma is as old as the church. It occupied an important place in the thought of St. Thomas, who fought

against two eternal and opposite inclinations to error: on the one hand, against the *accumulative inertia* of a backward scholasticism which clung to the accidental and passing elements of the Christian tradition; and on the other, against an instinct of *spendthrift disassociation,* represented in his time by the Averroist movement and which came to its full flower in a later era in the anthropocentric humanism of modern times. . . .

To-day, in that order of the philosophy of culture or of civilisation we are dealing, on the one hand, with conceptions due to a univocal inertia which clings precisely to what is dead and done with in the temporal ideal of mediaeval Christendom; and on the other, with a whole ideology of revolutionary destruction, which rises in opposition to the very idea of Christendom.[24]

The need, asserts Maritain, is to preserve the principles of "authentic Christendom" without spendthrift dispersion, but still realizing the exigencies of a modern temporal life which will not allow modern problems to be solved by medieval methods. Entirely apart from his value judgments, which are not a logical concern of this volume, Maritain has made a brilliant analysis of the church-sect dilemma. That religious group is most effective which maintains a balance between these two "opposite inclinations to error." That is as true today (see Chapter V) as formerly.

The Social Sources of Denominationalism

The great difficulty in maintaining this balance is that a religious organization is never purely religious, or even largely religious, in its functions. The various groups and tendencies within Christianity represent different secular groups, interests, and needs. Each religious group emphasizes, rather than a balance of all the elements in Christianity, only those particular elements which serve to reinforce its claims, justify its position, or fulfill other needs of the individuals who compose it. Religious divisions, in other words, have secular correlates. An investigation of this concept of the "social sources of denominationalism"[25] will throw additional light on our typology of religious groups. Just as "the dilemma of the churches" is responded to by more than one kind of action, making a classification into types of reaction a prerequisite of analysis, so also do the social sources of religious group behavior create a variety of responses. This second important factor, which is closely related to the first, must be taken into account in the development of an adequate typology of religious groups.

The division of Christianity into hundreds of separate groups is usually explained by differences in doctrinal belief. A closer examination of church history, however, will show that ethics, polity, and theology have their roots "in the relationship of the religious life to the cultural and political conditions prevailing in any group of Christians." No purely economic or political interpretation of theology is justified, of course, but "the religious life is so interwoven with social circumstances that the formulation of theology is necessarily conditioned by these. . . . Regarding theology from this point of view one will discover how the exigencies of church discipline, the demands of the national psychology, the effect of social tradition, the influence of cultural heritage, and the weight of economic interest play their role in the definition of religious truth."[26] With the breakdown of ecclesiastical unity at the end of the Middle Ages and the rapid differentiation of the social structure, it was inevitable that a great variety of religious groups should spring up. The first great schism of the church, which divided East and West, can be explained more adequately by political factors than by religious motive.[27] In the Eastern branch, as the Byzantine political power declined, Slavic national churches appeared: Greek, Serbian, Rumanian, Bulgarian, Russian. In the Western branch a kind of unity, due to common political control of the various nationalities by the church, persisted. This unity was soon threatened by rising nationalism, however, and the Roman Church was forced to fight a series of "political" battles. In Spain Ferdinand and Isabella won the decisive influence in choice of Spanish church princes. France, under Philip the Fair, witnessed the "Babylonian captivity" of the pope, and later there was a forty-year period with two popes. That struggle continued down to modern times, church and state not being separated in France until 1905; but the Concordat of 1516 had virtually separated the French Church from Rome and made the Reformation unnecessary. In Germany, however, the

Catholic Church remained under papal dominance: the cause of nationalism required the Reformation (see Chapter III); but the religious division continued and was an important cause of the failure of German nationalism. A national church came to England simultaneously with the growth of national unity and was practically independent of the papacy as early as the fourteenth century. By the time of Henry VIII the sharper break was relatively easy.[28]

The Reformation and other national churches accomplished political purposes, but they failed to meet the needs of the "disinherited" groups.[29] The new churches became the religion of the fortunate, and the lower strata again found themselves religiously expatriated despite their support of the Reformation. Consequently the Protestant sects, as distinct from the churches, constituted largely of the politically and economically disinherited, spread over Europe: note the Peasants' War and the Anabaptist movement in Central Europe, the Jacquerie in France, Quakerism in England—to mention some of the more important developments. These illustrate further the social (in this case largely economic) meaning of denominationalism.

Among the wealthier classes there were also religious divisions. Note the case of seventeenth-century England, where the preferences of Anglican and dissenter were a reflection of social divisions. The Established clergy supported the aristocracy; dissenters were the protagonists of the rising bourgeoisie. "Where the two main divisions converged, or were about to converge, in the persons of capitalists who allied themselves with the aristocracy, there also the attitudes of Churchman and chapelman tended to unite."[30]

The social sources of religious divisions could be illustrated at much greater length, with reference, for instance, to the American scene. The same causes which produced political, economic, and social conflict and differentiation also brought division in the churches, which persisted beyond their secular counterparts. Among the important influences were frontier life, the Civil War, immigration, race.[31] For our purposes, however, it is necessary to discuss only one more phase of the social sources of denominationalism, with reference to its significance for a typology of religious groups—the tendency for sects to shift toward the church type. This shift is partly simply a matter of age, partly the result of a different interpretation of the best way to meet the dilemma which faces the search for influence, and partly a reflection of a changing socioeconomic position in the group. These are closely related, of course, for it is to be expected that a sect which, in the process of development, finds itself in an improved and favorable economic position, should revise its earlier tendency to contradict sharply the *status quo* in which it found that improved position. If that is not enough to cause a shift in emphasis, the disappointment of reformist hopes in dealing with recalcitrant human beings forces the group to withdraw more completely from the world or else to adopt church tactics of reconciliation and compromise. The history of the church abounds with the stories of radical sect groups which shifted gradually into "respectable" denominations or churches.

> . . . one phase of the history of denominationalism reveals itself as the story of the religiously neglected poor, who fashion a new type of Christianity which corresponds to their distinctive needs, who rise in the economic scale under the influence of religious discipline, and who, in the midst of a freshly acquired cultural respectability, neglect the new poor succeeding them on the lower plane. This pattern recurs with remarkable regularity in the history of Christianity. Anabaptists, Quakers, Methodists, Salvation Army, and more recent sects of like type illustrate this rise and progress of the churches of the disinherited.[32]

Since the emphasis of a sect group is, at the start, very strongly religious, its implication for the secular life is far from unambiguous. Like the primitive church itself, most new developments are shaped by the conditions in which they evolve. We shall trace this sect-to-church transition briefly with reference to Methodism, as illustrative of a rather general tendency.

Quakerism in England had been prevented from becoming an

inclusive church for the disinherited by the persecutions which drove it back upon itself, by economic success, by the succession of generations with less fervor than the founders. The poor were once again without a dynamic religious sponsorship. Methodism in the late eighteenth century was the religious revolution which attempted to fill this need. It was a church of the poor, with an emotional quality which furnished them "with a psychologically effective escape from the drudgeries of an unromantic, unaesthetic life."[33] It had a lay character; its ethics distinguished it from the middle-class churches. Some writers have maintained that the Methodist movement, because of its democratic character, had the same significance for England that the Revolution had for France. Philanthropy, popular education, humanitarian legislation were stimulated. Methodism was the religious manifestation of the great revolutionary movement which, in the eighteenth century, placed the individual in the center of things.[34] But that is not the whole story. "The seeds of radicalism and reaction lay together in Wesleyanism of the first fifty years, awaiting the nurture of events."[35] Wesley's death and the increasing association of radical ideas with irreligion were factors forcing the sect toward conservatism. More middle- and upper-class people came to be associated with Methodism. Employers joined the movement because it encouraged those traits of industry most esteemed in workmen: industry, carefulness, disappearance of drunkenness, trustworthiness. This shift in class character inevitably influenced Wesleyanism. Wesley himself had stressed the dangers of wealth and insisted upon economic equality. "But the record of the growing prosperity of Methodists all over England is the story of the progressive rejection of the principle and the gradual disappearance of the social evaluations which it represented."[36] Wesley's interpretation of "right judgment" and "right relations," which were supposed to be the basis of individual morality, was not the interpretation of his middle-class followers of a generation or two later. Hammond and Hammond wrote: "Amidst the groans and tears of the poor, a new industrial world arose. . . .

Methodism, naturally engrossed in her work of spiritual regeneration of the individual . . . hardly had eyes or heart for what was happening; . . . her mood was ecstatic and transcendental. She forgot the new Manchester in the New Jerusalem."[37]

That is perhaps to put the case a little too strongly, but it is clear that the preoccupation with individual salvation which may be effective with a great religious leader and at the time of his dynamic influence is less effective among those not so religiously inclined. Faced with the dilemma of compromising with secular interests and crystallizing its own organization, or losing out, Methodism chose the former path, surrendered its early flexibility and the relatively radical implications of its teachings. That meant declining influence as an initiating power. For, as MacArthur writes, any institution must outgrow the ideas of its founder if it is to continue to be useful. "Perhaps in a very real sense, a great institution is the tomb of its founder. . . ."[38] Wesley's concept of a "providence of moral purpose" was seized upon to justify vested interests and sanctify social inequalities. There was an increased doctrinal rigidity. And the movement's political record became more and more conservative. In 1819, during a period of great unrest, a conference of ministers adopted a resolution entreating the workers to patience: "Fear God and honour the king . . . , submit to magistrates for conscience' sake. . . ."[39] Some of the working-class leaders looked upon the Methodists as enemies. Cobbett declared that "the bitterest foes of freedom in England have been, and are, the Methodists. . . . The friends of freedom have found fault, and justly found fault with the main body of the established clergy . . . but, hostile to freedom as the established clergy have been, their hostility has been nothing in point of virulence compared with that of these ruffian sectarians. . . ."[40]

Thus Wesleyanism moved from sect to church and illustrated again the secular significance of religious groups. A lay element which did not take part in the shift stimulated a series of secessions, largely over the political issue, starting with the New Connexion in 1797.[41] Once again the cycle started, with the poorer classes hunting for a religious group that would not only satisfy their religious needs, but give them hopes of a better position in this world. While this was not entirely a vain hope, the chances for a very great success were not large. It was not likely that persons controlling the other sources of power in the world would not attempt also to control as much of the power of religion as they were able to seize. A great many of the poor, disillusioned of the attempt to win a happier position on earth through religion, were to turn to the secular salvation of communism. It is hardly to be expected that this attempt to overcome human egocentrism can be any more successful, except in so far as the poor have gained an effective power position through organization.

Religion and Social Change

The net result of the above discussion may be to put into too sharp a form the dilemma of the churches. It may give the impression that religious groups have one of two equally ineffective alternatives: either to hold closely to their ideal, and have few people listen and fewer follow; or to disregard their ideal in favor of a place of power in maintaining the *status quo*. The evidence of the history of Christendom requires a modification of this position. Since this whole essay, in a sense, is a study of the connection between religion and social change, and since direct attention will be given to this problem in the last chapter, only a brief comment will be made here in order to forestall misunderstanding.[42] Although the sect seems to deny itself a place of influence by sharp attacks on the powers of society, it should not be forgotten that there are rather strong ideological connections between the sect and church. Even the most complete church-type group generates within itself some sect tendencies. In the early part of the twentieth century there were some socialist elements in the seminaries of the Greek Catholic Church in Russia. Moreover, the church does not necessarily completely capitulate to secular powers when it adopts a method of compromise. Although it accepts (of necessity) the main structure of society, within that structure it seeks to control behavior according to its ideal. It takes Herbert Spencer's advice and mixes "reformist zeal with philosophic calm." The dilemma is that in some cases the zeal outweighs the calm, without regard for the strength of the opposition. "The pulpit catches on fire, but the pew fails to ignite." In many other cases the calm smothers the zeal—to make the church scarcely more than a puppet. We have shown how difficult it is, because of the secular significance of religious divisions, to keep a balance between the two necessary elements. When that balance is maintained, however, religion makes a maximum use of its power, that is, of its ability to achieve the purely religious and ethical aims.[43]

Our Typology Illustrated

In order to put some of the formulations of this chapter in more concrete terms, it may be useful to trace briefly some sections of the history of the Catholic Church, where so many of the questions with which we are dealing are illustrated. This must take us back, first of all, to the very beginning of Christianity, for even the appearance of Christianity cannot be understood apart from the setting in which it was formed. The destruction of the polis in the ancient world, the extinction of freedom in a bureaucratic sovereign state, involving the destruction of many treasured ideals and traditions—these turned men's thought to religion and spiritual aims. The religious crisis which marked the close of the ancient world was a part of a vast social crisis in which, as Troeltsch shows, it had become clear that the social ideal of the Hebrew people was not to be realized by human thought and effort. The belief that the kingdom of God was to be of this world began to give way. This was not done rapidly, nor was the process carried to completion in Christianity. It seems likely that some of the immediate followers of Jesus thought of him as a social reformer—or at least hoped that he would be; and the later development of institutionalized

Christianity did not entirely exclude the purely social aspects which were an important part of its Hebrew prophetic background. Nevertheless, out of the centuries of frustrations and disappointments, culminating in the oppressions of Rome, religious thought lost much of its optimism concerning the possibilities of reordering the affairs of this world. The order established by the Roman Empire came to be accepted. ". . . henceforth the conduct of external affairs was left to the rulers, while men sought and cultivated individual and spiritual freedom. This applies to the later development of Platonism and Stoicism; it applies to countless new religious movements, and in particular it applies to the establishment of Christianity as well as to the preparation for it within Judaism."[44] Christianity was not primarily a program of social reform. The early church, particularly under the leadership of Paul, had an almost purely religious orientation; it emphasized personal salvation, not the reorganization of society. Jesus himself was not a reformer, although those who describe him as a proletarian leader have a part of the truth: they recognize some of the *implications* of his teachings for the life of this world. Moreover, as John MacMurray rightly points out, to describe the work of a religious leader as concerned *either* with social reorganization *or* with purely spiritual ends is to misinterpret the nature of his thinking, for the religious person does not make such a distinction; he thinks "monistically." Life is a unit with a religious purpose at its center, and this purpose is thought to apply to *all* behavior.[45] Troeltsch writes:

> . . . Christianity, along with all the radical equalizing of men in the sight of God and with all the penetration of this idea in the whole life of the soul, and in all personal relations of men to one another, is yet at the same time very cautious towards any attempt to carry over this equality into the sphere of secular relationships and institutions, which have nothing to do with the real religious basis of this equality.[46]
>
> . . . the message of Jesus is not a programme of social reform. It is rather the summons to prepare for the coming of the Kingdom of God; this preparation, however, is to take place quietly within the framework of the present world-order, in a purely religious fellowship

of love, with an earnest endeavor to conquer self and cultivate the Christian virtues.[47]

If this is true, what is the significance of Christianity for the secular world? Here Troeltsch makes the important observation that tied together in the original Christian doctrine is a dualistic ethic which is split apart under the pressures of the secular world. Both in the teachings of Jesus and in the other sources of Christianity there run these two currents: a thoroughgoing religious asceticism, emphasizing the universalism of love; and an ethical-prophetic strain, with its radical religious individualism. The former is conservative and traditionalistic in its effects; when it becomes especially dominant it has a definite quietistic tendency. The latter is radical and, when it receives an impetus, makes a direct challenge to traditionalistic society. The ethical teachings come in rather large measure from the Jewish prophetic background; the religious asceticism is an outgrowth of centuries of frustrations. They bind an implicit challenge to the injustices of the world together with a quiet acceptance of the social order. *Thus in the very origin of Christianity is found the dilemma to which we have referred, a dilemma that is inevitably forced into the thought of any religion which has tried to mold human behavior.*[48] Religious persons themselves resolve the dilemma in one way by transcending it. In dealing with the lives of the great majority, however, religions find the solution infinitely more difficult. The conservative and traditionalistic aspect of the doctrine usually dominates, because it contains a more profound understanding of the disappointments that must be faced and because the religious interest runs hard against man's more immediate material interests and for the most part is defeated by them. The radical, tradition-breaking forces in Christianity break loose only in times of unrest and rapid change.

The history of the church seems to reveal two situations in which the sect protest arises: After a period of cumulative disregard of the sect element within the dominant religious body, there will arise among those who suffer from this disregard—the poor and powerless—a reformist program, aimed at reasserting the radical implications of the original gospel. This program vastly exaggerates, of course, the original radical tendencies. It may have an immediate significance in changing some of the more obvious difficulties, largely by strengthening the religious orientation which has gradually declined in the church—in other words, by encouraging a monistic view of life which ties together belief and action. But because it is not backed by any power other than the purely religious one, this movement is soon absorbed and diluted.[49] A different kind of "sectarian" protest arises when a new emerging power group finds the church in the hands of its competitors and so accommodated to the *status quo* that it blocks the appearance of the new situation in which their position promises to be more favorable. Under these circumstances the church adjusts its doctrines in favor of the new elite, and/or the sect protest creates another church (see Chapters III and IV).

The first organization of Christianity, largely under the leadership of the Apostle Paul, moved rather rapidly toward the church type. Paul, a Roman citizen, prized the state which preserved order and justice. Although there were no rankings within the early church, the group did not fight slavery. Even in later years there was no rejection of slavery in principle; it was, in fact, expressly accepted. Out of the duality of the Christian ethic, those aspects which harmonized with the prevailing politico-economic system were emphasized, and received expression in the institutionalized form of the religious life—the church.

Despite its conservatism, however, the church contained energies of a revolutionary nature. The otherworldly emphasis was dominant, not so much because it was nearer to the inherent nature of Christianity itself, but because it was able to catch hold in the social setting of the time. The radical elements were backed by no other power.[50]

The enormous energies of Paul established the church in many important cities of the Mediterranean world, and it soon became a force to reckon with. At that point Rome forgot its earlier tolerance, and started on a program of persecution of the church. But this new movement was in tune with the times, and the persecution served only to increase its solidarity. We cannot trace here the march of the church, even into Rome, and its emergence in the twelfth century as ruler of the Western World, a comprehensive, unifying social whole, including both the circle of religious life and the social and political organizations. This rapid spread was due not simply to the inner power of the religious idea, for in its final manifestation the church included not only expressions of religious life, but all of society. The church succeeded in dominating medieval life in large measure because of the effects of the universal change to feudalism. Troeltsch writes: "It was thus at first actually due to pure coincidence that the social, economic, and political conditions of mediaeval life made a comparatively thorough and direct Christianization of civilization possible."[51] The return, in the early Middle Ages, to a settled agricultural way of life, with patriarchal authorities and mutual loyalty and respect among classes; the lack of a money economy; and the dominance of a traditional way of life were conditions favorable for the achievement of a unified society centered in the church.[52]

The ecclesiastical unity of Europe reached its climax in the thirteenth century,[53] and attained its highest expression in the work of St. Thomas. The church could not eliminate the inconsistencies between its ethic and the actual conditions of the world, but it did not allow this fact to destroy the unity of society. It reconciled the difference by giving to the conditions in this world a relative place. Aquinas accepted the Aristotelian idea of progress. The established society was to be defended because it represented the highest stage of man's development toward the absolute values. If the church was to dominate the world, it had to make room for the conditions and values of the world. They were given, however, only a relative place; from these the church led up to absolute values. Thus the church accepted slavery as part of the "relative natural law,"[54] yet it also contained an implicit criticism of slavery because it was *only* relative. It accepted everything it had to accept—war, slavery, the power of the secular life—but its acceptance was not unconditional, as it often is among churches of the second modal type, for it gave them only a relative place. That is, in this concept of relative natural law the medieval church accepted many things which contradicted its ethic, but it also challenged the life of the world, after the fashion of the sects. Thus neither its acceptance nor its challenge was unconditional. Of the two tendencies, Thomism, as was inevitable in its place of power, leaned more toward the church-type reaction to the dilemma which it faced. In the thought of St. Thomas, everyone's class and position in society were an expression of the will of God. No one ought to sink below his natural class, or try to rise above it. There was no place, in his thought, for the elevation of the masses to a higher status or class. His social ideal was thoroughly conservative. The medieval church looked upon society as a divinely appointed harmony, and the relative approximation of social institutions to the ideals of the church as a natural and logical world order which needed only to be checked by the church and constantly referred to the vitality of the religious principles.

The conservative retreat before the dilemma was not so complete, however, as this would imply. We have already noted that the concept of "relative natural law," although it can accept practically anything, can also challenge practically anything, if there is any possibility of success. In the hands of able strategists—of whom St. Thomas was the greatest, but of whom there have been many—this concept becomes a powerful weapon for keeping the church in power and yet still striving for its ideal.[55] Moreover, the radical sect tendency itself was at least formally enclosed within the church organization, in the monasteries. "The pure realization of the Absolute has to be entrusted to a particular class—that of the ascetics—who actualize it vicariously for the rest, and maintain its power and influence, so that from this ascetic class the primitive Christian energy once more radiates fresh vitality into all merely relative approximations to the Christian standard."[56]

Thus Thomism was a masterpiece of reconciliation. But the dilemma was still there, even if at a deeper level. It reasserted itself, when conditions became ripe, by a resurgence of sect reactions of both types. The all-inclusive system inevitably involved contradictions; it could not conquer the material aspects of life by encompassing them. The harmony of the ecclesiastical system could be maintained only by constant appeal to the divine authority of the papacy, which continually reconciled the failings of society by appeal to the idea of relative natural law. More and more the church became a secular power. ". . . it was inevitably diluted by the mass which it absorbed." It became implicated to the hilt in the economic system, especially on the side of land tenure. "Itself the greatest of landowners, it could no more quarrel with the feudal structure than the Ecclesiastical Commission, the largest of mineral owners today, can lead a crusade against royalties."[57]

Nevertheless, the accommodation of the church to society and the state was never perfect; there was always a disintegrating force in the partnership, associated largely with the fraternal orders. The monasteries had served to segregate the explosive element in Christianity; but the monastic life had the tendency to intensify the religious convictions in many cases, and created a pressure toward separation from the church and a demand for a purification of the church, for the restoration of its religiosity.[58] This was the first sect problem. Though the church was not revolutionary, it carried within it this explosive—the tendency toward constant conflict with the existing order. Thomism had encompassed the sect elements, but they began to break away when the situation permitted. The tendency to form sects was associated especially with the decline of feudalism and the development of a differentiated city civilization. Then the ecclesiastical unity of the Middle Ages began to break up, and the sectarian, uncompromising interpretation of the religious ethic began to crystallize. One must emphasize again that the appearance of sects was not simply a result of the resurgence of an original radical element in Christianity. It reappeared both because there were many people suffering from the growing failure of the church to incorporate that aspect into its teachings (in other words, the concept of relative natural law was being used more and more to justify things as they were, and less and less to challenge the *status quo* precisely on the grounds of its relativity) and because there was a new group gaining some power in society. Here were the beginnings of a major break in the ranks of the church.[59]

Thus even the medieval church was unable to solve the dilemma that faced it; and as society became more differentiated, its thirteenth-century synthesis began to break down. The social sources of denominationalism became apparent when religious groups of all types began to appear. Nevertheless, one should not underestimate the influence of the medieval church. It was something that men should think of themselves as one body. Though the church acquiesced in much and was heir to the weaknesses of men, it also made many demands. Tawney writes:

> The truth was that the very triumph of the church closed its mouth. The church of the third century, a minority of believers confronted with an alien civilization, might protest and criticize. But when the whole leaven was mixed with the lump, when the church was conceived of, not as *a* society, but as society itself, it was inevitably diluted by the mass which it absorbed. The result was a compromise—a compromise of which the critic can say, "How much that was intolerable was accepted!" and the eulogist, "How much that was intolerable was softened!" And both critic and eulogist will be right.
>
> For if religious opinion acquiesced in much, it also claimed much, and the habit of mind which made the medieval church almost impotent when dealing with the serried abuses of the land system was precisely that which made it strong, at least in theory, in dealing with the economic transactions of the individual.[60]

Although the struggle for power broke the societal unity which prevailed to quite a great degree at the time of St. Thomas, his system of thought was far from destroyed; it remains today, in fact, the center of Catholic doctrine. Catholicism still defends the general social and political structure upon which Thomism was raised. It pictures a society of classes and grades, just as the universe itself is graded—an architectonic theology and philosophy in an architectonic society. The various ethical motives of the different classes are unified and controlled, in Catholicism, by the supreme binding authority. Without any attempt at a complete discussion, we shall conclude our illustration of religious typology with a few references to modern Catholicism.

Although the contemporary Catholic Church is the heir of the method of St. Thomas, it has a far more difficult task, because the continuous flow of new elements into our society makes their incorporation into Catholic theory almost impossible. Nevertheless, the church has amazing success within the circle of its influence. Its strategy is not to let science, rationalism, humanism, or whatnot independently accomplish anything if the church can possibly step in to show that the new development is really a fundamental and established part of the church program. The power of the church must be preserved by encompassing all really crucial and inevitable elements in society, for then all of life can be included within the church, and the religious orientation—which is the meaning of the church's existence—can be maintained.[61] This principle of "plenitude" is a guiding rule of the modern Catholic, as it was of the medieval, church. The maintenance of a unity centered in the church is carried out not only by an appeal to tradition, but also through the work of contemporary scholarship. The process of preserving unity requires brilliant pedagogy and ingenuity, particularly in some instances where the former Catholic position is put in sharp, unambiguous language. The modernist movement, for instance, was sharply suppressed by Pope Pius X. That does not mean that it will not someday be accepted as orthodoxy, however, for if it proves to be important to any large number of constituents, the church will gradually admit the validity of the movement. As Van Vleck writes, this may become another example of the strategy of the

Vatican: ". . . the official quashing of any movement within its fold is likely to be followed by the eventual acceptance of its recommendations, and the result will be a continuation of popular belief in the perpetuity of church doctrines paralleled by their actual modernization."[62] The church-type Protestant groups also follow this procedure, although perhaps less skilfully (see Chapters V and VI); and within Protestantism there is the additional process of the appearance and decline of separate religious bodies which reflects new developments and keeps the total religious picture somewhat adjusted to the social structure. In Catholicism this adjustment must be carried on within an established institution, and there even mutually contradictory elements are at least partially accommodated. Sidney Hook writes:

The greatness of Catholicism as a movement, leaving aside the historical reasons for its varying fortunes, consists in its theoretical adaptability and practical resourcefulness. The extent of its theoretical adaptability may be gauged by the fact that in its struggles against other forms of totalitarianism, it sometimes assumes the vestment of ideological liberalism even though its authoritative spokesmen have on occasions held that the logical consequences of doctrinal liberalism is Bolshevism. Despite Jefferson's outspoken Deism, Catholic writers insist that his inspiration was Thomist. And if we are to judge by the writings of the outspoken apologists of Catholicism in Europe and America, they are just as ready, if necessity arise, to baptize Marx as they once baptized Aristotle.

The practical resourcefulness of Catholicism is exhibited, to mention one of many things, in the skillful use it can make of everyone. It has a place and function for all who accept the Catholic dispensation—for every type of mind and personality, for every interest and talent. Soldier or social worker, scholar or man of action, poet or astronomer, converted Jew or converted Protestant—the virtues of each individual's excellence can be made to serve the purposes of the Church. Its base of common dogmas is sufficiently broad to permit of a wide and *controlled* variation. It has countenanced a modernist and fundamentalist wing in politics, a realistic and nominalist tendency in philosophy, a rationalist and mystic emphasis in theology. In the past it has found use for a St. Francis Assisi and a Torquemada just as today it can find uses for a Maritain and a Coughlin.[63]

The recent history of Mexico well illustrates the adaptability of the Catholic Church.[64] The Mexican Revolution obviously made necessary a great shift in the church, for the clash of symbols and claims of power inevitably demanded that either the state or the church should yield. The constitution of 1917 seemed to shift every province of life into the domain of the state: the church has no legal standing; it can own no property, no schools, or residences, or churches. The church can control no schools, nor can clergymen be connected with schools. Catholic children must attend public schools. The position of the state in Mexico is not that religion has been eliminated, but that it has been restored to its purely religious functions. The church, of course, cannot accept this definition of religious "freedom," for freedom must include availability of instrumentalities to teach as well as freedom of conscience. It is clear that the church could not simply bow to this outright seizure of her former power. Government control of education is a particularly irreconcilable difficulty, for the church sees her children getting "impious and corrupt training," and finds itself unable to give what it considers sufficient religious instruction. The church probably regards the present situation, not as a solution, but as a truce.

Nevertheless, on March 28, 1937, the Pope sent an Apostolic letter outlining a new program for the church in Mexico, a program that involved three substantial shifts from the earlier position of the church. This letter shows that after twenty years Catholicism can accommodate itself at least partially even to so sharp a competitor for power as the Mexican Revolution. The three shifts, according to James, were these:

1. The Catholic laity, not the clergy, must secure change. The change must come by means of Catholic citizens exercising political rights, not by means of pressure from the church or a specifically Catholic party.

2. ". . . action must be flexible, according to circumstances, 'more or less opportune, more or less energetic'; and, what is important, relative—not ultimate and absolute—ends are to be

sought. The objective is thus to be not the immediate repeal of all the philosophy and acts of the Revolution as they impinge on religion—which was the position of the Church as late as the Appeal of the Bishops to President Cardenas in 1935—but such progressive modifications as practical circumstances permit."[65]

3. The church must prove itself not indifferent to social problems: agrarian reform, living conditions of the workers, problems of the Indians, and the like, should be given careful attention. "Such interest and work would be designed to put the Church as a force behind certain social objectives of the Revolution acceptable to the Church—at least as to ends, if not means—and remove any basis to the charge that it is a reactionary power seeking only restoration of an old order."[66]

It is doubtful if the church can wholly digest the revolution—there are too many mutually contradictory elements in the two movements—but the struggle in Mexico is an interesting example of the way the church deals with secular powers: if the present constitution remains in force in Mexico, we can expect to see even more elements of the revolution become part of the "relative natural law."[67]

This process of keeping adjusted to the contemporary world is also being carried out on a broader front. Many writers, of whom Jacques Maritain is perhaps the most outstanding contemporary, are trying to enfold in the Catholic doctrine the legitimate —i.e., the inevitable—elements of Marxism and humanism, and to show that the crucial and civilizing elements in these movements are even already a part of the teachings of the church, that they were important in the thought of St. Thomas, that the secular, anti-Catholic expression of these developments will kill the kernel of truth which they contain. The sources of contemporary humanism, Maritain asserts, are classical and Christian; the great weakness of the movement is its anthropocentrism. Integral (Catholic) humanism

is able to save and to promote, under the terms of a fundamentally different synthesis, all the truths affirmed or brought to light by socialist humanism, by uniting them in a way which is vital and organic with numerous other truths [i.e., religion]. . . .

However grave its errors and illusions have been, Socialism in the nineteenth century was a protest uttered by the human conscience, and of its most generous instincts, against evils which cry to heaven. It was a noble work to bring capitalist civilisation to trial and to waken against powers which know no pardon, the sense of justice and of the dignity of labour: and in this work it took the initiative. It has fought a hard and difficult battle at the cost of innumerable sacrifices, filled with the most moving of human qualities, the self-sacrifice of the poor. It has loved the poor. We can only criticise it effectively while remaining at many points in its debt. Yet the deception it has caused among men is for all that only the more bitter. It is pitiful to record how the errors in the metaphysic and the social philosophy on which it originally depends have spoiled such rich resources and how they have grown and aggravated with its growth and create, as long as they endure, so deep a separation between socialism and Christian thought.[68]

Anthropocentric humanism, says Maritain, can only defeat its own end, and finish in the same errors as the system it opposes: ". . . however different this new type may be, if it is formed apart from God and the climate of love, created by purely external and social or technical means, it will but end, after a certain expenditure of heroism (such as there is in all revolutionary periods and where part of the treasure of Christian mysticism is wasted), in a new pharisaism in place of the old: a pharisaic pride in the collectivity or the means of production in place of the old bourgeois honour and individual enterprise."[69] Maritain would preserve that which is absolute in this relative expression of truth by allowing for the primacy of transcendental and eternal principles. The church can never achieve any more than this theoretical acceptance of some of the principles of socialism, of course, until it is recognized as the final arbiter of the absolute, if not of the relative, in life.[70] Most contemporary expressions of socialism are quite absolutist in their own right.

That the thought of Maritain is not an exception to some of the tendencies of Catholic doctrine, although it may be more extreme than the writings of most churchmen, is amply demonstrated by the collection of documents edited by Ryan and Husslein, *The Church and Labor*. The volume "contains practically every document of present importance issued by any Pope or bishop on these subjects since the Industrial Revolution."[71] While we must postpone any complete discussion of this topic until Chapter V, a word concerning the general point of view of the Catholic Church concerning questions of labor will illustrate the church-type reaction to this powerful development: "The moral aspect of industrial relations, the necessity and limitations of private property, the indestructible right of labor to the means and conditions of decent living, the duty of the State to remove industrial evils that can be abolished in no other way, and the right of labor to organize—, may be regarded as the main propositions expounded and defended in these papers and documents."[72] The church in the nineteenth century was faced with a new power which was winning the allegiance of the working class. Churchmen soon recognized that they could not accomplish their religious aims if they stood out against a movement which was important in the lives of millions. If they did not sanction the demands of labor, secular interests would profit by the new power, and religion would suffer. The church did not create the labor movement; churchmen did not make the original discovery that the demands of labor were Christian justice: that only followed as a necessary consequence of the fact that those demands were crucial in the lives of a great many people:

> We appeal to all hearts of good will. The sons of darkness are forming associations, we too must form them. They found revolutionary clubs, we must found Catholic clubs. It will cost a hundred thousand francs, five hundred thousand, a million. No matter! Did it not cost more to recapture Paris from the Commune?[73]
>
> "Interest yourself in the laborer," warns Ketteler, "or others will do it in your stead who are hostile to the Church and to Christianity."[74]

One must not suppose from this brief reference to liberal tendencies in Catholicism that the Catholic Church has gone completely over to the cause of labor. Far from that being the case, one may be certain that so long as there are other secular powers to deal with she will make her support only tentative, as to part of "relative natural law." Still faced with the dilemma of the churches, she will make a place for an inevitable power, but will also make demands upon it. The church is still at great pains to show how important is the role of capital. St. Thomas's brilliant attempt at reconciliation of all secular powers is rivaled by Leo XIII in his famous *Rerum Novarum:*

> The great mistake that is made in the matter now under consideration, is to possess oneself of the idea that class is naturally hostile to class; that rich and poor are intended by nature to live at war with one another. So irrational and so false is this view, that the exact contrary is the truth. Just as the symmetry of the human body is the result of the disposition of the members of the body, so in a State it is ordained by nature that these two classes should exist in harmony and agreement, and should, as it were, fit into one another, so as to maintain the equilibrium of the body politic. Each requires the other; capital cannot do without labor, nor labor without capital. Mutual agreement results in pleasantness and a good order; perpetual conflict necessarily produces confusion and outrage. Now, in preventing such strife as this, and in making it impossible, the efficacy of Christianity is marvelous and manifold. First of all, there is nothing more powerful than Religion (of which the Church is the interpreter and guardian) in drawing rich and poor together, by reminding each class of its duties to the other, and especially of the duties of justice.[75]

This is by no means a complete survey of the varied activity of the Catholic Church. Its adaptability to wholly different contemporary powers could be shown by a study of the relation of the Vatican to Italy and Spain, or its activity in South America. We shall deal with some of these problems in Chapter V. Perhaps enough has been said here to show how well Catholicism illustrates the church-type response—accommodation to the powers that be, but never complete assimilation. Given time it can at least partially adjust to socialism (Mexico), democracy—although perhaps none too well—(the United States), or fascism

(Italy, Spain). If it has become more and more poorly adjusted to Nazi Germany,[76] the reason is perhaps that the church has met there an absolutism which challenges its own absolutism.

In the following chapters, the nature of our typology of religious groups will be further developed as we test its usefulness in interpreting and predicting religious behavior.

Chapter III

THE REFORMATION

Having arrived at a formulation of sociological religious types, we turn our attention to some concrete historical situations in order to interpret, sociologically, the reaction of religious groups to a series of new developments. In the next two chapters we shall deal with the Reformation and the much debated relationship between Protestantism (and more particularly Calvinism) and capitalism. This ground has been covered so often that some brief explanation of still another reworking may be justified. First of all, the very exhaustiveness of the treatment of this subject by many writers, from all points of view, makes it a fruitful place for the development and illustration of a theory of religious group behavior. In fact, the investigation of the relationship between Protestantism and capitalism, the study of the extensive and often brilliant literature on the subject, has been one of the chief sources of the theoretical formulations in this volume. Not only are there numerous interpretations, but the historical evidence is quite ample. Despite this, however, the treatment of the subject appears to be inadequate in most instances. The fact that controversy still surrounds the problem is evidence of the failure to solve it. It is our aim to give a meaningful interpretation of the relationship between Protestantism and capitalism by relating it to an adequate theory of religious group behavior. Max Weber's *The Protestant Ethic and the Spirit of Capitalism* continues to be the center of much of the discussion and will receive a great deal of attention in the next chapter.

Background of the Reformation

Before going to the problem of the relationship of Protestantism to capitalism, however, we must say something, by way of background, of the history and interpretation of the Reformation. Although it is customary to think of the work of Luther as the starting point of the Reformtaion, it is clear that the antecedents of his work reach far back into the history of the church. The revolt, in fact, is partly a logical outcome of the original "primitive" traits of Christianity that we have already discussed, and it awaited only the appropriate historical circumstance to bring it forth. The social pressures making for divisiveness in the religious group (because of different socioreligious needs), although kept brilliantly under control by the genius for reconciliation of St. Thomas and some of his predecessors, gradually became too strong. The tendency toward schism was correlated with the weakening of the "organic unity" of feudalism and the growth of social differentiation, largely as a result of the increase in culture contact and trade. We find, that is, a reflection of the tendency toward greater social, political, and economic differentiation in the increasing instability of the ecclesiastical world unity and in the tendency toward schism. These are the roots of the Reformation. The forces which had made the medieval church and the forces which the church had made began to combine to break the power of the ecclesiastical empire even as it reached its height. Most important of these movements of revolt were the rise of territorial churches and the rapid expansion of sects.

Only enough will be said of the first to show that the development of territorial churches or *Landeskirchen* grew from the pressure toward statehood in the late Middle Ages. These national churches were not an inevitable result of some purely religious development. In fact, they contradicted the basic idea of unity on which Christendom had been built. The movement toward the development of states in Western Europe, which was the other side of the picture of disintegrating feudalism, was largely the reflex of political and economic conditions. The growth of cities, the expansion of trade, and the consequent necessity for larger and more peaceful political units were some of the factors involved. Out of this situation came the territorial churches, designed to buttress the young states against the claims of the ecclesiastical order.

During this same period, there was a challenge to ecclesiastical unity coming from the church's own religious doctrines. It was an element that could not be completely contained within the existing system, even in the fraternal orders, for within these orders only the otherworldly aspects of Christianity could receive adequate expression. As a result, just as Thomism reached its highest development in the unifying of society in the church, numerous sects began to appear and to challenge that unity. That "element in Christianity which defies institutionalization," which had forced the church to include and even to encourage fraternal orders for the purpose of controlling the element which the orders embodied, now broke loose from the church altogether.

The Gregorian Reform, strangely enough, was one of the starting points for the medieval sects. The Universal Papacy arose against the territorial churches, whose priests were working hand-in-glove with the national nobles (of whom, indeed, they were often a part). In order to fight this tendency, the papacy encouraged the lower classes in their struggles against the territorial churches. These struggles, however, were inspired by wholly different reasons from those of the papacy. The laymen opposed the church because of its corrupt clergy, its exploitation through tithes. They were scarcely interested in the fight for power between the growing states and the ecclesiastical world order. As it happened, Gregory, in encouraging the laymen to oppose the national priests, made them skeptical of the priesthood in general. They became, therefore, willing listeners to the semi-Christian Gnostic-Manichaean sect of Cathari which spread across Europe from the East. In its Christianized form, this sect became a lay religion, criticizing the institutionalized church, refusing to swear in court, denying the duty of tithes, testing all things by the ethical standards of the primitive church. This heresy was connected with the rise of the new classes in towns, and appeared first, therefore, in Southern France, Lombardy, and Italy. Christianity descended to the people, across whom swept a wave of enthusiasm. Here again one must emphasize that the pressure toward lay religion and the implications of the radical Christian ethics are always present, but that they become strong enough to cause important currents in history only when favorable conditions arise. The corruption of the priesthood, the encouragement of Gregory, the growth of cities, were among the factors which made it possible for the Gnostic-Manichaean sect to unite with the latent radicalism of the Christian ethic and thus to cause a wave of sects to sweep across Europe.

Gregory himself, of course, and the church did not long remain sponsors of the movement. Seeing the dangers of her connection with the social movement of lay religion, the church severed her relations with the democratic tendencies that she earlier had encouraged in order to fight the territorial churches. The Gregorian "reform" then reversed itself: the right to examine the priests was withdrawn from the laity; it was decreed that only the priests could participate in public services; ecclesiastical taxes and tithes were demanded in full.[1]

The sect movement, however, was not thus brought to an end. The Waldensians became prominent in Southern Europe. These were mainly a group of traveling religious ascetics, vowing poverty and celibacy. They demanded the giving up of indulgences, opposed capital punishment and war, emphasized personal good works. St. Francis was probably influenced by the Waldensians; and though his sect was incorporated into the church, which sought thus to smother its radicalism, it continued to stimulate lay religion and opposition to ecclesiasticism.

In Italy the sect movement became entangled with the political situation, and finally was reduced to eccentricity and extravagances. Humanism and the Renaissance discouraged the Reformation, and the dominance of the papacy blocked its development in Italy. In the North, however, sect influence was stronger and paved the way for the Reformation, not because of inherently greater vitality of the sects in the North, but because of their more favorable environment. By the fourteenth century, numerous expressions of discontent with the papacy were to be found in England; many classes were united in the desire "to remove the popes from off their backs." Bishop Grosseteste emphasized the Bible as the primary authority—a principle with explosive possibilities. And most significant, Wycliffe, perhaps the foremost schoolman of his day, made a sharp attack on the medieval church. He brought his arguments home to the people by his vigorous pamphlets written in the common tongue. He challenged the efficacy of pardons, indulgences, absolutions, pilgrimages, the worship of images, and many of the sacraments. He rejected the dominant place of the priest and upheld the Bible as the chief authority. Milton was so impressed by the vigor of Wycliffe's protest against the medieval church that he exclaimed: "Had it not been the obstinate perverseness of our prelates against the divine and admirable spirit of Wyclif, to suppress him as a schismatic and innovator, perhaps neither the Bohemian Hus and Jerome—no, nor the names of Luther or of Calvin—had ever been known: the glory of reforming all our neighbours had been completely ours."[2] This is probably to oversimplify the forces at work against Wycliffe at the time; nevertheless, many would agree in calling him "the Morning Star of the Reformation." The cause of his failure, as Workman rightly observes, was the absence of a suitable environment for the spread and development of his ideas.[3]

The influence of Wycliffe was not confined to England, for it spread to Bohemia through the work of Huss. Although Huss was a less severe critic of the medieval religious pattern than Wycliffe, his attacks on the church led to a martyr's death, which gave impetus to the movement of revolt. Many of his ideas came directly out of the work of Wycliffe. Together they defended most of the significant principles that have come to be considered crucial to the later Reformation. This was recognized both by contemporaries and by Luther himself. Buddenseig tells of a remarkable picture that he has seen in a Bohemian Psalter of 1572. Wycliffe is seen striking a spark, Huss is kindling the coals, while Luther is brandishing the lighted torch.[4] In his *Address to the Christian Nobility,* Luther wrote: "It is not my intention here to judge John Huss's belief and to defend his errors, although my understanding has not been able to find any error in him. . . ." In February, 1529, Luther wrote to Spalatin: "I have hitherto taught and held all the opinions of Huss without knowing it. With a like unconsciousness has Staupitz taught them. We are all of us Hussites without knowing it. I do not know what to think for amazement."[5] As Workman points out, Luther did not mean by this that there had been any direct connection between him and Huss, in the sense of a continuing organization, or even that Huss had been the source of his beliefs, for in the same letter Luther had written that "Paul and Augustine are Hussites to the letter." He meant rather that there was close agreement in doctrine.

In view of these two facts—the greater success of the sect movement in Northern Europe and the fairly close doctrinal similarity between the early reformers, whose work did not lead to a reformation, and Luther, who was the spearhead of the Reformation —it is well to note again that there is a sociological, as well as a religious, significance in the appearance and in the success or failure of sects. Though the pre-Reformation sects expressed tendencies which were contained in the early Christian radicalism, "it is clear that the causes of this Christian revolution were not theoretical ideas, but, in the last resort, practical conditions and social tendencies."[6] That is, it is not enough to explain the medieval sects by the power of the radical and individualizing ideal present in Christianity. They cannot be accounted for without describing the political and economic currents of the times, which encouraged the radical ideals to appear; nor can their relative failures to produce a reformation be explained without reference to secular as well as religious conditions.

We have mentioned the challenges to the medieval ecclesiastical world unity that were made by the territorial churches and the sects. There were, of course, other changes, entwined together and connected with the strictly religious changes, which challenged the medieval church. There were peasant risings, based on democratic, equalitarian natural law, buttressed by radical Christian doctrine.[7] There appeared a literature of popular sovereignty, such as the work of Marsiglio of Padua, who called for the dominance of the secular state with the church limited to religious functions.[8] The growth of town civilization created an independent lay culture which competed with the ecclesiastical world of thought, limited its power, and reduced the objective side of religion. Literature, art, and science began to pass from the church to the laity. All of these changes are not in contrast with, but part of, the current which carried both the religious and the secular revolt.[9]

Thus the groundwork for the Reformation was laid. No effort will be made here to deal exhaustively with this movement except in those phases that pertain to our problem: the significance of Protestantism for the appearance of capitalism. Many of the antecedents of the Reformation were, of course, secular, and they are the factors which concern us. The history of the papacy itself was a story of increasing secularization.

> At Rome the popes came to occupy the position of princes of one of the Italian states, and were elected, like the doges of Venice, by a small oligarchy. Within seventy years the families of Borgia, Piccolomini, Rovere, and Medici were each represented by more than one pontiff, and a majority of the others were nearly related by blood or marriage to one of these great stocks. The cardinals were appointed from the pontiff's sons or nephews, and the numerous other offices in their patronage, save as they were sold, were distributed to personal or political friends.[10]

History also records the political murders of Sixtus IV (1471-1484), the bribes paid by Innocent VIII for his election, the evil associated with Alexander VI and his son Caesar Borgia and his daughter Lucretia, all of which testify to the extreme secularization of the papacy before the Reformation. The public conscience was not indifferent to the situation. Sects gained much of their following from resentment created by the abuses; it was a period when a number of preachers of repentance appeared, notably Savonarola (1452-1498). Only with the revolt, however, was the situation radically changed.

The corruption of clergy was not, however, the main cause of the Reformation. That had been opposed for centuries, and was probably no worse in 1450—and may have been better—than it had been. Greater difficulties came from other abuses, many of them connected with money. "The common man's conscience," Smith writes, "was wounded by the smart in his purse."[11] The income of the church from tithes and taxes and ownership of land was enormous. Many church offices were filled by sale, and dues were often levied on the first year's income from an ecclesiastical appointment. These charges were ultimately passed on to the constituents of the parish. It is not difficult to believe that such abuses would weaken the "faith" of a group of persons who were becoming more and more involved in a rapidly expanding commercial enterprise, or of the traditionally sacred laity in peasant and small-artisan circles, both because of the violence done to their religious beliefs and the material hardships that the abuses caused. Nor is it surprising that both groups should welcome and sponsor a movement which sought to check these practices.

The sale of indulgences was another rich source of ecclesiastical revenue which became more and more an ordinary means of raising money for the curia. "How thoroughly commercialized the business of selling grace and remission of the penalties of sin had become is shown by the fact that the agents of the pope were often bankers who organized the sales on purely business lines in return for a percentage of the net receipts plus the indirect profits accruing to those who handle large sums."[12] These agents usually received approximately 10 per cent of the net profits of the enterprise. An equal amount was given to the civil ruler of the territory, and commissions were paid to the local bishop and clergy as well as to the peddlers of the pardons. From 30 to 45 per cent of the gross receipts was turned into the treasury at Rome. Thus the territories were drained of vast resources. It is not difficult to see therein a strong pressure toward revolt. One phase of the revolt was religious; and much of the rest was covered over with religious symbolism, both because it was the dominant symbolism of the time and because the situation was seen as a struggle against the papacy. In 1372 the monasteries of the Rhineland entered into a compact to resist the levy of Gregory XI, who was demanding a tithe of their revenues. They wrote: "In consequence . . . of the exactions with which the Papal Court burdens the clergy, the Apostolic See has fallen into such contempt that the Catholic faith in these parts seems to be seriously imperilled. The laity speak slightingly of the Church, because, departing from the custom of former days, she hardly ever sends forth preachers or reformers, but rather ostentatious men, cunning, selfish and greedy. Things have come to such a pass that few are Christians more than in name."[13] Many rulers forbade the sale of indulgences in their territories, "because, as Duke George of Saxony, a good Catholic, expressed it, before Luther was heard of, 'they cheated the simple layman of his soul.' "[14]

Closely associated with these economic antecedents of the Reformation was the development of the nation-state system in Europe. For all of the division in Germany in 1500 there was a certain national consciousness, based largely on common language. The people were well agreed on their opposition to the rule of the Italian Curia. Year by year lists of grievances were drawn up at the Diets, demanding reform, refusing to be taxed for a crusade, opposing indulgences, appealing against the appointment of foreigners. "When such was the public opinion it is clear that Luther only touched a match to a heap of inflammable material. The whole nationalist movement redounded to the benefit of Protestantism. The state-churches of northern Europe are but the logical development of previous separatist tendencies."[15]

Luther and Emerging Nationalism

Thus the appearance of a Martin Luther was not a sudden or unexpected phenomenon; in many ways his work was a logical development of the sect movement. Although his genius carried the revolt beyond all earlier manifestations, the explanation of why this sect movement could prosper where others failed rests upon an understanding of the setting in which it grew. Power arrangements were shifting from the hands of those who held it by virtue of their position in the traditional feudal hierarchy and their inheritance of prestige symbols to those who were equipped by aptitude, interest, and freedom from traditional restraints to take advantage of the emerging modern commercial situation. Symptomatic of this shift was the realignment of religious forces, for no new elite could afford to have the power of the church set against it. In so far, therefore, as the interests of the emerging elite and the Italian Curia were in conflict (and we have shown that they were in conflict at many points), a severe challenge to the religious monopoly of the papacy was inevitable. That is not to say that Luther's religious ideas were simply a reflection of a politico-economic situation. There is some truth in Troeltsch's statement that "Luther's religious ideas were not due to the reflex action of social, or even of economic, changes; they were based essentially and independently upon the religious idea. . . ."[16] But regardless of the immanent development of Luther's religious ideas (and even there is involved a very subtle social-psychological problem regarding the social influences on his purely religious concepts—a problem for which the sociology of knowledge must furnish us some hypotheses), one must say that the *effects* of those doctrines, the very fact of their rapid acceptance, and their modification, can be interpreted only with reference to the social situation. When Troeltsch writes: "Luther's religious ideas were . . . based essentially and independently upon the religious idea, *which alone gave rise to the social, economic, and political consequences,*"[17] he slips into an idealism which does not do justice to his usual capacity for taking into account the whole interactional process. Weber does not always escape this same difficulty, as we shall show later. It is a kind of mind-body dualism which sees the life of the intellect, or of the spirit, as something independent of life as a whole. Troeltsch himself, in other passages, points out not only the immanent development of Luther's religious ideas, but their social conditioning, their relation to the emergence of cities, to the growing importance of national states, and to economic interests.[18] Important changes in the environment in which the church was working were necessitating a corresponding change in the doctrines of the church. A religious movement which was not committed to the support of the old social order held a great advantage in winning the allegiance of the new. That does not mean that secular changes create new religious developments, but it does mean that the success or failure of a doctrine, whatever its source, is closely related to secular conditions. And there is a further influence: as we have stated above, the purpose of every religious movement is to inject into a situation, whatever it may be, the moral and religious principles for which it stands. Since it has no monopoly of power and has to deal with an often contradictory world of "nature," it not only has to rewrite its doctrines and symbolism to correspond with the age, but also has either to compromise some of its sterner judgments with an often intractable world of nature, or else be content with a small following and influence. Luther rewrote some of the religious doctrines, and he also accepted the basic structure of the society in which he was trying to work. His desire was not to remake the social organization, but within the limits of that social organization to bring individual behavior closer to his interpretation of the Christian life.

Perhaps the most significant shift in doctrine was that from salvation by works to salvation by faith only.[19] Although this doctrine was not new, the emphasis Luther gave it contained the germ of revolution. It was not a remote religious question, but intensely practical, for in the sixteenth century the church claimed the right to rule over every detail of men's daily lives. Until this claim was broken, there was a great barrier to the emergence of modern society. The idea of justification by faith alone was a powerful force in breaking that claim. The conception of absolute truth, which formerly had centered in church dogma, tradition, and the hierarchy, was made by Luther and his adherents to center on the Bible. The Decalogue, not the Sermon on the Mount, took a central position in the Lutheran ethic. It is not altogether true that Luther rejected the traditional doctrine of the church as a means of salvation, but he did weaken church influence, for with salvation dependent on faith alone the church no longer had a monopoly as the dispenser of saving grace. If an individual were possessed of faith, the ministrations of the church were unnecessary; if he lacked faith, they were useless. This doctrine also greatly weakened the place of the clergy, who now, far from being indispensable, were unnecessary to the laity.[20] Luther wrote:

> . . . if a little company of pious Christian laymen were taken prisoners and carried away to a desert, and had not among them a priest consecrated by a bishop, and were there to agree to elect one of them, born in wedlock or not, and were to order him to baptise, to celebrate the mass, to absolve, and to preach, this man would as truly be a priest, as if all the bishops and all the popes had consecrated him.[21]

This is clearly a sharp attack on the ecclesiastical domination of the Middle Ages. It is not difficult to see economic and political, as well as religious, consequences in this freedom from the hierarchy. It should be noted, however, that Luther, especially in his later years, came to differ from Wycliffe and Huss, and other more complete Protestants, in seeing the church as an indispensable means of salvation—not because, as with the Catholics, it dispenses grace, but because it teaches the gospel.

As one aspect of his protest against the selling of indulgences, it is not surprising that Luther accepted the doctrine of predestination. This was closely associated with his opinion concerning justification by faith alone and his modification of the importance of the church. Predestinarianism, which was already clearly expressed in Paul, is a "logical" way to reconcile "equality before God," as a declared belief, and manifest inequality on earth in terms of rewards, sinfulness, faith. (Another reconciliation is achieved in the "organic" theory, which holds that even the lesser tasks are essential to the Christian unity.) Although in a weakened form this doctrine tends to fall to a rather low ethical plane, in its most rigid interpretation this is not true, for the idea of predestination permits the development of a disinterestedness in one's own needs, a pure selflessness in charity—for if one is already saved, his concern for others need not hide a deeper concern for himself. "No one can give himself in self-forgetful love to the service of his neighbour so long as he is anxious and troubled about his own fate."[22] The doctrine is subject to other interpretations, however, and we shall see later the importance of the ways in which it was used.

In his later years Luther modified his doctrine of predestination; and it was not until the advent of Calvinism that it became crucial in Protestant theory. Luther's whole orientation, in fact, underwent a shift as he grew older. His first great challenge to church authority forced him out of the church as a genuine revolutionary; there was a strong early emphasis on the sect-type religion. His famous early essays, *Address to the Christian Nobility of the German Nation* and *Concerning Christian Liberty,* probably even more than the Ninety-five Theses, contained much of what came to be thought of as the essence of Protestantism. In later years, however, he came to support more and more the territorial church system, and re-established most of the mediaeval ideas of church and religion, until, as Milton expressed it, "New presbyter was but old priest writ large." This shift was largely due to the fact that the rising rulers of the German states supported the new movement which would help free them from ecclesiastical dominance. This meant that the church came strongly under the influence of the political situation in which it was found. Luther supported the state as part of the God-ordained world. He held that "if in any town Catholics and Lutherans are teaching diverse doctrines and attacking each other, the municipal government is to interfere, to take the matter under consideration, and to stop the mouths of those who are not preaching in accordance with the Scriptures. This involves a connection between Church and State, and a subjection of the former to the latter not recognized under Catholicism."[23] Thus the emerging state escaped from the dominance of the church—with a vengeance.

It is clear that the early Lutheran theory of individual religion could not exist under such circumstances. As a result, the consistories were formed—ecclesiastical organs of government, ordered by the prince and governed by the church—which upheld purity of doctrine and Christian behavior by penalties and controls. In doctrinal rigidity Lutheranism became even more severe than Catholicism. Although it was in contrast with the early Lutheran position, the state-church conception was a unifying influence which allowed the movement to prosper. It could not have prospered as a radical sect movement.

Thus Lutheranism came to involve the dualism inherent in the Christian doctrine. As we have frequently pointed out, there is an inevitable tension in Christian thought, arising from the opposition between the Christian ethic and secular interests, which every religious body must resolve. Luther does this by positing the social order as God-given. "In place of the earlier and more spiritual point of view, in which Luther formulated the purpose of life from the point of view of the absolute religious end, and of the opposition to the world to which that gave rise, Luther insisted more and more upon the necessity for obedience to positive authority."[24] Peace and order, with a slow development, will bring prosperity. Luther was opposed to any kind of revolutionary scheme. He almost paralleled Machiavelli in glorifying authority; but always in the front of his mind was the belief that the harshness of authority was to be modified and softened by the application of Christian principles, for he interpreted life religiously. "The thread of pure idealism . . . constantly reappears" (Troeltsch). Lutheranism came to be an almost completely church-type group, with very few sect elements. Its ability to change, to adapt to the new, was greatly hampered. In terms of Reinhold Niebuhr's vocabulary, Luther succumbed to almost complete pessimism regarding this world—the world of nature—and transformed his earlier sect tendencies into transcendental optimism.

This being the case, it is not surprising that many of his earlier followers began to desert, for the desire for reform and change in *this* world loomed large. The intellectuals who were with him at Worms were alienated by his opposition to science and learning and his increasingly narrow dogma. Humanists like Erasmus had seen in Luther a symbol of the break from the oppression of Rome; but this hope soon faded, for he proved to be no less tyrannical. Luther dissociated himself from the extreme radicals and the peasants, whose uprisings he condemned in violent terms in the pamphlet *Against the Thievish, Murderous Hordes of Peasants*. The lower classes moved toward the Anabaptists, who were demanding reforms. Schism, which focused on the question of the sacraments but which had many social implications, also split his ranks, largely under the leadership of Zwingli. On the other hand, Luther's churches gained in coherence and discipline, and there was a gradual increase in the support by the middle and governing classes in Germany. Luther was an extremely able pamphleteer and swung state after state to his support. "The appeal was to the upper and middle classes, sufficiently educated to discard some of the medievalism of the Roman Church and impelled also by nationalism and economic self-interest to turn from the tyranny of the pope."[25] Within fifty years Scandinavia, most of Germany, parts of Hungary, Poland, most of Switzerland, and Great Britain had declared for the "gospel"; then the sudden expansion stopped, and actually began to reverse itself, as the Counter-Reformation, under the leadership of the Jesuits, gained strength.

As suggested above, Luther's intellectual orientation was entirely medieval. Although many of his contemporaries were beginning to question traditional doctrines, "he remained entirely without intellectual difficulties, finding no trouble with the most extreme supernaturalism and the crassest superstitions of the current faith."[26] His views on economic questions were equally traditional. He emphasized the idea of the just price and opposed usury more vigorously than the canon law itself. He waged war on the early manifestations of capitalism—large-scale commerce, the luxury trade with India, financial speculations, commercial companies—championing in their stead, frugality, love, and trust in Providence.[27] It is clear that the energy and business rationality of the capitalist are not trust in Providence. (But the church also discovered that trust was not enough to secure the satisfaction of earthly needs: in view of the obvious plight of the poor, it had to return to the practice of charity.) Luther wrote:

> I do not see many good manners that have ever come into a land through commerce, and therefore God let the people of Israel dwell far from the sea and not carry on much trade.
>
> But without doubt the greatest misfortune of the Germans is buying on usury. . . . The devil invented this system, and the Pope has done an injury to the whole world by sanctioning it. . . . Doubtless we should also find some bridle for the Fuggers and similar companies. . . . I am not skilled in accounts, but I do not understand how it is possible for one hundred guilders to gain twenty in a year, or how one guilder can gain another, and that not out of the soil, or by cattle, seeing that possessions depend not on the wit of men, but on the blessing of God. . . . All I know is that it were much more godly to encourage agriculture and lessen commerce; and that they do the best who, according to the Scriptures, till the ground to get their living. . . .[28]

To understand Luther's position with respect to trade, however, one must remember that the economic setting in which he lived was far from modern. There were only beginnings of modern capitalism, and these did more to disrupt the "natural economy" than to bring wealth to the masses. Production was for a small market, money was unimportant in the traditional rural economy, commerce and finance were occasional incidents rather than the key elements in the economic system.[29] Against departures from this "natural state of things" Luther spoke with vigor. The greed, the restless competition for gain which was beginning to appear, upset the stability of the existing order and left confusion.

Luther was conscious of his hostility to the tendencies of his age in economic matters, but he was convinced that the medieval economic ethic was the only one that harmonized with the Christian ethic of love, trust in God, and renunciation of the world. Competition, a calculating spirit, and individualism, he felt, were opposed to it. "Luther's revolt against authority," writes Tawney, "was an attack not on its rigor, but on its laxity and corruption." Like some contemporary Catholics, he was a "reactionary radical," not seeking to establish a new equalitarian society, but to solidify the old against the disorganizing effects of new developments. He completely accepted the traditional social hierarchy, "though he knocked away the ecclesiastical rungs in the ladder."[30]

Lutheranism made no direct attempt to mold society according to Christian ideals. It retired behind the battle line of external events into a citadel of religious freedom. When Luther heard of a declaration that serfs ought to be freed, he wrote:

> There ought to be no serfs because Christ has set us all free. What then is that? This means Christian freedom would be quite carnal—did not Abraham and other patriarchs and prophets also have bondmen? Read St. Paul and what he teaches about the servants who in his time were all slaves! Therefore, this article is clean against the Gospel and sheer robbery, for every man who considers his body thus his own has stolen it from the master . . . a serf can, indeed, be a Christian and have Christian freedom. . . .[31]

Luther was not simply bowing to the ways of this world: he thought religiously and therefore was not concerned with the dualistic interpretation of acts. At first his thought had much in common with the sect-type; but gradually, amid many contradictions, he came to support the church. Radical Christianity, from his point of view, emphasized good works instead of grace, and that was what he was opposing: ". . . divine grace is only obscured by human effort." It is clear to see that such a position could lead to a kind of quietism, an unquestioning acceptance of the *status quo*. "The happy and docile humility which accepts the grace of the forgiveness of sins increasingly resembles the humility which accepts the conditions appointed by God. . . ."[32]

It is not to be supposed that Lutheranism, because it was so strongly influenced by its environment and yet detached from it, had no influence in turn on social currents. Lutheranism prospered because it appeared at a time when it harmonized—or could be made to harmonize—with the political tendencies, and because, by its extreme religiosity, it did not conflict openly with prevailing powers. It became an almost pure church-type with practically no radical sect tendencies, and thus became a great bulwark to the sixteenth-century *status quo*. That Luther's situation was not conducive to some kind of a church-sect reconciliation (such as existed in medieval Catholicism, and to a degree in Calvinism) has not been unimportant in the later history of Germany. The frequent appearance of sects and the relative slowness of Germany to develop beyond the feudal period are both partly associated with this fact.[33] A church, once established, is an important factor in a social situation. The original success of Lutheranism may have been made possible by the sixteenth-century German environment, but once established it exerted a counterinfluence. Its emphasis on spiritual individualism, according to Troeltsch, is traced in a great deal of German thought, in Kant and Goethe. Though Lutheranism prospered under the tutelage of the growing state, it in turn reinforced the position of states by deifying government and renouncing ecclesiastical independence. In economics it helped to preserve middle-class traditionalism. In the main, Lutheranism worked to preserve established society and did little toward achieving a new social order.

An important distinction, with reference to the power of religious groups, must be repeated at this point. These influences of Lutheranism were not primarily religious. There is no denying the power of religious symbolism and feeling to reinforce the secular *status quo* or even to implement the emergence of new secular powers. But that is quite a different thing from power to control the behavior of men according to the religious idea. On this score, the power of Lutheranism, as of other churches, assumes much smaller proportions.

The Early Development of Capitalism

Before going further with the interpretation of the development of Protestantism (particularly in its important Calvinistic phase), we must retrace our steps in order to outline very briefly the early developments in what was to become "modern economic society." Although our primary task is to interpret the relationship between the emergence of Protestantism and the emergence of capitalism, it is clear that each of these movements had elements which were quite independent of the other. We have already noted this in connection with Luther's work; certainly no less can be said regarding the evolution of capitalism. No competent scholar—above all, not Weber—has tried to correlate the appearance of capitalism solely with the influence of Calvinism. We shall be at pains to interpret the significance of the area in which these two movements do overlap. But in order not to be misunderstood, we list here some of the many important sources of capitalistic development which have nothing to do with religion.

There are almost as many prime causes given for the origin of capitalism as there are authors dealing with the subject. Sombart, who lays great stress on the development of accurate calculation, in *Der Moderne Kapitalismus* wrote that if he were to give a definite birth date for modern capitalism, he would choose 1202. In that year Leonardo Pisano's *Liber Abbaci,* a book which made exact business calculations possible, appeared. In the same year Venice began the attack on Constantinople and thus opened up an era of exploitation and the accumulation of money. This suggests also that the Crusades were important in developing capitalism. They required large capital to equip the band and were, in fact, a commercial undertaking in part; they brought in booty which was one of the chief sources of capital stores at the time. The rise of a financial science which the Crusades stimulated allowed capital to become impersonal and abstract; the accountant provided the rational basis for making capital mobile. Because the transportation of specie was dangerous and difficult, the development of the bill of exchange, which was widely in use before the Reformation, was a big advance. Double-entry bookkeeping, bills of lading, and drafts came to be widely used, especially by Italian merchants. Robertson, drawing from Sombart, writes:

> It was only by means of the clarifying process brought in by systematic book-keeping that the various elements of a man's property came to be distinguished and the amassing of wealth was seen to consist in the alterations of these elements one to another—the very conception of capital as "lucrative possessions" practically depends on the analysis of scientific accounting: "One can define capital straight away as the wealth set aside for gain comprehended by means of double-entry book-keeping."[34]

Systematic bookkeeping made clearer the acquisitive ends of commerce; it swept away the mercantile traditionalism which overlay the "natural" propensity to barter. Of course the question immediately arises: Is the appearance of accurate accounting techniques a cause or a result of the development of capitalism? Undoubtedly the development of accounting methods is in part an expression of the needs of an already existing economic situation. The point that Robertson is making is that accounting, once developed, had a reciprocal effect on economic change.

Preserved Smith, noted historian of the Reformation, gives a different factor as the most important one in the appearance of capitalism. He stresses the purely mechanical influence of the increase in the production of precious metals: "Wealth could not be stored at all in the Middle Ages save in the form of specie; nor without it could large commerce be developed, nor large industry financed, nor was investment possible. Moreover the rise of prices consequent on the increase of the precious metals gave a powerful stimulus to manufacture and a fillip to the merchant and to the entrepreneur such as they have rarely received before or since. It was, in short, the development of the power of money that gave rise to the money power."[35] With the appearance of money, banking developed, and along with it came great fortunes. The Genoese bankers, who invented the first substitutes for money in the form of circulating notes and bills of exchange, made huge profits and won a position of power in the growing commercial enterprise.

Certainly one may list as important causes of the growth of capitalism the invention of printing, the development of rational structures of law and administration and of modern science (points which Weber emphasizes), and more directly the discoveries. Out of this last there came a greatly augmented supply of precious metals, and an increase in trade, as new markets and a new source of supplies were opened. The opening of the Atlantic and Indian oceans after the discoveries did for England what the reopening of the Mediterranean after the Crusades had done for the nations on its shores.

Although this list is in no way exhaustive, it suggests some of the factors operating in the development of capitalism before the appearance of Protestantism. Regarding these there is very little dispute. Weber has changed the level of the argument, however, by making a distinction between these objective factors and what he has called "the spirit of capitalism." He did not assume that the Protestant ethic was the only source even of the capitalistic spirit; and it may be well to discuss briefly some of the nonreligious influences that contributed to the capitalist mentality before we investigate the religious influence. (Thus we postpone once again coming to grips with the heart of the argument regarding the relation between capitalism and Protestantism. We are still dealing with relations which are fairly well agreed upon and in harmony with sociological concepts.)

It is a widely accepted generalization among sociologists that migration and culture contact are an important cause of a "secular" mode of thought and a stimulus to the development of rationality, as contrasted with the "sacred," traditional thought patterns of an isolated culture group.[36] The relationship between culture contact and the breakdown of social control and the loosening of traditional restraints was not lost on many ancient thinkers. The Hebrew prophets, Plato, Aristotle, Lucretius, to mention only a few, saw, usually with regret, the secularizing effects of contact with other peoples. The history of Greece is made meaningful in the light of this concept. One may go so far as to say that no one generalization has received so much brilliant confirmation and aided so much in interpretation in the whole of sociology as the concept dealing with the progressive "secularization" of human life, under the impact largely of the contact (and conflict) of cultures. One need only mention the names of Comte, Spencer, Maine, Tönnies, Weber, Durkheim, and others, to substantiate this statement. It is not surprising, therefore, that the greatly accelerated pace of culture contact after the Crusades and the discoveries should have stimulated the appearance of a secular and rational mode of thought among the people affected. And in so far as these qualities of thought are part of the "spirit of capitalism," one may trace its origin to the purely mundane factor of culture contact.[37]

This relationship has not been missed by those who are trying to trace the origin of the spirit of capitalism. Robertson writes:

> . . . the consequent expansion of commerce meant a necessary expansion of ideas. An alteration in the typical attitude towards making

one's living had to follow an alteration in the typical ways by which important sections of the population actually earned their living. When Florence, Genoa, Venice and the other Italian cities were busily engaged in expanding trade in the Mediterranean they were centres of a capitalistic and individualistic movement of which the Renaissance formed a part. It seems likely that the expansion of trade in the Atlantic and Indian Oceans was a prime cause of the growth of economic individualism in Western Europe in the sixteenth and seventeenth centuries. The emergence of economic individualism, making the spirit of capitalism a respectable basis for the organization of economic effort, rests upon the severely practical ground of the existence of forms of social organisation favourable to it.[38]

Fanfani takes quite a similar position, but adds his regrets concerning the effects of trade on belief: "It is the waning of faith that explains the establishment of a capitalistic spirit in a Catholic world, but in a certain sense it is the establishment of the capitalistic spirit that brings about a waning of faith."[39] St. Thomas did not exaggerate, in terms of his own values, when he saw in the merchant the greatest danger to "civil life," and his fear of trade was justified, for it brought in many foreigners, who, as Aristotle had observed, corrupt national customs.

> Faced with foreign customers, the merchant is withheld from pushing competitive methods to their extreme limit only by the power of law. . . . "No sooner did a city begin to break through the narrow circle that had hitherto circumscribed its life and the horizons of its citizens, no sooner did some of these dare the risks of the trade in far countries, where they found wholly new opportunities of gain, where their audacity opens new horizons to the produce of the city, bringing about the growth of industry for export, than the doctrine of the just mean, of blessed mediocrity, loses all its force." . . . It was the international trade ventures that did most to favour the rise of the capitalist spirit. . . . The characteristics of capitalism are precisely the following: the adoption of an economic criterion as criterion of order; failure to consider third persons; a quest for purely individual profit.[40]

Here, indeed, is an important source of the capitalist spirit. Later we shall see in what measure this interpretation contradicts and in what measure supplements Weber's thesis regarding the origin of the spirit of capitalism. The "extension of the market" theory, meanwhile, is given support from an entirely different direction in the well-known article of John R. Commons[41] on the history of the shoemakers in the United States. The purpose of this article is to illustrate the wedge which was driven between the journeyman and the master shoemaker and finally between the merchant-manufacturer and the worker as a result of the extension of the market.[42] While Commons seeks thus to describe the origins of modern trade unionism, his article also brilliantly illustrates the inevitable business rationality which is forced on the emerging capitalist by the pressure of out-of-town, out-of-state, and finally out-of-country competition.[43]

Thus briefly we describe some of the many sources of modern capitalism and the spirit which surrounds it. The question now emerges: How are the two movements, Protestantism and capitalism, related? This will be the central concern of our discussion of Calvinism. A brief account of some of its doctrines will complete our survey of the evolution of Protestantism and introduce us to its relation with capitalism.

Calvinism

Although in terms of the origination of Protestant Reformed doctrine, Zwingli ought probably to be given a more important place than Calvin, for our problem of the development and influence of that doctrine, Calvin is more significant, for he was the great organizer of the church. There is very little in his teachings, however, for which ample authority cannot be found in his predecessors. Not only did he retain a strong measure of pure Catholic traditionalism, but he also borrowed from Luther, Zwingli, Bucer, and even Erasmus. It is not necessary for our purposes to undertake a statement of his theological system; we are interested only in certain doctrines which had special importance for the secular life of his time, particularly economic activity. Consequently, we shall deal with only those aspects of his system which will serve to introduce us to the problem of the relation between Calvinism and capitalism.

At the center of Calvin's teaching was the doctrine that the sole purpose of the universe was the glorification of God, who was known to man only by divine revelation. God had created the world and put man in it only that he might be glorified. To carry out this doctrine, Calvin worked out an elaborate casuistry, which defined the proper rule for every act in rather great detail—a new legalism which restored in part the dominant place of the church, so much weakened by early Lutheranism. In many ways Calvin became the St. Thomas of Protestantism: he demonstrated the same genius for balancing opposing tendencies in Christian doctrine that St. Thomas had shown three centuries before, and thus was able to develop the second great Christian social system. Calvin combined the principles of authority and individualism, compulsion and initiative, aristocracy and democracy. The result of this combination was to give the system great influence and great flexibility, for like Thomism, though perhaps less successfully, it combined the main ideas of both church and sect.[44] In his famous *Institutes of the Christian Religion,* Calvin succeeded in summing up most of Protestant doctrine and practice. Its comprehensiveness and clarity, its attempt to develop a complete and infallible dogma gave to the work a place in Protestant theology very similar to the place of the *Summa* of Aquinas in Catholic doctrine.

Calvin took over from Luther, with modifications, a new idea of asceticism. From the start, asceticism had had a dual significance: metaphysical condemnation of the world and rational control of the senses. Both aspects were present in Catholicism, which placed the life of the ascetic along side and above the life of the world. Protestantism, however, discarded this dualism. (At a later stage we shall discuss the significance of this discarding.) Its ideal became spiritual detachment from the world combined with victory over it, *while remaining in the world:* every man became a monk. Protestantism recognized all secular means, but only as means, as valuable to the achievement of the holy community. It insisted, however, that all of these activities be kept under control by rigorous discipline and limitation of the sense life; for Calvin's ideal of the Christian life was exceedingly stern. There were, in Calvin, both a strong emphasis on other-worldiness and a demand for abstinence from the frivolities and luxuries of this world.

The doctrine of predestination was very important in Calvin's thought. This was not unique with him, of course, for most Protestants at that time considered it to be a necessary part of the doctrine of justification by faith alone and the only adequate safeguard against the Catholic theory of human merit. The important thing about Calvin's use of the doctrine of predestination was that he made it an integral part of a complete system of theology. By itself it might have been modified rapidly, as indeed it was in Lutheranism. "But Calvin gave it an essential place in a system whose controlling principle was the majesty and might of God. As a result to reject or even to minimise it seemed to limit God and throw contempt upon him."[45]

Calvin stood on common ground with other Protestant leaders in his defense of the Bible as the final authority, his claim that the true priesthood is the priesthood of all believers, his contention that justification by faith can alone bring salvation. His use of this last doctrine, however, gave it a new significance, for he coupled it with the idea that good works, although not a means to grace, were yet proofs of its presence: "We are justified not without, and yet not by works." In an age when the most important thing in life, as Weber points out, was the assurance of eternal salvation, these teachings of Calvin inevitably had important consequences for the secular life as well as for religious behavior. These consequences are by no means easy to trace, and must be studied as parts of an interacting situation involving many factors. The study of their role in the development of modern capitalism—which is our next problem—can throw a flood of light on the problem of causation in history, the place of ideas in social change, and more particularly on the typical behavior of religious groups when confronted with a new situation. Weber's *Protestant Ethic and the Spirit of Capitalism* will be a valuable point of focus in this discussion, because of its insights and its mistakes, and also because of the controversial literature which has been written with reference to it. It should be noted that our aim is not so much to refute Weber, or to validate his thesis—for we are interested in a somewhat different problem—as it is to show the value of our conceptual scheme in clearing up much of the confusion which surrounds his thesis, both in his own treatment and that of his critics, and also to develop further our typology of religious group behavior. In the discussion other elements of Calvinist doctrine that relate to our problem will be developed.

Chapter IV

CALVINISM AND THE RISE OF CAPITALISM

Weber's thesis, in brief, is this: Capitalism, defined as the pursuit of profit and the use of roundabout methods of production, is of course practically universal. The kind of capitalism found in the Occident since the sixteenth century, however, is quite distinct from this general type. It is the pursuit of profit and ever renewed profit by means of rational enterprise, the organization of (formally) free labor, and a careful system of accounting, all initially accompanied by a rigorous asceticism, self-control, and rationalism. Weber holds that it is not sufficient to explain the technical conditions which made capitalism possible, but that one must, if he is to understand the special quality of modern capitalism, also explain the ideological conditions. It is to solve this phase of the problem that Weber studies the Protestant ethic. He concludes that the Protestants developed an ascetic economic rationalism because of the "permanent intrinsic character of their religious beliefs," as well as their temporary external historico-political situation. He supports this conclusion with several carefully reasoned arguments.

Weber points out that business leaders and owners of capital, technicians, commercially trained people "are overwhelmingly Protestant." This may be explained historically: those sections of Europe which were most highly developed economically, especially the wealthy towns, went over to Protestantism in the sixteenth century. But why, asks Weber, were these highly developed communities favorable to the Reformation? It did not mean less church interference in life, but more, for Protestantism extended to all departments of life—"the unexampled tyranny of Puritanism." Why were the rising middle classes heroic in its defense? Weber attributes this rather surprising fact to the nature of Protestantism, particularly Calvinism, which not only has an affinity for the modern business world, but actually furnished economic enterprise with a dynamic which accounts for the peculiarly ascetic and vigorous quality of its rationalism.

In his essay Weber seeks not so much to explain the origin of capitalism as to account for the ethical and philosophical presuppositions which give the system its special character. To accomplish this task, he makes a distinction between capitalism and the capitalist spirit. The spirit is characterized by great energy and initiative. It makes work an end in itself and seeks to bring it under the control of rational judgment and precise calculation. Every minute is considered valuable, and scientific advances are esteemed for their contribution to efficiency and rationality. Such a point of view is quite in contrast with the spirit of traditionalism, which regards work only as a means to the achievement of various ends—the enjoyment of ease, the maintenance of status, and the like. On noting the prevalence of the capitalist spirit in Calvinist countries, Weber was led to the hypothesis that it was precisely the religious ethic which encouraged the new spirit, and that, therefore, the ethic was important in the development of an ideological foundation for capitalism.

Like Sombart, Weber uses Benjamin Franklin as the prototype of his Calvinist capitalist. Aside from a possible injustice to Franklin (for Weber apparently draws only from *Poor Richard's Almanac* and some parts of the *Autobiography*), this serves as a good typological description. With Franklin, time was money; waste of either time or money was not simply foolishness; it was a sin—forgetfulness of duty. His morality was utilitarian, however: Be honest because it is thrifty to be honest, and if the appearance of honesty suffices, one need do no more:

> . . . all Franklin's moral attitudes are coloured with utilitarianism. Honesty is useful, because it assures credit; so are punctuality, industry, frugality, and that is the reason they are virtues. A logical deduction

from this would be that where, for instance, the appearance of honesty serves the same purpose, that would suffice, and an unnecessary surplus of this virtue would evidently appear to Franklin's eyes as unproductive waste. And as a matter of fact, the story in his autobiography of his conversion to those virtues, or the discussion of the value of a strict maintenance of the appearance of modesty, the assiduous belittlement of one's own deserts in order to gain general recognition later, confirms this impression.[1]

In this rigorous pursuit of gain, however, there was no hedonism, according to Weber; that lack was its most distinguishing trait. Acquisition per se was the *summum bonum.*

Now how, asks Weber, could such an ethic arise in face of the entirely contradictory traditional ethic? In medieval theory, all economic activity was for a moral end; trade was counted necessary, but dangerous to the soul; finance, if not immoral, was at best sordid. The trader was surrounded by restriction; the middleman was the focus of persecution and public indignation. The medieval doctrine held that the craftsmen who made the goods and the merchants who transported them were entitled to a payment. But the unpardonable sin, as Tawney says, "is that of the speculator or the middleman, who snatches private gain by the exploitation of public necessities. The true descendant of the doctrines of Aquinas is the labor theory of value. The last of the schoolmen was Karl Marx."[2] In the Calvinist regions, however, in contrast to this traditional view, it appears that pursuit of private wealth is not only permitted, but encouraged, and the traditionalism that restricted enterprise is gone. How is this to be explained?

One must not think that in attempting to solve this problem of the breakdown of the traditional viewpoint, Weber disregarded all the important economic factors which contributed to the development of capitalism. He states in his Introduction:

> It is . . . our first concern to work out and to explain genetically the special peculiarity of Occidental rationalism, and within this field that of the modern Occidental form. Every such attempt at explanation must, recognizing the fundamental importance of the economic factor, above all take account of economic conditions.[3]

Capitalism certainly would have appeared without Calvinism. Moreover, the stimulus which the religious ethic gave to business activity, according to Weber, was entirely unforeseen and unintended.[4] He does not try to equate the growth of capitalism simply with Protestantism. His task is to ascertain "whether and to what extent religious forces have taken part in the qualitative formation and the quantitative expansion of that spirit [capitalism] over the world."[5] Would the modern economic system have had the ascetic self-discipline, the freedom from so many traditional restraints, the utilitarianism, had it not had the religious sponsorship of Calvinism? That is his question.

Weber directed his attention to this side of the picture because he believed that one-sided historical materialism was giving a distorted view of the historical process. He contended that the development of economic rationalism depends not only upon favorable technical or material conditions but also upon the disposition to adopt certain types of conduct.

When these types have been obstructed by spiritual obstacles, the development of rational economic conduct has also met serious inner resistance. The magical and religious forces, and the ethical ideas of duty based upon them, have in the past always been among the most important formative influences on conduct.[6]

. . . the religious valuation of restless, continuous, systematic work in a worldly calling, as the highest means to asceticism, and at the same time the surest and most evident proof of rebirth and genuine faith,[7] must have been the most powerful conceivable lever for the expansion of that attitude toward life which we have here called the spirit of capitalism.[8]

Magic is one of the "spiritual obstacles" that may block new developments. The absence of almost all magical beliefs from Calvinism, according to Weber, is one of the reasons for its congeniality with capitalism. Note the opposite effects of Hindu religion:

Every new technical process which an Indian employs signifies for him first of all that he leaves his caste and falls into another, necessarily lower. Since he believes in the transmigration of souls, the immediate significance of this is that his chance of purification is put off until another re-birth. He will hardly consent to such a change. An additional fact is that every caste makes every other impure. In consequence, workmen who dare not accept a vessel filled with water from each other's hands, cannot be employed together in the same factory room. Not until the present time, after the possession of the country by the English for almost a century, could this obstacle be overcome. Obviously, capitalism could not develop in an economic group thus bound hand and foot by magical beliefs.[9]

In Christian countries the capitalistic spirit also had to fight its way through the traditionalism that opposed it. Sombart gives as the two leading principles in economic history, needs and acquisition. The former, observes Weber, is traditionalism; the latter is capitalism; and one destroys the other. For instance, production in the textile industry on the Continent was traditional prior to 1850; price, quality, hours of work were matters of custom. There came into the scene, however, some traders who were looking for profit (acquisition, not needs); they took large orders in advance, supervised their worker-peasants rigorously, cut prices. Others were forced to do the same, with the result that the old leisurely way of life gave way to a hard frugality; the peasants became workers. In those regions where a spirit of traditionalism still prevails, raising a man's piece wage will not increase his output, but decrease it, for he will work only enough to maintain his traditional wage. It was this spirit that caused much of the dislike of Methodist workmen in the eighteenth century: they were willing to work long hours; they were "scabs" in the eighteenth-century trade union—which was traditionalism.

How was Calvinism so powerful in helping to break through the prevailing spirit of the times? Largely, says Weber, through the idea of a calling—one's place in God's ordained world, which one must fill with righteous ambition. Calling was given a secular significance by Luther, who, by evaluating the fulfilling of one's worldly duty as a moral activity, gave everyday activity a religious tone. Luther's view, however, was largely traditionalistic: God appointed man to a station in life that he should accept and fulfill. "Every man should abide by his living and let the godless run after gain." In Calvinism, however, it was the godly who ran after gain, for by the acquisition of worldly goods a man could both glorify God and prove to himself and the world that he was of God's elect. Work became important for its own sake. The ancient dualism in asceticism[10] (condemnation of the world and rational control of the senses) was dropped, for asceticism come to mean rational control of the sense in the world.[11]

Calvin's interpretation of the doctrine of predestination was also an important factor in stimulating worldly activity, according to Weber. While this doctrine can lead to quietism, it seemed to have had the opposite effect on Calvinists. In their eagerness to discover whether or not they were of the elect, whether they were in God's favor, they strove diligently at worldly tasks. Tawney observes:

> It is not wholly fanciful to say that on a narrower stage but with not less formidable weapons, Calvin did for the *bourgeoisie* of the sixteenth century what Marx did for the proletariat of the nineteenth, or that the doctrine of predestination satisfied the same hunger for an assurance that the forces of the universe are on the side of the elect as was to be assuaged in a different age by the theory of historical materialism.[12]

Thus Calvinism gave succeeding ages "an amazingly good conscience" in the acquisition of money. The modern asceticism which it stimulated was far removed, because of its rationalism, from the otherworldly asceticism of the Middle Ages. The feature which distinguishes Occidental civilization most sharply from all others is its rationalism; and this owes, according to Weber, much of its influence to this religious expression. He held that this ascetic, worldly rationalism, an outgrowth of religious ideas, was one of the most important factors in the development of capitalism.[13] Weber criticizes Sombart, however, for equating the rise of capitalism with the rise of rationalism as a whole, for in many Catholic regions the rationalism of Voltaire, for instance, was accepted without any accompanying capitalistic spirit. Although in the France of Louis XIV the economic techniques of production were developed, the capitalistic spirit did not arise. And there still exists in a France a *rentier* class, whose ideal of early retirement on a modest income is abhorrent to the Calvinist who glorifies work for work's sake. Weber noted that there are fewer Catholics in German higher education; and they are given a classical, not a technical, training for the most part. It is also strange, he says, that in Germany the Catholics, unlike most minority groups (the Huguenots, Jews, and Quakers), did not go into large-scale business. Note the proverbial piety *and* wealth of the Quakers and Mennonites.[14] Weber suggests that there is a relation between training in a pious home and commercial success (Cecil Rhodes, for instance). "Even the Spaniards knew that heresy (i.e., the Calvinism of the Dutch) promoted trade. . . ."[15]

Weber's whole thesis is made clearer when one understands that the essay was written, in part at least, as a protest against the widespread acceptance of historical materialism as an explanation of social reality. Weber was convinced that the Marxian formula gave a one-sided and therefore distorted view of the rise of capitalism. He insisted that the religious and ethical ideas of Calvinism, along with economic factors, must also be taken into account. These ideas, moreover, are not to be treated simply as reflexes of material conditions, but as immanent developments within the religious realm, and at least partially independent. Their conjuncture with the other forces making for modern capitalism was in the first place a "historical accident," to use Weber's phrase, which cannot be accounted for by even the most perfect analysis of the logical unfolding of the purely economic tendencies. The Protestant ethic "*through the processes of its own internal dynamic development* . . . , in a manner quite unforeseen by its founders, had the practical effect of creating attitudes which could not but powerfully further types of activity of the greatest importance to economic life."[16] The significance and implications of this conception of Calvinism's precapitalistic internal development will be shown later.

We should keep in mind that Weber's essay was not a general theory of the "cause" of modern capitalism, but simply an attempt to show that the Protestant ethic could be assigned an important place, along with many other factors, in the development of capitalism.

From Calvin to "Calvinism"

Having stated Weber's thesis briefly, without much comment, we must now see how well it can stand up under the scrutiny of historical fact and our conceptual system. It should be noted that our purpose is not so much to validate or refute Weber as it is to draw from the discussion an analysis of the relationship between capitalism and Protestantism that will test the usefulness of the theoretical structure we are using in the study of religious phenomena. For the most part, Weber's observations of fact appear to be accurate; our concern is with the meaning of those facts for the sociology of religion.

We have noted above that there is an implicit dualism in Christian teachings which prevents, except at rare moments in history, the achievement of a stable equilibrium in religious organization. This inherent disequilibrium, or tendency to schism, is least obvious in the work and teachings of the great religious leaders, because they, being almost wholly preoccupied with a religious view of life, tend to think in terms of only one standard of conduct for all of life, religious and secular. Among their followers, however, where religious loyalties tend to be less complete, the attempt of religion to inclose the secular realm, to control men's other interests, runs into severe difficulties. Activity is divided, by most individuals, into religious and secular spheres[17] —a division the prophet or other religious leader does not make in such a sharp way—and the influence of religion is limited by the other interests as they express themselves in the particular social setting. In other words, the religious power has to compete with other powers when it attempts to deal with the lives of any but the most religious. As we have shown, there are two typical methods of carrying on this competition. The more usual one is for the religious leaders to recognize the strength of secular interests, to avoid direct criticism of the *status quo* (even though it does not correspond to their fondest hopes), to accept it, instead, as "relative natural law" that must be dealt with and is essential for order. It is not surprising that those who are at the center of influence in a society should thus control the religious power as they control other powers. That control, however, does not eliminate the influence of religion. Religious tendencies are also part of man's "nature," as interpreted in Chapter I, or one of the "interests," to use Weber's term. Consequently even the church-type religious institution involves a continuous challenge to unethical (in its definition) behavior *within the basic structure of the society which it accepts.* Although it may not challenge slavery, for instance, the church will insist upon kindly treatment of slaves; it may not object to rational, competitive pursuit of gain, but it will demand generosity and personal frugality from the rich. The religious power is captured by the ruling class, but only after they have paid—and continue to pay—some heed to its demands.[18]

If they pay very little heed to the ethical demands of the dominant religion of their society, the ruling class is likely to be faced with a sect movement, which appears among those who suffer from the failure. The sect is far less solicitous of the *status quo,* because it is composed of persons who have no great share in it. The strength of this sect movement varies with the extent to which those in power desert the ethical demands of the religion; it varies with the presence or absence of some kind of power for the disinherited (if historical developments are putting them into a position of greater power, the sect movement can grow into a veritable religious revolution which overthrows the church and establishes the sect in its place—the sect in turn becomes a church); it varies with the quality of its leadership; and it varies with the strength of religious symbolism at the time (Marxism might be called a nonsupernaturalistic sect movement).

Church and sect thus make opposite interpretations of the inherent dualism of Christian teachings. If a religious movement spreads to a larger and larger group and moves away from the religious preoccupation and fervor of its founders, to become involved as one factor among others in the daily lives of its members, it becomes adjusted to suit the needs of the people who come in contact with it. The nature of the adjustment is of great importance in determining the influence and further spread of the movement.

These two choices—the paths of church and sect—were open to religious groups in the sixteenth century, a time of significant social change. A study of the nature of the choice made by Calvinism and of the process by which it was made—for it was a process and not an instantaneous decision—reveals a great deal of the essential relationship between religious groups and social organization. The church-sect dilemma is not at first apparent, and the leader of a movement may not recognize it. But it is revealed in the process of interaction with the social situation of the time. It is essential in connection with our problem, therefore, to study not only what Calvin taught, but what happened to Calvinism. Only in that way can we understand its relation to the development of capitalism. What was Calvinism in the sixteenth century was not Calvinism in the eighteenth, and we must know the reasons for the difference. Moreover, we cannot wholly accept the Weber-Troeltsch assumption that at the start Calvinism was largely independently determined out of an inner dialectic of religious phenomena. We must inquire into the socioeconomic setting out of which came some of the very assumptions with which Calvin *starts*. It is not likely that he would reason from premises contradictory to his time and place and still be successful. Capitalism was already fairly well under way in Geneva; or, at the least, many of the forces which were to produce capitalism were operating. It is not surprising therefore that his thought was somewhat less medieval than his predecessors'.

When Troeltsch writes: "I would rate still higher the difference which *Weber* emphasizes between Calvin and Calvinism . . . ,"[19] he is putting the case mildly, for Weber gives it too little attention.[20] As Troeltsch rightly points out, there are contradictory currents in every mass movement. This is scarcely less true of Calvinism than of the primitive church. The Geneva movement was at the same time traditional and radical, collectivistic and individualistic; it contained a sober prudence and a divine recklessness. "Primitive Calvinism is the daughter of Lutheranism." It emphasized obedience to the word of God revealed in the Bible, and stressed its connection with the primitive church. Like Lutheranism, it accepted secular culture and the idea of a calling which was the fulfilling of one's place in the divine scheme. It identified the Decalogue and law of nature. In other regards, however, primitive Calvinism had distinctive features. It had a strong element of individualism. For Luther, happiness because of the assurance of the forgiveness of sin was the important thing; but expression of the glory of God was central with Calvin—therefore, let there be activity. As we have seen, Calvinism also emphasized predestination: pure, unmerited grace as an expression of God's absolute will. And this grace fell only to the few. Luther, who had held to this doctrine in the early days, never wholly abandoned it; but under the pressure of conditions he was forced to adopt a creed which taught that grace was revocable, and able to be won and rewon by humility and faith.

Now it is of the utmost importance to discover what influences selected the teachings of Calvin that were to survive, what teachings were reinterpreted, what new doctrines added, as well as to understand the original setting which may have influenced the nature of this religious development. By means of the concept of the "church" as a type and a comprehension of the sect-to-church process, one can begin to understand the development of Calvinist teachings.

The doctrine of predestination, for instance, underwent a rather important change and development. With Calvin himself, the elect were God's invisible church. For ordinary men, however, the *recognizability* of the state of grace was of supreme importance; all men did not have Calvin's self-assurance—they wanted a visible sign of salvation. There were also institutional reasons for wanting to know who the elect were. Who were to take and administer the sacraments? For the laymen it came about, therefore, that self-assurance was the chief proof of divine grace. How could God's favor better be demonstrated to businessmen than by success in this world's activities? Worldly achievement and good works came to be, not the technical means of winning salvation, as in Catholicism, but the best way to get rid of the fear of damnation. We get, therefore, in place of the humble sinners to whom Luther promises grace, a group of self-confident saints. It is not difficult to see how, as Weber shows, this kind of doctrine leads to enterprise. In practice it becomes: God helps those who help themselves.

It is of great importance to ask at this point, however: Why did this particular solution to the problem of salvation—a solution which is not necessarily the logical development of original Calvinism—appear, in contrast to the Lutheran and Catholic solutions of the same problem? Why is it that among the various tendencies within Calvinism, those which were favorable to the rising economic system were "sorted out," so to speak, and emphasized to the minimization of other tendencies which were just as important in early Calvinism? Why did not the quietistic tendencies, to which predestination can as logically lead, prevail instead of its stimulating effects?[21] This may be explained in terms of the origin of Calvinism and its setting. What could be more convincing to a businessman, who also was seriously interested in his eternal salvation, than that worldly success was a sign of God's favor? (Just as vast numbers of the poor had been taught for centuries, and continued to be taught by Calvin, Baxter, and other churchmen, that their salvation was the better because of their worldly "failure.") It was not inevitable in the logic of the idea nor in Calvin's use of it that the doctrine of predestination should become a stimulus to worldly success. The earlier teachings in Geneva had put severe restriction on the businessman. Calvin and the church in general preached unceasingly against unjust moneylenders and avarice. The Council of Geneva, who were businessmen, heard the ministers on thrift and simplicity, sent their children to catechism, and supported the church. On business matters, however, they were obdurate. They were glad to invoke the sanction of religion on traits which their secular activity found valuable—honesty, industry, sobriety, as well as the dynamic interpretation of predestination. But, as H. R. Niebuhr points out, the less useful virtues of solidarity, sympathy, and fraternity were ignored.[22] The ministers did not capitulate to the businessmen; but those who emphasized the elements in the all-embracive Calvinist doctrine which were in tune with the times secured an audience and prospered. Calvin himself, unlike Luther, was a man of affairs. His movement was an urban movement. Although he preached against the dangers of riches and commerce, he started with the assumption that they were an acceptable part of the Christian order. ". . . the Geneva situation helped determine Calvin's political, social, and economic ideal. . . ."[23]

> As was to be expected in the exponents of a faith which had its headquarters at Geneva, and later its most influential adherents in great business centers, like Antwerp, with its industrial hinterland, London and Amsterdam, its leaders addressed their teaching, not of course exclusively, but none the less primarily, to the classes engaged in trade and industry, who formed the most modern and progressive elements in the life of the age.
>
> In doing so they naturally started from a frank recognition of the necessity of capital, credit and banking, large-scale commerce and finance, and the other practical facts of business life. . . . It is not that they abandon the claim of religion to moralize economic life, but that the life which they are concerned to moralize is one in which the main features of commercial civilization are taken for granted, and that it is for application to such conditions that their teaching is designed.[24]

Misuse, not the accumulation, of riches was declared to be the enemy of religion. Only by such a stand could Calvinism hope to have a practical influence in Geneva. Therefore, as Barnes and Becker point out: "The ethic of Protestantism was quickly and thoroughly *adapted* to the spirit of capitalism and business enterprise."[25]

Whenever the external order of society and moral precepts are in strong contrast, men seek solutions. The German reformers preached a return to primitive simplicity; the Humanists looked for the gradual victory of reason over superstition and avarice; the Calvinists tried to bridge the gulf by dedicating the qualities which economic life demanded to the glory of God, thus to put a check on individual self-seeking. This last is the church-type reaction to a moral problem—encompass any new social development within the "relative natural law," for then the church will be in a position to require that it pay heed to her teachings. The church does not thus desert its job: if it is to have any voice, it must speak to the age in which it is found. Such "compromises" as may be found in the acceptance of the existing power arrangement are simply a recognition of the possibility of only relative success.[26] The process of encompassing a new movement is not, of course, a conscious one for the most part. It is the natural result of the efforts of religious leaders to appeal to their own age and to harmonize their religious beliefs with a social organization which their own experience has led them to think normal. Robertson and others are correct in pointing out that the Catholic Church also relaxed its restrictions on a life of trade and its rules against usury.[27] We have already noted Luther's complaint that the Pope had sanctioned usury. The weight of historical evidence, however, seems to show that this relaxation was less complete in Catholic policy than among certain Protestant churches. This incompleteness may be explained by the fact that the Catholic Church was appealing to a more varied congregation, many of whom continued to live in a medieval world. As a result, she had to speak more ambiguously in order to maintain unity of principle and still appeal to all. The emerging Protestant churches, with more unified congregations from a class point of view, could afford to speak more directly in favor of the modern world.

Calvin himself shared the Lutheran view of the value of work, emphasizing its moral qualities, the need for moderation in wealth, and even the value of poverty in fostering Christian virtues. By preaching rigorous self-denial and condemning greed and profit, Calvin, especially in his early years, restricted trade and sponsored disdain of this world scarcely less than did Luther. In the *Institutes* he writes:

> With whatever kind of tribulation we may be afflicted, we should always keep this end in view, to habituate ourselves to a contempt of the present life that we may thereby be excited to meditation on that which is to come. . . . There is no medium between these two extremes, either the earth must become vile in our estimation, or it must retain our immoderate love. Wherefore if we have any concern about eternity, we must use our most diligent efforts to extricate ourselves from these fetters. . . . But believers should accustom themselves to such a contempt of the present life, as may not generate either hatred of life, or ingratitude towards God. For this life, though it is replete with innumerable miseries, is yet deservedly reckoned among the Divine blessings which must not be despised. . . . It should be the object of believers, therefore, in judging of this mortal life that, understanding it to be of itself nothing but misery, they may apply themselves wholly with increasing cheerfulness and readiness to meditate on the future and eternal life. When we come to this comparison, then indeed the former will be not only securely neglected, but in competition with the latter altogether despised and abhorred. For if heaven is our country, what is the earth but a place of exile? If the departure out of the world is an entrance into life, what is the world but a sepulchre? What is a continuance in it but an absorption in death? If deliverance from the body is an introduction into genuine liberty, what is the body but a prison? If to enjoy the presence of God is the summit of felicity, is it not misery to be destitute of it? But till we escape out of the world "we are absent from the Lord." Therefore, if the terrestrial life be compared with the celestial, it should undoubtedly be despised and accounted of no value.[28]

How far this is from a call to vigorous worldly activity to prove one's divine election! And surely if it is claimed, as Weber does, that it was not the intention of the reformers, but the unconscious and quite unexpected effects of their teachings which were crucial in producing the capitalistic spirit, then it is quite meaningless to say that the religious ethic "caused" the spirit, for in truth it was the interpretation given to the ethic that is associated with the spirit. The important question becomes, therefore, as we have been trying to show: Why was the original meaning of Calvinism interpreted in the way it was, rather than in other possible and equally "logical" ways?[29]

The process of adjustment to external circumstances is well illustrated by the English churches, which were so largely under the influence of Calvin.[30] The doctrine that Calvin himself taught differs from the doctrine of seventeenth-century England. "It is this second, individualistic phase of Calvinism, rather than the remorseless rigours of Calvin himself, which may plausibly be held to have affinities with the temper called by Weber 'the spirit of Capitalism.' The question which needs investigation is that of the causes which produced a change of attitude so convenient to its votaries and so embarrassing to their pastors."[31]

The Puritan before the Civil War in Great Britan would have been as astounded as his opponents to learn that he has been labeled a friend of unbridled economic activity. The contrast between Calvin's rigorous teachings on the one hand and the impatient rejection of traditional economics on the other was at first, as we have seen, extreme. There were tendencies in Calvinism, however, which favored capitalism, and these were encouraged by the economic and political situation. ". . . the Puritan conscience lost its delicacy where matters of business were concerned."[32] Calvin himself had fused two elements: ascetic discipline and activity. In Geneva, a small, homogeneous city, the restraining hand of discipline had dominated, although even there there was conflict. In Britain, however, a civil war gave evidence of the irreconcilability of these two aspects of Calvinism. What had been held together in the work of Calvin, because of the domination of religious motives, proved to be an unstable union in the lives of the less intensely religious. The Civil War was not a conflict between a state committed to one view and Puritanism defending another; it was the expression of a conflict within Puritanism itself. It revealed the secular divisions within the group which had temporarily been brought together in opposition to the control of the Catholic Church.

We have not undertaken, in this study, a systematic analysis of the complicated religious and political situation during the period of the Civil War in Great Britain. This in itself would prove to be a major task, but one which would certainly yield abundant rewards to the sociologist of religion.[33] The complicated alignment of religious loyalties—Catholic, supporter of the Establishment, Presbyterian, Independent, Sectarian—was by no means unrelated to the secular conflicts of the day. At first, as we have suggested above, there was a kind of unity among the groups that opposed and feared Catholicism, but when this fear was largely removed by the destruction of prelacy, the internal dissensions among the Protestant groups came to the surface; they were found to comprise both church and sect elements. The Civil War had made certain, as Petegorsky writes, "that neither an absolute king nor an absolute Church would ever again impede economic progress." "The Restoration was essentially a compromise between the aristocracy and the middle classes for the exploitation of the economic opportunities an expanding society presented."[34] Out of this compromise came a thoroughly churchlike acceptance of the new social structure. Then the lower classes became aware that they had not won a share during the long struggle of the English reformation. Puritanism had an essential inequalitarian aspect: the poor were demonstrably the nonelect. To this doctrine the disinherited raised a strong religious protest. Drawing partly on the tradition of Wycliffe, which had never been stamped out, but far more from the more radical teachings of Winstanley and others, a sectarian movement developed which has not yet spent its force. The anwer of the sectarians to the predestination doctrine of the Calvinists was to declare the equality of all persons before God. The religious doctrines of Winstanley, perhaps the most important sectarian leader of the time, were implicitly and in some ways openly class weapons: "True religion and undefiled is this, to make restitution of the Earth which hath been taken and held from the common people by the power of Conquests formerly and so set the oppressed free."[35]

In this situation, as in others, we find conflicting groups using religious arguments to support their demands. We cannot understand the sanction of later Puritanism for economic activity without seeing it in relation to the support, on the one hand, that the Establishment was giving to the king and the landed gentry and the claims, on the other hand, of the sectarians for a radical humanitarianism. Aristocratic landlord and rising bourgeoisie were as separated in belief as they were in material interest, and whenever those interests tended to merge, so did belief.[36] All of this demonstrated again "the social sources of denominationalism."

These secular divisions and conflicts were reflected in the growing inability, during the seventeenth century, to enforce the canon law. Although conservative writers denounced business as soulless individualism, their renunciations were "as futile as they were justified." The state law against usury was repealed in 1571; and even the doctrine of the Establishment was modified by the crown, which was also supreme head of the church. Churchmen fortunately were able to recall Calvin's statement that interest could not be condemned before the terms of the loan were considered. All liberal theologians declared that it was not the letter but the spirit of the law that counted. A common gibe in those days of religious conflict was, ". . . the Presbyterians, the Bank and other corporations" (Tawney).

In this struggle in England the canon law was not abolished, but nationalized, under the pressure of commercial interests, the state's own financial needs, and the logic of economic development, all of which made it impossible for the state to pursue the rigorous discipline demanded by the clergy. Tawney reports:

"When the Rev. David Jones was so indiscreet as to preach . . . a sermon against usury on the text, 'The Pharisees who were covetous heard all these things and they derided Christ,' his career in London was brought to an abrupt conclusion."[37] Capitalizing on the idea of a calling, it appeared to the businessmen that "a man can serve two masters, for—so happily is the world disposed—he may be paid by one, while he works for the other."[38]

Under such pressures, churchmen also expounded a new medicine for poverty. Penalties on the vagrant were doubled; less emphasis was put on the obligation of charity and more on the duty of work. Distress became a sign of dismerit. If character is everything, as bourgeois Calvinism found it convenient to declare, and circumstances nothing, the poor are to be condemned, not pitied, and success is to be praised. "A society which reverences the attainment of riches as the supreme felicity will naturally be disposed to regard the poor as damned in the next world, if only to justify itself for making their life a hell in this."[39] Marx asserted in the *Communist Manifesto:* "The bourgeoisie, wherever it has got the upper hand, has put an end to all feudal, patriarchal, idyllic relations. It has pitilessly torn asunder the motley feudal ties that bound man to his 'natural superiors,' and has felt no other nexus between man and man than naked self-interest, than callous 'cash payment.'"[40] In brief, individual responsibility, not social obligation, was the main trend of Puritan teaching.

Now it is not surprising that Weber, in studying this situation, should see an affinity between this kind of religious teaching and capitalism. While he may overstate his case, the relationship seems to be real. What we are attempting to investigate, however, is the process by which an early Calvinism—which we have seen was scarcely less otherworldly and restrictive on economic behavior than Catholicism—came to permit and stimulate business. This was a gradual process, involving a long struggle between traditionalism in the church and the desire to retain influence over an emerging power group. In this struggle, the traditional element continued to offer the same solutions for the resolution of human ills.[41] It tried to moralize economic relations by having every transaction treated as a case of personal moral conduct. But in an age of impersonal finance and capitalistic organization, this was often meaningless. Late Calvinism was made to reinforce capitalism, because other aspects of Calvinism tended to wither away or went unheard. Richard Baxter, whom Weber cites frequently, stands midway in the process of transition from early to late Calvinism, and consequently refutes Weber's claim as often as he validates it. ". . . he was constantly wavering between the two opposing camps of Puritanism on the one hand and its deadly enemy at that time, 'Independency,' on the other. His very influence was to some degree based upon his blowing neither too hot nor too cold to displease any, and even in Anglo-Catholic circles he was read and enjoyed."[42] Baxter, who was a man of great practical experience, is an excellent example of the way churchmen attempt to moralize from within a social order. He did not want to alienate an important group who had taken to a life of trade, with or without the church's permission, for England had already gone far toward capitalism, but neither did he give up the task of trying to control their behavior. He stressed the dangers of trade and wealth, but did not condemn them. Baxter allowed lending upon pledges, pawns, and mortgages for security, provided that it was not against something necessary to a poor man's livelihood. And the mortgage might be taken if the pledge is "among merchants and rich men." Taking of interest is also lawful when the borrower has profited by the use of the money; it is unlawful when it violates justice and charity.[43] The two great principles of justice in trade he held to be love of neighbor and self-denial. "When the tempter draweth you to think only of your own commodity and gain, remember how much more you will lose by sin, than your gain can any way amount to."[44] One gets the impression in reading his "directions for the rich" that Baxter is preaching to a group who are already, willy-nilly, involved in a life of business and wealth: he seeks only to enfold that group within the Christian doctrine.

To the poor he counsels patience, eyes on the next world, content with one's status, lack of covetousness. There the traditional element in his preaching looms large, and is a long way from giving the dynamic impetus to the capitalistic spirit that Weber held was in *the* Protestant ethic.

> We are like runners in a race, and heaven or hell will be our end; and therefore woe to us, if by looking aside, or turning back, or stopping, or trifling about these matters, or burdening ourselves with worldly trash, we should lose the race, and lose our souls. O sirs, what greater matters than poverty or riches have we to mind! Can these souls that must shortly be in heaven or hell, have time to bestow any serious thought upon these impertinencies?
>
> . . . "Stedfastly believe that, ordinarily, riches are far more dangerous to the soul than poverty, and a greater hindrance to men's salvation." Believe experience; how few of the rich and rulers of the earth are holy, heavenly, self-denying, mortified men? Believe your Saviour, "How hardly shall they that have riches enter into the kingdom of God! For it is easier for a camel to go through a needle's eye than for a rich man to enter into the kingdom of God. And they that heard it said, who then can be saved? And he said, The things which are impossible with men, are possible with God." So that you see the difficulty is so great of saving such as are rich that to men it is a thing impossible, but to God's omnipotency only it is possible.
>
> . . . Also you will be tempted to be coveting after more; satan maketh poverty a snare to draw many needy creatures, to greater covetousness than many of the rich are guilty of; none thirst more eagerly after more; and yet their poverty blindeth them, so that they cannot see that they are covetous, or else excuse it as a justifiable thing. They think that they desire no more but necessaries, and that it is not covetousness; if they desire not superfluities. But do you not covet more than God allotteth you? And are you not discontent with his allowance? And doth not he know best what is necessary for you, and what superfluous? What then is covetousness, if this be not?[45]

How far all this is removed from ascetic rational pursuit of gain! Baxter is a direct descendant of medieval doctrine. "The Christian avoids sin rather than loss." He modifies his teachings only enough—and that rather reluctantly—to bring the businessmen within the fold of the church, for only then may it have a claim upon their conduct. Baxter's work may be somewhat contradictory and ambiguous, although of the utmost sincerity; but what effective "political" action is not?

Other clergymen of the time, less subtle or sincere, or less alive to the movements of history, preached a far sterner traditionalism, calling down fire from heaven on those who called attention to abuses of landownership, declaring that they were stirring up class hatred.[46] That kind of traditionalism was disregarded for the most part, however, and those elements in Calvinism which supported the rising tide of industry received more and more attention. "Tillotson was eloquent in a sermon on the *Advantages of Religion,* proving that God increased the wealth of the godly, both by special Providence, and by making religious graces conducive to worldly success."[47] The church-type mind, having accepted the legitimacy (inevitability) of trade, was devoted to the task of controlling the new activities. Baxter's work was soon followed by a series of books attempting to encompass the economic life of the time: *The Religious Weaver, Navigation Spiritualized,* Defoe's *The Complete English Tradesman,* and Steele's *The Tradesman's Calling.* It is apparent that these men were by no means entirely successful in their aim. As Bates observes, they sought to idealize commerce, not to materialize religion, but that was not always the result: "Calvin's legalization of interest 'took with the brethren . . . like polygamy with the Turks,' and the injunction to exact interest for the sake of widows and orphans appealed to 'divers zealous ministers who themselves desired to pass for orphans of the first rank.'"[48] What interests us here, however, is the fact that religious doctrine changed, under pressure of social conditions, in an attempt to keep the church in a position where it would be heard.

This struggle between traditional economic morality and rising political and economic interests was not, of course, limited to England. Holland, the center of European commerce, witnessed a sharp controversy as a result of the refusal to admit usurers to communion. The theological faculty of Utrecht performed "prodigies of zeal and ingenuity" to solve the problem, by declaring that the church was not concerned with questions of banking.[49]

It should not be forgotten, in this discussion of the evolution of Calvinism, that the later developments in Calvinism were based on elements of the original which contained possibilities of adaption to the bourgeois-capitalist situation which Catholicism and Lutheranism possessed to no great degree. Bunyan's Mr. Badman is a medieval villain "who ground the poor with high prices and short measure," but the sanctions with which Baxter and Bunyan[50] sought to enforce their teachings were not medieval. They were not ecclesiastical discipline and sacraments, but individual conscientiousness and personal responsibility. Thus the emerging Calvinism may not have sponsored the modern world, but its approach to religious problems was such that neither did it prevent its appearance. It sought only to moralize it.[51]

Moreover, we must emphasize again that churchmen were not simply capitulating to the demands of the rising middle classes. If they were "retreating," it was a strategic retreat which had elements of victory. Schlatter, in his careful study of *The Social Ideas of Religious Leaders, 1660-1688,* makes an excellent statement of the meaning of shifts in religious doctrines:

> . . . religious leaders did not abandon the world to the world, dividing the realms of business and religion into two separate kingdoms. Looking squarely and realistically at the structure of society in seventeenth-century England, they attempted to spiritualize and control it in the interests of the Good. Experience and reason, they thought, had taught them that they could not remake that social structure, nor did they wish to do so. What they could do was maintain it, and try to alleviate whatever minor, or irremediable, defects caused injustices.
>
> In short, ministers of God wanted to see justice done within the framework of the *status quo*. . . . Since they did not wish to rebuild the house, they were not critical of the foundations. They but-

tressed the base, and gave good advice for keeping the superstructure in repair. For example, they did not condemn that usury which was a normal part of business life and which could not have been abolished without remaking the economic system; they did condemn that usury which was not so essential, and which seemed to be the result, not of impersonal economic laws, but of the rapacity of immoral men. . . . A national clergy, one of whose practical functions was to inculcate the moral rules necessary for the very existence of their society, could not be at the same time utopians or revolutionaries.[52]

Thus through a process of evolution as well as because of a measure of original congeniality, Calvinism came to be the religion of the new elite to a rather large degree, a religion which did justice to their role in life but which also put demands upon their conduct.

This discussion of the gradual modification of Calvinism through two centuries requires at the least a restatement of Weber's thesis. It is not that the relationship which he observes between Calvinism and the spirit of capitalism is nonexistent (although he probably states the case too strongly). The important thing is that when one interprets the meaning of this relationship in connection with the development of Calvinism, he finds nothing surprising about the harmony between the spirit of capitalism and Calvinist ethics. Moreover, there are limitations to the assumption of Weber and Troeltsch—and it is scarcely more than an assumption in the essay under discussion—that original Calvinism was a product of an inner religious dialectic, and that it became conjoined with capitalism only by a historical accident (the crossing of two theretofore independent causal systems). This assumption is absolutely crucial to their argument, and yet by the nature of the case it is very difficult to validate.[53] In fact, there is more than a little tendency to get this assumption in, in the early stages of the debate, as a kind of first premise, and thus to beg the whole question under dispute. That is pehaps to put the case a little too strongly, for Weber's concept of the inner development of religious ideas is part of a carefully worked-out religious typology. According to his conception, the immanent

Carl A. Rudisill Library
LENOIR RHYNE COLLEGE

development of a religion is largely the result of "prophecy," which is the religious aspect of the destruction of traditionalism, carried on under the claim of charismatic authority. This break with traditionalism is the result of a religious "interest" in interpreting the meaning of the world. The genuine prophet, according to Weber, establishes *new* obligations; he repudiates the past. His claims cannot be reduced to various secular interests; they are a primary revolutionary force.

Clearly it is very difficult to prove the immanent quality of the development of religion by prophecy. At least two questions are involved: What might be some of the social factors conditioning the appearance and the nature of prophecy? And how is the purely religious development transferred into a realm of secular influence? Weber, of course, was not unaware of these problems. He noted that the appearance of prophecy was itself dependent upon social conditions. Social crises, in which traditionalism was already being challenged, encouraged the development of prophecy. Moreover, in a differentiated society, the interpretations of the meaning of the world will vary with the interests and problems of the various classes. And the likelihood of prophecy's having a dominant influence depends upon the power of the group who become its principle adherents. On the other hand, says Weber, the prophecy would not enter the field of interaction at all were it not for a religious "interest." It cannot, therefore, be reduced to conditions which influenced it.[54]

With reference to the last point, we should accept Weber's formulation (cf. Chapter I). The other statements, however, from Weber's own presentation, seem to restrict greatly the idea of "historical accident." Is it an accident, if Calvinism appeared as a "prophecy" due to the same social unrest that was breaking down feudalism and was interpreted with reference to Geneva middle-class interests and problems, that the new doctrine should harmonize with the emerging way of life? The argument of a "historical accident" might be more convincing, moreover, were it not necessary to explain the fact that at the time Calvinism was emerging there also appeared a new legal situation, a political revolutionary tendency, a new theory of poverty and its treatment, individualistic theories in philosophy, all of which also harmonized with the capitalistic spirit. Are we to assume that these connections are the result of an amazing series of historical accidents? Or are these human products to be seen as on a different level from religious phenomena? Until these problems are more fully solved, no argument can rest solidly on this premise. It is easily conceivable that the appeal to moral action on the basis of individual character, which is characteristic of Calvinism, is the expression of the same forces that created other kinds of individualism.

We must not, however, exaggerate the extent of our criticism of Weber. It may be that he would accept most of the above discussion of the evolution of Calvinism. It is not entirely clear how large a part of the total explanation of capitalism he intended the Protestant ethic to fill. When he says only: To all other sources of capitalism Calvinism added a peculiarly rigorous and ascetic discipline and furnished ready at hand a religious dynamic that *could be made into* a stimulus of enterprise: if that is his thesis, the idea of a "historical accident" is more readily established. There is perhaps very little in the pre-Calvinistic development of capitalism that would have enabled one to predict the emergence of this peculiarly ascetic rationalism, although indeed there are some instances of it in earlier times. Such a limited interpretation of the essay, however, scarcely fulfills the herculean task of disproving the economic interpretation of the rise of capitalism, as some of its supporters claimed. Nor does it establish the basic role of Calvinism in the development of the spirit of capitalism, for it must be seen in relation to the many other factors which stimulated that spirit. Above all, one must not forget the important ways in which Calvinism was molded to fit the needs of the class who had found in it the possibilities of the kind of religious sponsorship that they required in their struggle for advancement. They would have advanced in any event; they probably would have found a religious sponsor in any event. Nevertheless, it is not unimportant that Calvin's formulations appeared when and where they did. Without them capitalism would have evolved along somewhat different lines.

The Question of Usury

In addition to the matter of the origin and evolution of Calvinism there are other related questions which can throw light on the nature of the relationship between religious teachings and secular interests. While Weber gives scant attention to the question of usury, it is not unimportant for our problem, for the development of religious doctrine on interest-taking demonstrates the adjustment of churches to new secular situations. In a local economy where self-sufficient production is the rule, persons borrow only in unusual circumstances—when they have suffered some loss by fire, theft, crop failure, and the like. Lending for gain under such circumstances was almost synonymous with extortion and oppression.[55] The Aristotelian theory that money was barren was not only accepted but largely true. It is not surprising that the church condemned all interest as sinful, although it overlooked, and thereby accepted, the transactions of merchants and governments and even of church officials, whose borrowings were obviously not expressions of immediate need.

With the growth of trade and large-scale enterprise, however, credit came to be, not an exception to the usual practice, but a normal part of business, and the old restrictions seemed more and more unreasonable. ". . . it was clear that a man who borrowed in order to speculate or take advantage of some opportunity for profit was not being oppressed."[56] How did the church deal with the new developments? The first reaction was to make the original prohibition more emphatic and universal. The Lateran Council of 1179 issued the first of a series of stringent prohibitions of usury.[57] Gradually, however, modifications appeared in the pronouncements of the church; they came as the granting of exceptions rather than the abandonment of the principle. In the early stages the taking of interest was allowed by the overlooking, if not the actual permission, of rent charges and triple contracts.[58] This did not mean, of course, the complete abandonment of the rulings against interest, but it allowed interest payments to be made where there seemed to be moral justification. This permitted the church to maintain unity of principle at the same time that it allowed flexibility of practice. It was an adjustment to the development of trade while still preserving the basic condemnation of interest-taking as it applied to the traditional economy. This is the kind of reconciliation that one would expect from the church of St. Thomas, because it had as many moral problems to solve as there were classes of people to whom it wished to appeal. If it did not capitulate quickly and easily to the demand for justifying interest-taking, the reason was that the church had among its members the vast number who still borrowed only for consumption purposes, to whom interest was a genuine injury. Medieval teachings were repeated, in spite of new economic developments, because economic conditions continued, over a wide range, to be what they had been when the teachings were first formulated.[59] Like an effective political party, the Catholic Church tried to balance the demands and needs of its various contradictory groups, so that justice would be at a maximum and so that none would be tempted to desert the fold. This is the inevitable program of any group that tries to appeal to all people.

Further modification of the doctrine of the church was made as the external situation changed, although the process of transition was very slow.[60] Calvin appeared in the midst of this process of modification of the principle of usury. It is not surprising that as a citizen of the commercial center of Geneva, as a man of affairs and associate of businessmen and traders, Calvin did not oppose the modification of principle. He wrote: ". . . by no testimony of scripture am I resolved that usuries are altogether condemned . . . we do not see usuries simply forbidden to us, unless so far as they are repugnant both to justice and charity."[61] Calvin examined the idea that money does not breed money, and decided that money lent created more, just as did money invested in a farm. To the taking of interest, however, he laid down these seven restrictions: it is wrong to exact usury from the needy, to exact from the poor more security than they can afford, to violate natural justice, to take payment for a loan that does not equally benefit the borrower; contracts must be for the benefit of the state, with no higher interest than civil authorities allow; and the fact of common usage is not justification of usury.[62]

Even this moderate justification of interest was not quickly and easily accepted by the followers of Calvin. Interest was legally prohibited in England until 1571, although there were exceptions for borrowings of the crown. Of the writers against usury listed in Blaxton's *English Usurer* (1634), most were Puritans. It was the second decade of the seventeenth century before any important Protestant writer dealt with the problem of usury in a way at all comparable with Calvin's letter of 1545. Then Johann Gerhard, a Lutheran, published his *Loci Theologici,* in which he discussed the subject at length, coming to the conclusion that only an immoderate rate of interest was usury. Not until 1631 did a Calvinist pastor (Ames) make a thorough review of the subject of usury and decide in the liberal favor.[63]

Baxter, a century and a quarter after Calvin, stands on about the same ground. Usury is a sin in most cases when it violates principles of charity, when it takes advantage of another's need. When borrowed money is put to productive use, Baxter holds that interest is justifiably taken. In the main, he holds that moral issues cannot be judged in the abstract, but only with reference to practical experience:

> As all oppression and unmercifulness must be avoided and all men must do as they would (judiciously) be done by; so it is a bad thing to corrupt religion, and fill the world with causeless scruples, by making that a sin which is no sin. Divines that live in great cities and among merchandize, are usually fitter judges in this case, than those that live more obscurely (without experience) in the country.[64]

While Catholic teachings are seldom so forthright as this regarding the necessary flexibility in moral judgments, in practice, as we have seen, they too adjusted to the new situation regarding interest. Although Calvinist churches adjusted more quickly and easily perhaps, it should be remembered that they had a far higher percentage of businessmen in their congregations. Any religious group which hoped to influence the increasingly powerful business class was forced to accept the legitimacy of interest-taking as a moral principle, for business enterprise depended more and more on credit.

Business Becomes a "Calling"

The investigation of another problem will sharpen the analysis of the relation between Protestantism and capitalism. One of the chief sources, according to Weber, of Protestant influence on the spirit of capitalism is in the concept of the calling. The religious connotations of this word are not unique with Calvinism. The whole spirit of the traditional idea that each man is in his God-appointed place, whether he be slave or king, is in harmony with the concept of the calling; thus it is part of Catholic teaching. When Cortadillo (in Cervantes's *Rinconete y Cortadillo*) remarks to the Servillian thief that he never heard of thieving by the grace of God, the thief replies: "'Sir, I am not up in theology, save that everyone can glorify God in his occupation.'"[65] The medieval Catholic concept, however, carried less of the idea of worldly duty than the modern interpretation. Luther was important in freeing the doctrine of the calling from ascetic and monastic limitations. His treatment of the subject, however, was far from revolutionary; it was tied closely to a class system, and tended to keep each individual in his class. He wrote:

> What you do in your house is worth as much as if you did it up in heaven for our Lord God. For what we do in our calling here on earth in accordance with His word and command He counts as if it were done in heaven for Him. . . . Therefore we should accustom ourselves to think of our position and work as sacred and well-pleasing to God, not on account of the position and the work, but on account of

the word and faith from which the obedience and the work flow. . . . It looks like a great thing when a monk renounces everything and goes into a cloister, carries on a life of asceticism, fasts, watches, prays, etc. . . . On the other hand, it looks like a small thing when a maid cooks and cleans and does other housework. But because God's command is there, even such a small work must be praised as a service of God far surpassing the holiness and asceticism of all monks and nuns.[66]

The importance of this emphasis given to the idea of the calling by Luther was that it gave everyday activities a religious significance; worldly activities were no longer subordinated to ascetic ones.

Now without denying that Catholic doctrine regarding the meaning of a calling underwent, as many writers claim, a transformation which fitted it also for a modern individualistic society, one can see that Calvinism, especially in its later stages, had a peculiarly dynamic conception of the calling. Weber's point here is that Calvinist doctrine was not merely negative—permitting industry, but positive—encouraging it as a religious exercise and duty. This idea of the calling which Weber calls the *conditio sine que non* of modern capitalism is a trumpet call to activity. It gave rise to the doctrine of work for work's sake. ". . . the saint of Calvinism has a roving commission, entailing unlimited liabilities and risks before God. . . . This is not, as with Luther, the stewardship of a job, of the things that are. It is not static, it is a tremendously dynamic thing. It means literally to make the best of one's self and of the world. . . . Where the calling concept of Luther demands continuous traditional performance, that of Calvin entails a principle of continuous initiative."[67]

A question of crucial importance at this point, however, concerns the consistency of this Calvinist doctrine. Weber was well aware of the evolution which the idea of the calling underwent, but he did not analyze sufficiently the sociological significance of the fact. The whole discussion above of the significance of the transition through which Calvinism went applies here. The sixteenth-century doctrine was much nearer the medieval spirit of ordered status than eighteenth-century teaching. Early Puritans used the concept of the calling ". . . almost invariably in reproof of covetousness and ambition." It was employed to combat capitalistic ambition in many cases. "It was an invitation to live the orderly and settled life ordained for one by God. . . ."[68] Weber himself notes the relatively traditional conception of Calvin on this subject:

> How far in the background of Luther's thought was the most important idea of proof of the Christian in his calling and his worldly conduct, which dominated Calvinism, is shown by this passage. . . : "Besides these seven principal signs there are more superficial ones by which the holy Christian Church can be known. If we are not unchaste nor drunkards, proud, insolent, nor extravagant, but chaste, modest, and temperate." According to Luther these signs are not so infallible as the others (purity of doctrine, prayer, etc.). "Because certain of the heathen have borne themselves so and sometimes even appeared holier than Christians." *Calvin's personal position was, as we shall see, not very different, but that was not true of Puritanism.*[69]

For our purposes it is of the utmost importance to explain this difference between Calvin and later Puritanism. Baxter as usual occupies a halfway mark. He justifies business, but holds that it should not be given too much attention and must be accompanied by generosity. As Robertson rightly observes, Baxter's treatment of the fitness of business as a calling gives the impression that Baxter's readers are already much influenced by the spirit of capitalism, and he is "trying to show good businessmen the importance of being also good Christians. . . ."[70] Baxter was trying to bring the life of commerce under the control of Christian doctrines:

> ". . . may I change my calling for the service of the church when the apostle bids every man abide in the calling in which he was called?"
>
> The apostle only requireth men to make no unlawful change . . . nor any unnecessary change. . . . No man must take up or change any calling without sufficient cause to call him to it; but when he hath

such cause, he sinneth if he change it not. . . . God nowhere forbids men to change their employment for the better, upon a sufficient cause or call.[71]

Not until the eighteenth century did the commercial ethics of English Puritanism reach the point expressed in the *New Whole Duty of Man,* and even there, and in DeFoe, there is condemnation of overstepping one's calling. Only after a long process of evolution did the doctrine of the calling cease to be "a Puritan antidote against the temptations of ambition."[72] Thus the Puritan conception of the calling and of the validity of trade as a calling seems to be, not so much an original stimulant to the development of the spirit of capitalism, as the product of two centuries of change in which the bourgeois individualism itself became traditional and a center of power. In terms of our frame of reference, the new idea of the calling was a natural result of the appearance of a great many new secular activities. Religious groups, in order to keep their influence in spite of and in face of the new developments, which they could not stop, were required to make the calling, or the worldly activity itself, imbued with religious significance. This is precisely the way the church deals with every new situation. It was the way the Catholics had already dealt with the concept of the calling; but because of the vast increase in independent secular activities after the fifteenth century, the idea had to be reinforced so strongly as to be almost different in kind from the medieval Catholic idea.

Calvinism in Many Settings

In pursuing further our study of the relationship between Protestantism and capitalism, it is fruitful to investigate the examples which Weber gives. Here again our object is not to refute Weber's thesis—although it is necessary to criticize it at many points—but to make the historical relationship which he observes (after it has been freed from his exaggerations) more theoretically adequate by comparing the behavior of the churches with their theoretically "expected" behavior.

With reference to the ascetically rational spirit of capitalism, Weber observes that

> in the most highly capitalistic centre of that time, in Florence of the fourteenth and fifteenth centuries, the money and capital market of all the great political Powers, this attitude was considered ethically unjustifiable, or at best to be tolerated. But in the backwoods small bourgeois circumstances of Pennsylvania in the eighteenth century, where business threatened for simple lack of money to fall back into barter, where there was hardly a sign of large enterprise, where only the earliest beginnings of banking were to be found, the same thing was considered the essence of moral conduct, even commanded in the name of duty. To speak here of a reflection of material conditions in the ideal superstructure would be patent nonsense.[73]

The ideas of eighteenth-century backwoods Pennsylvania may not reflect the material conditions of the place and time, but neither are the ideas an immanent religious development of the territory. To discover the reasons for their appropriateness there, we must once again raise the question of the circumstances under which those ideas emerged. Weber's original thesis held that the "permanent intrinsic" Calvinist doctrine furnished a great stimulus to the development of the capitalist spirit; and now he is talking about a doctrine which, after two hundred years of modification, has been transported by commercial-minded people to a country which was being developed, at least in part, as a business enterprise. Despite the traditional picture of early American history, which gives the impression that this country was formed largely by people who sought little else than religious freedom, a good deal of contemporary research shows that one dominant motive was a search for livelihood.[74] The most naïve historical materialist does not deny that ideas are forces in history; he denies only their intrinsic, immanent character. Weber certainly does not prove his case by referring to eighteenth-century Pennsylvania, where the Calvinist ideas were neither new nor indigenous. The whole story of the *modification* of these ideas must be read into his statement.

Some reference must also be made to Weber's statement regarding the lack of a capitalistic spirit in Florence. While it might appear that the traders of Florence in the fifteenth century could have functioned more freely without the restricting pronouncements of the church, and thus, according to a materialistic interpretation, could have been expected to seize avidly at the Protestant ethic that would free them, one must take note of the ecclesiastical situation in Italy at the time. The papacy itself was the greatest financial institution of the Middle Ages; it had a privileged position which made it to its advantage to maintain the institutional manifestations of the traditional ethic. In Italy a large part of the emerging business class was working with and within the ecclesiastical system. The new power group which was arising outside the church in Italy was not so strong as in the northern countries, and consequently was not in so powerful a position to demand the reinterpretation of religious principles. At the same time, the papacy itself could not suppress business and trade. Tawney writes:

> The Papacy might denounce usurers, but, as the center of the most highly organized administrative system of the age, receiving remittances from all over Europe, and receiving them in money at a time when the revenue of other Governments still included personal services and payments in kind, it could not dispense with them. Dante put the Cahorsine money-lenders in hell, but a Pope gave them the title of "peculiar sons of the Roman Church."[75]

That is, the church, despite its pronouncements, was not suppressing usury and enterprise. Once again unity of doctrine was accompanied by flexibility of practice wherever that flexibility enabled the church to influence more elements of society. Business was being freed in Italy without the Protestant ethic, within the traditional ethical system. Weber is not justified in assuming that because the pronouncements of the church condemned the scramble for profit, the Florentine traders were not thus scrambling. The church could not suppress enterprise because it was itself implicated in the system of profit. Moreover, in the commercial cities, where violations of doctrine were most likely to occur, the interference of the churchmen was not regarded with favor.[76] The traditional religious doubt of the moral validity of trade was not suppressing its growth, but it was weakening the hold of the church over the expanding and powerful group who worked at commercial enterprises. As a result, canon law on the subject of moneylending and trade underwent a steady development. "Italian canonists performed prodigies of legal ingenuity" (Tawney) to reconcile the law with actual practices and needs.

Why, then, if this interpretation is correct and the pressure of circumstances was freeing economic enterprise from traditional restrictions in Italy, did the Protestant revolt succeed in the North but not in the South? Because with the center of authority in Italy, the emerging states were restricted in their political, economic, and religious development. They were eager for a religion that would free them from the ecclesiastical dominance of Rome. It appears, therefore, that the explanation of conditions in Florence as due to material considerations is not "patent nonsense." Nor, on the other hand, is Weber's thesis, when he does not try to explain too much by it. Once a church system is established (even as Catholicism was established in Florence), and notwithstanding that the course of its development is not immanent but depends upon the surroundings, it becomes itself a conditioning factor.

Thus once again we find that our ability to understand religious conduct is increased when we realize that the church-type reaction, of which both Catholicism and late Calvinism are examples, is not to contradict movements in history which are proving to be centers of power, but rather so to interpret religious principles that the new power group may be brought under church influence, and thus moralized.

The criticisms that we have made against Weber's interpretation of the situation in Pennsylvania would also apply to his statement that the spirit of capitalism was present in Massachusetts before the capitalistic order, and was far less developed in the later

Southern States of the United States "in spite of the fact that these latter were founded by large capitalists for business motives, while the New England colonies were founded by preachers and seminary graduates with the help of small bourgeois, craftsmen and yoemen [*sic*], for religious reasons. In this case the causal relation is certainly the reverse of that suggested by the materialistic standpoint."[77] His conclusion does not necessarily follow from the facts. Economic historians would have something to say about the failure of economic enterprise to appear in the South. And before attributing the capitalist spirit of the New Englanders to their religious training and beliefs, one would certainly have to control other variables, taking carefully into account the economic and political situation.[78] Perhaps the necessity for thrift, a good geographical position with regard to trade, the class origins of the population, and the social setting in Europe out of which their economic ethics had grown would be among the important factors.

Many recent historians, as we have already noted, have minimized the role of religious motives in the development of New England. W. W. Sweet points out that until the third decade of the eighteenth century the lower classes in the American colonies "were little influenced by organized religion." Even in the Puritan colonies a small proportion of the population were church members. ". . . there came to be more unchurched people in America, in proportion to the population, than was [*sic*] to be found in any country in Christendom."[79] The upper classes, however, had quite strong church connections. There can be little doubt that, as Weber observes, their religious doctrines furnished many of them with a powerful stimulation and convincing justification for their business activities. But that was a later Calvinism molded to a rather great extent in decades of conflict in Great Britain and Western Europe to fit the modern commercial scene. Weber is right in noting the significance of that religious doctrine for the life of trade; he is led into exaggerations, however, and overly sharp conflicts with "the materialist interpretation" by failing to stress the significance of the evolution of Calvinism.[80] Puritan doctrine is not a purely religious stimulation that is making business enterprisers out of "preachers and seminary graduates." It was the church-type expression of accommodation to a powerful new group, part of whom came to America for greater business opportunities, bringing with them a religion that was quite well adjusted to their needs. Even the Massachusetts Bay Colony, where so much of the tradition of early colonial religiosity is centered, was in many ways simply a commercial undertaking.

These examples tend to show that it is not "Calvinism" which is the ethical stimulant of capitalism, but a descendant of Calvinism which has been appropriated by a business class and molded to suit their ethical and religious needs. Hall declares that the main effect of Calvin's teaching was quite different from that described by Weber. He contends that the asceticism, the demand for self-discipline and simplicity which characterized early Calvinism are traits of all "primitive" religions, and that they represent the influence of "Old Testament desert prophetism" on Calvin.

> Far from finding in Calvinism, as Max Weber does, the spirit of capitalism, a glance at the map will show that just as capitalism advanced, Calvinism declined. The country districts of Holland remained true to Calvin long after Amsterdam and the Dutch towns had adopted Arminianism.[81] It is not in Glasgow but in the Highlands of Scotland that one looks for pure Calvinism,[82] and it is almost alone in the mountains of the South that Calvinism in its purity, untouched by "revisionism" or higher criticism survives in the United States.[83]

This observation of the primitive element in Calvinism is justified. It must be noted, however, that the rigorous asceticism can also have an affinity for enterprise. Hall can give examples that show no relationship between enterprise and Calvinism, but Weber can give examples which show a close relation between the two. The significant thing is that original Calvinism is far from unambiguous, and being appropriated by different groups for different motives, it evolved along more than one line, according to the needs of each group. Thus Weber in his more cautious statements and the more adequate critics of Weber are both right. The two interpretations are reconciled by a theory of the conduct of religious groups.

The whole history of the spread of Calvinism teaches us to beware of facile generalizations regarding its influence, for it could evolve in many directions. Its rigorous asceticism could be a tonic to those who stood to gain by vigorous activity. But the doctrine of the depravity of the flesh, taken emotionally, could lead to a deadening of earthly activity. This was manifest in some aspects of Pietism, which emphasized that aspect of asceticism which meant withdrawal from the world, in contrast to the activist tendencies of Calvinism in general.[84] As we have shown above, it is of great importance to know why these tendencies toward withdrawal were not dominant. Weber himself noted that "the doctrine of predestination could lead to fatalism if, contrary to the predominant tendencies of rational Calvinism, it were made the object of emotional contemplation."[85]

One may note too, alongside the main emphases of Calvinism, a kind of Christian socialism, which taught that goods ought to be inexpensive, interest rates low (Calvin held that 2.5 per cent was high enough), and regard for others the dominant ethic. Weber wrote: ". . . the desire to separate the elect from the world could, with a strong emotional itensity, lead to a sort of monastic community life of half-communistic character, as the history of Pietism, even within the Reformed Church, has shown again and again."[86] This is one of the sources of Christian socialism today; but it did not (and one may perhaps say does not) receive much attention because it was moving against contemporary developments. When one understands "the social sources of denominationalism," he is surprised neither at the infrequency of this interpretation of Calvinism, nor at its occasional appearance.[87]

These inner contradictions in Calvinism, these "radical" elements, were not able to swim upstream and hence remained obscured. The most powerful opponent of prevailing Calvinism, however, was that very capitalism which it helped to support. Calvinism recognized secular activities—political participation and economic enterprise—but only as means to a spiritual end—the glory of God and the demonstration of salvation. Material motives were kept under control by rigorous discipline and limitation of the sense life. Such asceticism, however, was not for most men. Anyone who could endure a sermon became a Calvinist. The new doctrine helped to free men from traditionalism but was unable to establish its own tradition of ascetic self-denial, until, as Weber says: "The people filled with the spirit of capitalism today tend to be indifferent, if not hostile, to the Church."[88] "In Baxter's view the care for external goods should only lie on the shoulders of the 'saint like a light cloak, which can be thrown aside at any moment'. But fate decreed that the cloak should become an iron cage."[89] The Puritans were well aware that their ideals tended to give way under the influence of wealth, once it was achieved. The genuine adherents to the doctrine always were found in the classes rising from a lowly status, while those who had gained wealth continually repudiated the ethic.[90] Monasticism underwent the same fate throughout the Middle Ages: penniless monks were outspoken and sincere; but wealthy monasteries, with large financial interests, lost some of their ardor.[91] The Christian ethic needed constant regeneration from the bottom. Methodism, says Weber, may be regarded as a kind of monastic reform of Puritanism. It furnished a religious basis for ascetic conduct after the doctrine of predestination had been given up. Wesley was well aware of this contradiction into which the Puritan church fell: "I fear, wherever riches have increased, the essence of religion has decreased in the same proportion. Therefore I do not see how it is possible, in the nature of things, for any revival of true religion to continue long. For religion must necessarily produce both industry and frugality, and these cannot but produce riches. But as riches increase, so will pride, anger, and love of the world in all its branches."[92] The form of religion remains, but its spirit swiftly vanishes.

Thus we see that Protestant asceticism was molded by "the totality of social conditions, especially economic" (Weber). While recognizing that a fully developed Calvinism became a powerful ideological weapon for the business classes, we must avoid misinterpreting the significance of this fact for the sociology of religion. We do not have a complete understanding of the importance of a religious ethic until we study the process by which it developed.[93]

Critical Summary of Weber's Thesis

From this long discussion of Weber's essay, it is apparent that a large body of controversial literature has grown up around it. It may be valuable at this point to restate the sense in which the study may be regarded as valid, to point out in summary its weaknesses, and to draw together some of the explicit criticisms that have been made against it. As a critic of naïve historical materialism, Weber has forced upon all students of social causation the necessity for working out with great care the precise role of ideas in history. Even sociologists, who profess to be students of the influence of tradition, belief, and ritual on behavior, sometimes fall into an easy "economic" interpretation of social change. Weber's essay makes it clear that there is an affinity between Calvinism in some of its phases and rational, ascetic, commercial activity. This is a legitimate historical and sociological investigation.

When one tries to draw from this study, however, more than is in it, he is bound to misinterpret the relationship between Calvinism and capitalism. Since Weber set as his task the explanation of only one side of the causal chain, he made little effort to explain the origin of Calvinism. This limitation of the problem has been a source of confusion to his critics and in some ways a source of inaccuracies in his own work. Much of the difficulty is a result of a misunderstanding of the nature of causation. We do not propose to enter here into the discussion of the validity of the use of the concept of causation. Criticisms of its use have resulted in more explicit recognition of its heuristic nature and have helped to free it from metaphysical connotations. Once that is done, there is no sharp conflict between those who insist on speaking of probabilities of co-occurrence or probabilities of one event succeeding another, and those who refer to causes: both are interested in prediction. On one level of causation it is entirely accurate to say that certain aspects of Calvinism are among the causes of energetic worldly activity. For certain other scientific questions, however, this statement would be quite meaningless, for causation is not absolute, but relative to a problem.

The relativity of any causal explanation in science can be illustrated by a simple example: In answer to the question, Why did a boy drown? one can say that his lungs filled with water, or that his boat overturned, or that a great storm came up. Each of these is correct on a different level and each is valuable for prediction. On the other hand, there are certain disadvantages to each statement. To say that the boy drowned because his lungs filled with water is almost a truism, because the filling of lungs with water is almost, if not quite, synonymous with drowning. Someone interested in something besides the physiological question would be tempted to say: Of course he drowned because his lungs filled with water, but how did he happen to get his lungs full? There might follow the explanation of the boat overturning as the "cause." Such an explanation as a "hypothesis" of drowning obviously has less predictive power than the first—the boy might have been a good swimmer, or in shallow water, etc.—but at least it is not a truism, and it does contribute to our understanding of the event. For the complete story, however, we should probably also inquire why the boat overturned, and hear about the storm as the "cause" of his drowning. As a hypothesis of drowning in general, this is obviously very poor: there might have been no one on the lake at all. We can reduce the "causal" explanation to the absurd by saying that the boy drowned because he was born—as true a statement as it is meaningless. These statements are progressively less "causally adequate," but each contributes something to the explanation, and all are necessary to the complete explanation.

To return to our problem, it is apparent that there are several levels on which the relationship of Calvinism to capitalism can be studied. The cause of Calvinism can be taken as a given, just as the overturned boat was a given in the first explanation of drowning. This was Weber's method, and it is clear that the study gives him certain predictive power regarding the appearance of a spirit of capitalism where there is Calvinism (although his ability to predict is badly reduced by his failure to distinguish several dated and localized varieties of Calvinism). His essay is not nearly so helpful, however, in answering the more general sociological question: What adjustment will a religious group make to a change in the distribution of economic power? Or, in other words, Why this concurrence between Calvinism and capitalism? Weber has partly not been interested in this more "specific why" (MacIver's term), and partly answered it inadequately. In so far as he has been interested in the "specific why," his explanation is not causally adequate, because different effects could, and did, follow from the original Calvinist stimulation. He does not adequately demonstrate that the elements in Calvinism which stimulated the capitalist spirit were the products of an independent causal system, yet this is absolutely crucial to his thesis. If he does not demonstrate it, at least in part, the relationship which he observes is reduced to nothing but correlation. We have shown that some phases of Calvinism adapted themselves precisely to fit the capitalist situation, and other phases were created in a semicapitalist situation. In so far as these are true, they reduce the force of Weber's argument of the immanent development of Calvinism. He would doubtless accept both of these points; and we, on the other hand, agree that the independence of Calvinism's stimulation to capitalism may be a factor which adds to the causal adequacy of any explanation of the spirit of capitalism.[94] With regard to relative weight to be given to these factors, however, we should give far more attention to the adjustment of Calvinism to the modern world than Weber does, and should restrict the emphasis given to the influence on capitalism of Calvinism's "original" tendencies. We have been led to this conclusion by the study of the evolution of church doctrine. It becomes meaningful in light of our hypothesis that the expected "church" reaction to a new situation is the gradual adjustment of doctrine in order to stay in place of influence.[95] In so far as the Calvinist influence on the spirit of capitalism was *not* due to an independently developed emphasis, Weber's essay is reduced almost to a truism. By the very nature of the case, it is very difficult to demonstrate how much is independent; we have tried to show how much is not.

It should not be forgotten, of course, that Weber was not interested, for the most part, in the cause of Calvinism; he did not plan to cover the many sides of a complex question, but sharply delimited his field in order to avoid the necessity for taking into account its many elements. Many of his critics have made irrelevant arguments because they accused him of not solving a problem he was not trying to solve. The essay became important in fact, not only because of its argument, but also because of the methodological implications, the great body of controversial literature that it stimulated, and the unhappy state of methodological unawareness that was often exposed in the criticism. On some occasions Weber himself forgot the limitations of his problem with consequent unhappy results. The danger of delimiting a field of study to "one side of the causal chain" is that one may argue from partially hidden assumptions to complete the picture. Weber's explanation of the cause of Calvinism was not a hidden assumption, but it was also not a carefully tested hypothesis. He sometimes failed to keep in mind the fact that the origin of Calvinism also has to be explained before the significance of his thesis, if not its accuracy, can be revealed.[96] Although he thought of the essay as a test and a limitation of the materialist conception of history, it can scarcely be that until one has carefully traced the origin of the ideas that are being studied in relation to the material conditions. Weber did not make that study. He substituted for it the assumption that the crucial factors in Calvinism were immanent religious developments. He shared with Troeltsch the idea that religious teachings are influential factors in history *especially at the beginning* of their careers, in opposition to the idea that they are most influential after they have become traditional.[97] The former conception interprets religious teachings as immanent developments within a religious sphere; the latter sees them as products of an interacting situation of which they then become a part, and a cause of future developments. Weber's position is implied in the statement that the original conjuncture of Calvinism and capitalism was due to a "historical accident"—the crossing of two (relatively) independent causal systems. He seems to mean that Calvinism was a precipitant, as MacIver has used that word. If it is not a precipitant, the significance of his thesis, even when established as true, is not great. Calvinism, if not a precipitant, is similar to one of a series of dominoes—it knocks down the one ahead of it, and in that limited sense is the cause of its falling, but it is scarcely more than an agent for transmitting a force. The term "cause" could be applied more meaningfully to the force which started the row of dominoes falling. A quotation from MacIver throws some light on this concept:

> The risk of the ideal type approach is that it may discount or ignore the tendencies to change already present in the situation. This risk is not absent from the treatment of the subject by Max Weber. He takes the position, for example, that the Protestant ethic was in a special way the solvent of the traditional restraints on business enterprise and monetary acquisition and thus a primary cause of the rise of capitalism in Western Europe and in America. But it might easily be claimed that the rise of the Protestant ethic itself, with its stern individualism, its "worldly asceticism," and its doctrine of stewardship, was the expression in the religious sphere of a pervasive change of social attitudes corresponding to and causally interdependent with a changing

socio-economic order. Unless this claim can be refuted—and I do not see how a claim of this sort admits of definite refutation—we cannot establish the fundamental role in the process of social change attributed by Weber to the Protestant sects.

Moreover, while a particular complex of social attitudes may enter very significantly into the causal process, it is difficult ever to assign to a factor of this sort the salience and immediate causal decisiveness suggested by our term "precipitant." . . . [A precipitant] may reasonably be regarded, at the hour of its occurrence, as not inevitably the outcome or expression of the conditions or forces inherent in the particular system it disrupts. There is an element of conjuncture, if not of sheer chance, in the mode and time of the occurrence. The most indubitable type is that in which the decisive factor comes wholly or essentially from outside the affected system. A war, for example, might precipitate important changes in the economic employment of women, in the credit structure of a country, or even in an artistic style. The settlement of missionaries or of traders among a primitive people may initiate profound changes in the life of that people.[98]

Weber looked upon Calvinism as something of an intrusive force from the outside, developed by its own inner dialectic, not simply a part of the socioeconomic system that was producing capitalism. The determination of the validity of this assumption is a problem the difficulty of which cannot be exaggerated. It is precisely the issue around which revolves the whole question of the causes of societal phenomena. There is not a precise distinction, of course, between a precipitant on one hand and a cause that emerges out of the interacting system in which it operates on the other. Calvinism can be both precipitant and "lesser cause." It might seem, for instance, that an "extension of the market theory" can account for much of the rationality and extreme competitiveness of the capitalistic spirit; but how account for its rigorous asceticism and religious dynamic? That might be a precipitant element in Calvinism. As a tentative hypothesis on the basis of our theoretical structure, we might state that while religious ideas may be precipitants or immanent religious developments, their ethical implications—in other words, their practical influence on secular behavior—are not likely to be precipitants, but are the product of the situations in which they have been gradually worked out and defined.[99]

It is easy to exaggerate, as Weber indeed does, the harmony of Calvinism with the rationalism and individualism which are so characteristic of the modern world. On at least one important front, Calvinism was criticized precisely for the lack of these qualities:

> Though in other respects entirely orthodox, Arminius and his fellow Remonstrants felt the irrationality of the traditional doctrine of total depravity and the injustice of the Calvinistic dogma of unconditional election, and attacked them both. The emphasis which they laid upon the justice of God is instructive, for it means a regard for the dignity and rights of man not felt by the genuine mediaevalists of the Reformation. To Calvin as to Zwingli, man is a creature who has no rights over against God. The Creator may do as He pleases with His own. But the spirit of the modern age, with its new estimate of man, was out of sympathy with such a doctrine. Man is not a mere cipher whose fate is of no importance; he is a rational being who may demand consideration and fair treatment from God.[100]

There have been other criticisms of Weber, from many points of view. Gordon-Walker holds that Weber is almost inevitably led into error by the use of a "unilateral" or "isolierendkausal" method, which, although capable of important discoveries, is likely to mistake a partial picture for the total one. Weber's critics who follow the same method, using, however, a different explanatory factor, get into the same difficulty.[101] While Gordon-Walker's paper is in many ways a very fine analysis of the methodological problem surrounding Weber's essay, he fails to note the gravest danger in the "unilateral" method. The method itself may be a legitimate and necessary analytic procedure. The difficulty with Weber's treatment was not that he took Calvinism as a "given" but that he assumed (necessarily for his thesis) an explanation of that given—internal religious development—without adequate demonstration. He should either have left the matter of the cause of Calvinism open or proceeded to a careful investigation of its origin.

Tawney is less critical of Weber's thesis, at least in his explicit comments, but in the present writer's opinion Tawney's own study of the rise of capitalism contains a great deal of implicit criticism of Weber's work. He holds that the argument is "over-subtle in ascribing to intellectual and moral influences developments which were the result of more prosaic and mundane forces, and which appeared, irrespective of the character of religious creeds, wherever external conditions offered them a congenial environment."[102] Tawney shared with See the feeling that Weber sometimes simplified and limited the meaning of the term "capitalism" "to suit the exigencies of his argument." "Over-subtle" is perhaps the key phrase in Tawney's criticism, for he does not deny the reality of the relationship between Calvinism and capitalism. He does question the source of Weber's knowledge on the influence of religious forces on everyday life. Are the teachings of the great divines definitive? In the first place, they are probably not representative of the general attitude of the lesser clergy, who are not so capable of rewording church doctrines to fit a new age. Moreover, a great variety of conduct can follow from the same maxim. Weber would argue that certainly it was not the intention of most of the clergy to stimulate the capitalist spirit. Once he has admitted, however, that an ethic can be interpreted, despite the intentions of the preacher, to suit the listener, what is to prevent one from assuming that any other ethic would not also have been thus reinterpreted—in which case Calvinism can be considered a cause of the spirit of capitalism in only a very limited sense. That, in fact, is the point of much of the discussion above.

As we have seen, Weber oversimplified Calvinism; he failed to trace the changes and evolutions within the sects. English Puritans of the seventeenth century, among whom he finds most of his examples, were unlike the Calvinists of the sixteenth century, with their rigorous discipline and abhorrence of individualism. We have tried to show why this change took place. Weber's essay is, at the least, subject to serious misinterpretation without such a statement.

Several critics have reduced Weber's thesis to the idea that Calvinistic capitalism appears among Calvinists. They contend that only by defining the spirit of capitalism in such a way that some of the noncrucial traits are peculiarly Calvinistic can one demonstrate that capitalism thrives in Calvinist communities. One should not be surprised that Calvinist capitalists should give capitalism a Calvinist twist. This is related to the argument that capitalism preceded the Reformation. Brentano holds that the great merchants and bankers since the days of Babylon have been standard bearers of capitalism. Pirenne writes: "Ce que MM. Weber et Troeltsch . . . prennent pur l'esprit Calviniste, c'est précisément l'esprit des hommes nouveax que la révolution économique du temps introduit dans la vie des affaires, et qui s'y opposent aux traditionalistes auxquels ils se substituent."[103] Robertson points out that Jakob Fugger the Catholic, or the nonreligious capitalist described by Milton in *Areopagitica,* did not need to be "called" to riches.

Other writers contended that Weber was right in giving a good deal of weight to "spiritual" factors in the appearance of capitalism, but held that he chose the wrong religious doctrine for the chief role. Sombart declared that the Jews were the chief source of modern capitalism.[104] Brentano held that Catholicism was more important than Protestantism (and himself had to resort to "historical accident" to account for the greater development of capitalism in Protestant lands). Each of these arguments has an element of truth in so far as it points out Weber's tendency to assume what he is trying to prove. By defining the spirit of capitalism in Calvinist terms, one can easily find that the two come together. When Weber demonstrates, however, an actual quantitative difference in capitalist enterprise under different ethical systems, none of these arguments applies; and the essay will have to be criticized on other ground.

With regard to the arguments that the Renaissance was a powerful solvent of traditional ethical restraints and that a vast number of economic and technical changes were necessary before capitalism could appear, it is clear that they do not refute Weber's thesis, although they point out the limitations of its scope. Weber discovered another element in capitalism, different from any that these other influences have created: it is not pursuit of self-interest, but selfless devotion to worldly tasks. "Under certain peculiar circumstances . . . this disinterested attitude may become devoted to the task of profit-making—*not* for the sake of enjoying the expenditure of the profits, but of earning as an ethical duty in itself. This is what Weber calls the element of 'rational bourgeois capitalism' as distinguished from the 'capitalistic adventurers.' It is this element, not the total concrete phenomenon of capitalism, which is the theme of the essay. . . ."[105]

MacIver notes that capitalism appeared in Japan in the late nineteenth century unsupported, of course, by the Protestant ethic, although many of the traders may have been Calvinists.[106] Weber had noted this fact, and attributed it to the lack of any traditional restriction on enterprise in the Japanese religion which would have blocked the growth. Moreover, there is a great difference between the possibility of accepting capitalism, imposed from without, and spontaneously developing it within a social structure.[107]

To sum up this discussion of *The Protestant Ethic,* we may say that the essay establishes the fact that on a rather "low" level of causation, the Calvinist ethic is properly seen as *a* cause of the capitalist spirit. Whatever the cause of Calvinism's interpretation of worldly activity, it is clear that it sponsored, even in the beginning, but especially after the middle of the seventeenth century, the activities of the new middle class. Although it did not create the new opportunities for trade and enterprise, it did furnish businessmen with an ideological weapon and a spiritual justification which were not unimportant in helping them come to power and in conditioning the nature of their activities.

Alongside these statements, however, it is necessary to note that the very success of the Reformation can be explained only from the standpoint of economic and political conditions. "The social position and relations of the sects reveal the hidden reasons for sudden changes of religious thought, which could not have been explained from their merely intellectual dialectic."[108] How could a religious leader in the commercial centers of the sixteenth century begin to succeed without starting from the assumption that trade was a valid Christian pursuit? And how could a religious doctrine continue to succeed in the emerging modern world without increasing recognition of the legitimacy of commerce and industry? It is not surprising that by the eighteenth century Calvinism was giving wholehearted support to economic activity, for a social structure is of a piece: dominant religious teachings are not likely to be in conflict with dominant economic practices and ideas. One acquainted with the theory of the behavior of religious groups would have been able to predict that if the businessman were coming into an age of power, religious doctrine would soon sponsor him. This is not a cynical statement (decrying the inconstancy of religious teachings), for once again we must recall the dilemma of the churches: only by such sponsorship could they begin to control the behavior of this powerful group.

Thus our theory of the action of religious groups helps us to interpret the relation between Protestantism and capitalism. This body of historical evidence leads us to the conclusion that the description of social change requires the eschewing of all one-factor deterministic theories to account for societal processes, and demands in their stead a careful analysis of the many interacting factors at work in every cultural setting. For our problem of types of religious-group conduct, we have found it necessary in this chapter to take into account a larger field of interaction, to include more of the links in the chain of causation, than does Weber. His study does not help us to predict on the level on which we are working. He has asked: What happens when Calvinism (and this term he did not sufficiently clarify) appears in a semimedieval economic setting? We have asked: What is likely to happen when *any* "church" group appears in that setting? He starts with Calvinism as a given; we have been interested precisely in the *why* of that Calvinism.

Chapter V

THE ECONOMIC ETHICS OF CONTEMPORARY CHURCHES

We turn our attention now away from early capitalism and the response that religious groups made, from the sixteenth to the eighteenth century, to the emerging industrial society, and focus our interest on the contemporary economic situation. Culture contact, trade, the development of large-scale industry, and many other factors continued to revolutionize society so that the churches were continually called upon to make new adjustments. Can our theory of the behavior of religious groups help us to interpret these adjustments? [Some will think it unjustifiable to apply the same concepts to the problems of the nineteenth and twentieth centuries that we have used to interpret the early development of Protestantism.] Scientific results can be the only test of that claim. It is our contention that the continuity of religious problems, and, more important, the basic similarity of the problem of power during the two periods make the application of one theoretical formulation both possible and valuable. The purpose of the present chapter is, therefore, to analyze sociologically some phases of the response of religious groups to "late" capitalism, to the labor movement, and to socialism. It is scarcely necessary to state that this analysis will be both incomplete and introductory, for there is an enormous amount of relevant data to survey and the problem is complex. It has seemed best for our investigation, nevertheless, to cover the ground extensively, even if lightly, rather than to cultivate a small area intensively. One of the chief tasks of this study is precisely to demonstrate the value of a sharply defined theoretical structure in furnishing guideposts through an unorganized mass of data. The formulations must, of course, have suggested themselves as a result of wide acquaintance with adequate empirical material. Moreover, we must be very careful about extending the generalizations beyond the data in which they were worked out. That is not to say that the extension of hypotheses beyond their empirical derivations is unscientific—precisely the opposite is the case: the value of an hypothesis rests squarely on its ability to enable one to "go beyond the facts"—i.e., to predict in a way which admits of proof and disproof. Until the time, however, when the whole field has been studied intensively, and/or a statistically valid sample obtained, all generalizations must be tentative and flexible. What is often not understood is the fact that representative sampling and statistical formulations are not the beginning of an investigation. The first rule of the statistician is "know your universe." Without such knowledge sampling is blind, and statistical precision is a façade to cover up theoretical inadequacies, for "facts" uninformed by well-articulated concepts do not speak for themselves.

In this chapter, then, we shall not get very far beyond "knowing our universe" and shall leave more precise demonstrations of our hypotheses to later research.

The Development of "The Social Gospel"

The roots of modern economic society go back, of course, to the industrial revolution and beyond. Specialization, increasing trade, the factory system, and high-cost machinery are perhaps the factors which are most crucial to our problem. These combined to force the reorganization of the lives of ever-increasing numbers of people. The central fact was the loss of self-sufficient handicraft and agriculture for vast populations: the worker lost control of the tools with which he worked and lost the skills which had enabled him to live relatively independently. On a great scale, men became interdependent with strangers. Under these circumstances, the former "primary group morality" was weakened; the *noblesse oblige* which had modified some of the severity of the medieval class structure was neither adequate to the new situation nor very strongly operative among the new "nobility." Despite a greatly expanded industrial output, the lower classes could not rise above a subsistence level. Depression, unemployment, insecurity, long hours and low wages, accident and disease, woman and child labor—these are a matter of record. They lie behind all working-class movements; they furnish a driving animus for the work of Marx, who lashed them with all his might.

We are not primarily interested in the appearance of socialism or the development of the labor movement, however, but in the reaction of religious groups to industrial society, with particular reference to the *timing* of that reaction. We refer in detail only to the United States, but we have already discussed briefly the abortive attempt of Methodism in England to appeal to the workingman (see Chapter II). The Church of England, with its upperclass clergy and state connections, made even less of a challenge to the existing power arrangement during most of the nineteenth century.[1] Christian socialism was largely a sectarian movement, and the influence which Maurice, Kingsley, Ludlow, and others had on such developments as the Fabian Society, for instance, became effective only after the labor movement in Britain had already won its way to a measure of recognition.[2] Nevertheless, the effectiveness of the state-church idea of organic unity, with the necessity it forces on the church of adjusting to new developments, is partially validated by the fact that the labor movement in England did not develop a powerful antireligious feeling. The Anglican Church, like the Catholic Church, once it was convinced that organized labor was a power, made concessions to it. It well understood the strategy of Sir Robert Peel: "If you see a move coming . . . *head* it." That, in fact, typifies the behavior of alert churchmen; and when—to give an opinion—the move harmonizes so well with the original Christian ethics as does the solidarity and mutual helpfulness, at least in theory, of the labor movement, the church has an added incentive to head it. The transition is not quick or easy at best. It is especially difficult for a religious institution, based so largely on symbol, ritual, and belief, to change. But the purely religious factor would seem to make the church more readily adjusted to collectivism than to liberalism. That is to assume, of course, that other power elements are held constant. They are not constant in reality, and therefore the church—not the religious—sponsorship of capitalism may have been more readily achieved than sponsorship of collectivism.

This brief statement concerning England may introduce us to some of the problems that we face in interpreting sociologically the response of religious groups in the United States to modern industrialism. The great acceleration of American industrialism began during and after the Civil War. Between 1860 and 1890 national wealth increased from sixteen to seventy-eight and a half billion dollars, but the increase was not universally shared. Forty thousand families, three tenths of one per cent of the population, held title to over half of the wealth. In the decade of the seventies, real wages, which had always been at the subsistence level, declined from an average of four hundred dollars to three hundred dollars. Women and children were forced by need into the factories. "The American industrial revolution, in the process of creating wealth such as the world had never seen or dreamed of, produced also a sullen proletariat resentful of the poverty it had obtained as its share of the bounty. . . ."[3] Labor organization, which had been on a small scale before 1860, began to gain strength. Socialism, particularly under the influence of Germans driven out by Bismarck, became more widespread. Most of the labor organizations were of a definitely radical disposition; their strikes were bitter, and harshly suppressed. Between 1881 and 1894 there were fourteen thousand strikes and lockouts in the United States, involving four million workers. Many of these have achieved notoriety as a thinly veiled industrial war. Technological unemployment, large-scale immigration, the closing up of Western lands, and other factors created a standing army of unemployed of over a million, although the labor supply had been inadequate in 1870.

The early labor organizations tended to make direct challenges to the existing distribution of power, but the leaders gradually learned, as religious sects learn, that little was to be gained by open conflict with the far stronger power of the industrialist, backed as he was by American tradition. After 1886 we witness, therefore, the ascendancy of the American Federation of Labor over the once dominant Knights of Labor. The Federation accepted the main structure of capitalism and worked only for a measure of control over working conditions and job opportunities. By 1890 it had one hundred thousand members, and by the turn of the century a half million. Organized labor began to wield an influence.

With this brief sketch in mind, we must now ask: What was the response of the churches, both to the hardships of industrialism and to the search for power that labor was making? The first thing to note is that religious conduct was defintely a *response:* except for a small radical sectarian element the churches accepted the sufferings of the masses in this world as inevitable. They were concerned with industrial conditions only so far as those conditions influenced belief; they opposed the irreligion and tradition-breaking of the labor organizations. That was the early reaction, and it was modified only gradually in a process which we shall trace below. The failure of American churches to make an adequate place for the common laborer is demonstrated by the vast decline in religious enthusiasm among the working class during the latter part of the nineteenth century. Powderly, head of the Knights of Labor, made the statement that if the Sermon on the Mount were preached without reference to its author, the preacher would be warned not to repeat such utopian ravings, and "the fashionable pews would be emptied." The *Workmen's Advocate* in 1887 reported the result of a questionnaire sent out by the Rev. A. H. Bradford. Although the sample is probably not adequate, the results are worth noting. In reply to the question, How large a percentage of the artisan classes in your region are regular attendants at any church? the responses for Protestants varied between one half of one per cent and ten per cent. In all but one case the ministers thought attendance was decreasing.[4] The disbelief that the workingmen expressed was not in Christianity, but in the church. As late as 1912 Rauschenbusch wrote:

> There is no doubt that in all the industrialized nations of Europe, and in our own country, the working classes are dropping out of connection with their churches and synagogues, and to a large extent are transferring their devotion to social movements, so that it looks as if the social interest displaced religion. But here, too, we must remember that solid masses of the population of continental Europe have never had much vital religion to lose. Their religion was taught by rote and performed by rote. It was gregarious and not personal. Detailed investigations have been made of the religious thought world of the peasantry or industrial population of limited districts, and the result always is that the centuries of indoctrination by the Church have left only a very thin crust of fertile religious conviction and experience behind. This is not strange, for whenever any spontaneous and democratic religion has arisen among the people, the established churches have done their best to wet-blanket and suppress it, and they have succeeded finely.[5]

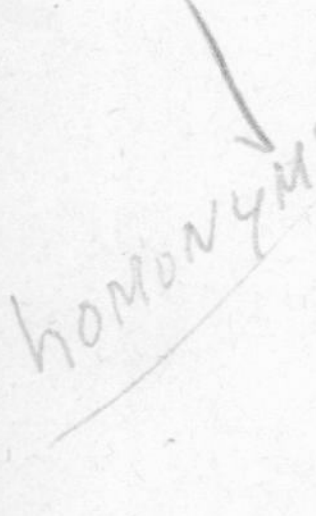

Washington Gladden reports one of his correspondents: "When the capitalist prays for us one day in the week, and preys on us the other six, it can't be expected that we will have much respect for his Christianity."[6] And Samuel Gompers wrote in 1898: "My associates have come to look upon the church and the ministry as the apologists and defenders of the wrong committed against the interests of the people. . . ."[7] In the main ranks of the church, the workingman was certainly not finding a place that suited him.

Meanwhile, the American churches were gaining in wealth and influence. Rockefeller, Armour, Hill, Morgan, and many other powerful industrialists and financiers were devoted church members. After the Civil War many church colleges were founded or backed by large gifts from wealthy men. "Places on the boards of trustees formerly held by ministers began to be filled more and more by wealthy laymen. . . ."[8] In the costly churches, the poorer classes felt alienated. As a result, many new "holiness" churches began to appear—at least twenty-five holiness bodies came into existence between 1880 and 1926.

There was within the American churches, to be sure, a small group who saw the failure to win the support of the laborer and sought to rectify it. Even before the Civil War there were liberalizing tendencies: Transcendentalism, an offshoot of Unitarianism, was somewhat hospitable to socialism; and the writings of Maurice and Kingsley had some influence in this country by way of the Protestant Episcopal Church. These were small minorities, however, and they continued to be small after the war. Moreover, they directed their attention, not to social organization, but to character. Their aim was to direct the philanthropic urges of church people toward the solution of the new problems without, however, changing the old doctrines. "Social reform was approached by way of the traditional conception of stewardship that was to be applied by individuals to business and industry, and the few radicals of the 1870's who demanded that the church enter the class struggle on the side of the workers were completely ignored, if they were at all understood."[9]

This emphasis on individual morality is a part of the "dilemma of the churches" which it is always difficult to transcend, and its limitations in the modern world are especially evident. Rauschenbusch was thoroughly aware of this difficulty. A man who may be willing to pay his workmen a living wage may be faced with competitors who are not willing. "Shall he love himself into bankruptcy?" "If a man owns a hundred shares of stock in a great corporation, how can his love influence its wage scale with that puny stick? The old advice of love breaks down before the hugeness of modern relations. . . . It is indeed love that we want, but it is socialized love."[10] Faithful use of funds is not enough to make Christian teachings operative in a modern world. The churches, by their inability to develop a new ethics and a new organizational principle for a new world, lost much of their ability to influence that world. By the late nineteenth century, a few church leaders were demanding that the church implement its teachings by helping to rebuild the social structure, but they were a small minority. Rauschenbusch writes:

> . . . the older brethren told us that the true function of the ministry was not to "serve tables," but to save the immortal souls of men. One told me that these were "mere questions of mine and thine," and had nothing to do with the Gospel. A young missionary going to Africa to an early death implored me almost with tears to dismiss these social questions and give myself to "Christian work."[11]

For our purposes, it is very important to inquire why the churches tended to emphasize the otherworldly aspects of original Christianity, with quiet acceptance of this world, rather than developing the implicit radical challenge to secular arrangements that contradicted its ethic. Rauschenbusch lists several reasons why the "social hope" of Christianity has generally been obscured: the extension of the church beyond the Jewish environment; the ascendancy of the otherworldly emphasis,[12] dominance of the institutional life of religion.[13] These seem to be surface explanations, however, for the crucial question remains: Why has the otherworldly emphasis prospered; why did the institutional aspects of religion become dominant? Here again our answer would be that the religious "interest" is only one among many in man, that it is not strong, except in its traditional—and therefore conservative—form, in the lives of most men, that it must compete with egocentrism and powerful material interests. Only in times of great unrest does the explosive element in Christianity come to the fore in the work of a few "prophetic" individuals.[14] They challenge tradition with a demand for literal obedience of the Second Commandment. Their success depends upon two things: an ability to stimulate the purely religious interest in others (this seldom lasts beyond the personal influence of the "prophet"), and the achievement of an organizational principle that will incorporate the new demand into the balance of power. In our instance this would mean, perhaps, the organization of labor rather than dependence upon appeals to the "character" of the industrialist or of the labor leader. Even the prophets with all their challenging of tradition seldom achieve this latter requirement, for they are scarcely ever concerned with profane existence. When they are "politically minded" and have organizational ability—men like St. Thomas, Calvin, and Wesley, for instance—religion makes the maximum use of its power.[15]

That the "social gospel" of the late nineteenth and early twentieth centuries did not manifest the organizational skill that was necessary, but was unrealistic and utopian in nature, is demonstrated by the tremendous popularity of such novels as Charles M. Sheldon's *In His Steps* (1898).[16] In this book a "dusty, worn, shabby-looking young man" arose in church one morning and told his story of privation and suffering, and then collapsed in the aisle. A few days later he died. Moved by this story, and under the encouragement of the minister, fifty members of the congregation—including an heiress, a college president, a railroad executive, a newspaper editor, a merchant—resolved never to do anything without first asking themselves the question, "What would Jesus do?" Needless to say, their lives underwent an abrupt change. By means of this novel, millions of people found to their satisfaction that the alleviation of suffering required only the personal conversion of persons in places of influence. Hopkins analyzes the situation well:

> . . . the utopian nature of these stories was doubtless the real secret of their success. They revealed how the simple adaptation of a familiar method would quickly accomplish the reforms for which the times so passionately yearned. A panacea such as that proposed by *In His Steps,* while realistic in its description of conditions, was at the same time utopian in its grasp of the forces producing those conditions, and in its prescriptions. Asking for charity while unaware of the need for

justice, this literature was a plea for a socialized Christianity, not for a Christian socialism—a distinction worthy of note. Fully awake to the social emergency, its evangelistic fervor yet failed to project social goals and techniques commensurate with the demands of the crisis. Nevertheless, the social-gospel novel brought social religion to the attention of millions of laymen who might never have heard of it otherwise.[17]

That the development of "social Christianity" was unrealistic is not the whole story, however, for its energy forced a readjustment upon the more realistic and politically minded churches. Their latent sect tendencies were stimulated; and although the churches continued to accept the basic structure of society—as of course they must—their attempts to soften some of the harshness of the system were increased. These attempts of the churches are, typically, very weak until the plight of the "religiously disinherited" has caused them to look for some profane salvation, and until the sect element in religious teachings recalls the church to its mission. In the situation which we are studying the workingman was gradually winning a measure of political and economic power. Under these circumstances, more and more churchmen "discovered" that strikes, when properly qualified, were just, that hours of labor should be shortened, that child labor was a menace, rather than a brace, to character. This phase of the development of "social Christianity" was an about-face for a great many churchmen and churches. For the most part it represents, not the triumph of radical Christian doctrine forcing society to justice, but the emergence of a new power to which the churches had to adjust—as they adjusted to the bourgeoisie in the seventeenth century—if they were not to lose what influence they yet maintained over a large group of people. This adjustment was not extreme, of course, because the power of labor was not great.

Thus both radical Christian doctrine and a new balance of secular power forced more and more elements of American Christianity toward the "social gospel." Perhaps the first important official church attempt to deal with the problems of labor was the Church Association for the Advancement of the Interests of Labor, organized by the Protestant Episcopal Church in 1887. The advancement of the Episcopalians in this regard probably demonstrates their connection with the British situation, where industrialization was ahead of the United States by several decades. The Episcopal Church was not alone, however. The Protestant seminaries began to offer courses in "social ethics" during the 1880's, led perhaps by F. G. Peabody at Harvard, but followed closely by Andover and Hartford. Sociology in its "social reform" aspect was offered in the Chicago Theological Seminary in 1892 by Graham Taylor, at the University of Chicago by C. R. Henderson, and at the Cambridge Episcopal Theological Seminary in 1895 by E. A. Woods. Yale, Meadville, and others followed.[18]

Official recognition of "social Christianity" had proceeded, before the World War, to the point where most of the large denominations, except only the Lutheran,[19] had appointed social-service boards or commissions. This does not necessarily mean that a majority of churchmen were demanding radical changes in society or even that they were actively working to soften the harshness of the existing arrangement (see below), but it shows that proponents of the "social gospel" had gained enough influence to compel their churches to recognize the movement officially. Somewhat paradoxically, the first Protestant church to appoint a full-time paid secretary concerned with social problems was the Presbyterian Church in the United States of America. Its Department of Church and Labor, under the leadership of Charles Stelzle, was a vigorous promoter of harmony between churches and labor organizations. Stelzle dealt directly with the labor unions and persuaded many ministerial associations to send fraternal delegates to central labor bodies. He wrote a syndicated press release, preaching an ethical religion, that went to three hundred labor papers with a circulation of over three millions.[20] That the work and point of view of this Presbyterian department was largely a result of Stelzle's individual conviction and ability, and not a revolutionary change in a conservative church, is shown by the fact that Stelzle was forced to resign in 1913.

In 1901 both the General Convention of the Protestant Episcopal Church and the National Council of Congregational Churches took preliminary steps toward the organization of official social-service committees. The Methodist Federation for Social Service (in the Northern church) was organized in 1907. The American Unitarian Association and the Northern Baptist Convention established agencies a year later. By 1912 eleven other denominations had given official recognition to the need for attacking "social problems."[21]

It is not to be supposed that any of these organizations were making radical challenges to the existing distribution of power: the creation of these agencies was entirely a church-type reaction. In coming to terms with labor (which was the significance of most of these agencies) the churches were simply recognizing a *fait accompli:* the labor movement was growing in power, and the working classes were deserting the churches which did not have time to concern themselves with their problems. The "social creeds" demonstrated that the churches were "for labor" by echoing some of labor's milder demands. These demands were put in somewhat ambiguous language, however, and their realization by conciliation, co-operation, and the development of character was emphasized. The churches were supported and attended, after all, by the middle and upper classes, who were often generous, but were always convinced of the legitimacy of the *status quo*—in other words, of their right to rule.[22] The Methodist Social Creed stated:

The Methodist Episcopal Church stands:

For equal rights, and complete justice for all men in all stations of life.

For the principle of conciliation and arbitration in industrial dissensions.

For the protection of the worker from dangerous machinery, occupational diseases, injuries, and mortality.

For the abolition of child labor.

For such regulation of the conditions of labor for women as shall safeguard the physical and moral health of the community.

For the suppression of the "sweating system."

For the gradual and reasonable reduction of the hours of labor to the lowest practical point, with work for all; and for that degree of leisure for all which is the condition of the highest human life.

For a release from employment one day in seven.

For a living wage in every industry.

For the highest wage that each industry can afford, and for the most equitable division of the products of industry that can ultimately be devised.

For the recognition of the Golden Rule and the mind of Christ as the supreme law of society and the sure remedy for all social ills.[23]

This piece of political fence-straddling would alienate the more extreme laissez-faire industrialists and disappoint all but the least ambitious workers. But in so far as an employer were seriously interested in religion, such a creed from his church would increase his willingness to concede some of the laborer's demands, and it would give the workmen a measure of hope and encouragement. A church federation for social service may not be a decisive factor in the balance of power, but before dismissing it as a mere reflection of material interests, one should recall the dilemma that the churches faced: Could religion bring society any nearer to its ethic by vigorously denouncing all social arrangements that did not measure up to its standard? Not only would the rulers not respond, but they would suppress such heresy, aided indeed, in most instances, by the traditionally minded masses. "Men," Rauschenbusch writes, "are impatient with the moral forces which are changing the social order, because they have never comprehended the terrible tenacity and vigor of the social forces that resist progress."[24]

Official recognition of "social religion" reached a climax in Protestantism with the organization of the Federal Council of Churches of Christ in America in 1908. The fact that the Council has only advisory capacity probably allows it to make more forthright pronouncements than could come from an executive body. Twenty-five Protestant denominations, representing three fourths of the Protestant membership of the country, joined the Federal Council through the course of several years. Its original statement on social problems was taken almost verbatim from the Methodist creed quoted above.[25] This formulation was somewhat liberalized in 1912 by the addition of references to "suitable provision for the old age of workers, and for those incapacitated by injury," a minimum wage, and other factors.[26] In 1932 the statement was made even more liberal by reference to such factors as subordination of the profit motive, control of the monetary system, social insurance, building of a co-operative world order, and maintenance of the basic democratic freedoms.[27]

Thus Protestantism adjusted to the contemporary world. A few leaders actively challenged the basic social arrangements; and though they had very little direct influence, they goaded the main church bodies into keeping fairly well abreast of social changes, at least in their official pronouncements. There seems to be very little evidence for an interpretation of the "social gospel" as a product simply of the inherently radical qualities of the Christian doctrine. It seems, rather, to be, at least on the part of the larger religious groups, a response to a changed environment in which new material powers and new ideologies were challenging the power of the churches.[28] We shall deal with this adjustment from a somewhat different point of view in a later section.

The Catholic Church and Modern Industrialism

The more highly organized and universalized Roman Catholic Church presents somewhat different problems for sociological analysis, although the basic theoretical formulations remain the same.[29] Despite a theoretically stable and consistent Catholic doctrine, one can find various and contradictory behavior carried on by the church in different situations. "In any crucial situation," Hook writes, "the behavior of the Catholic Church may be more reliably predicted by reference to its concrete interests as a political organization than by reference to its timeless dogmas."[30] Indeed, one will not find consistent Catholic behavior under different circumstances. Underlying the variety, however, is a unity of method—a method that is skilled in the art of encompassing any new societal development that gives promise of being of significance. By never making an absolute decision, Catholicism preserves its absolutes.[31]

We shall be concerned here only with some aspects of the reaction of the Catholic Church to the labor movement, but the analysis is at least partially generalizable. The Catholic synthesis was achieved under feudalism and is far more effective in some kind of a corporate society than in rationalistic individualism. The idea of an organic unity which binds together all classes and elements, each in its proper place, is fundamental to its teachings. Fanfani writes:

> . . . the Catholic conception cannot grant the individualism that is a postulate of capitalism, still less can it agree that society should be organized on an individualistic basis. That is why the Popes of the last two centuries have so definitely condemned liberalism, seeking to circumscribe its effects in the economic and social spheres by indirect and direct encouragement of social legislation, and looking forward to the time when it should give place to a corporative organization of society.[32]

Nor is that an isolated Catholic opinion. In a somewhat similar vein, Ryan observes:

> Pope Leo would have regarded copartnership and cooperation as the best practical application and realization of this policy. Considered as a fundamental and consistent industrial system, cooperative ownership has a greater claim to the title of Catholic than any other. For the system that developed and that seemed destined to prevail in the days when Catholic principles and the social influences of the Church were at their zenith, in the later Middle Ages, was that in which the masses of the workers both in town and country owned and managed the tools and the land. It is no longer possible for the majority of urban workers to become independent owners of separate industrial estab-

lishments. But they can exercise individual ownership and management through cooperation.[33]

This nostalgia for the days when church and society were synonymous makes Catholicism more responsive to the contemporary "interventionist" state than it has ever been to democratic individualism (capitalist or socialist). Its fondest aim is a religious corporatism, with the church in final authority.[34]

Under these circumstances we might expect the Catholic Church to be quite responsive to the labor movement, which in one of its aspects substitutes corporate solidarity for individual responsibility. This generalization, however, must be qualified because of several factors which influence the church's policy: the class location of laymen and clergy (Catholic clergy and laymen in the United States are predominantly of the lower classes, while in Italy all classes are included); the strength of the labor movement (German Catholics were far quicker to proclaim the demands of labor to be Christian justice than were those in Italy and Spain); and the religious orientation of labor.

Two of the foremost Catholics interested in the labor movement were Bishops Ozanam and Ketteler of Germany. They lived at a time when secular organizations of workmen were gaining rapidly in membership and power. Under this stimulus they discovered—what the church had not always recognized—that "the masses of the people . . . will judge the Church by the external works accomplished by her members. They will test the truth of our Faith by the sincere fulfillment of our duties towards our fellowmen."[35] Here was a political problem of the utmost importance to the church, for the profane parties of socialism and trade unionism were winning more and more of the votes of the people. Bishops Ozanam and Ketteler warned their fellow churchmen that if they did not attempt to solve the problems of labor, the belief of the workingmen in the church would be broken. It is significant to note that the problems long preceded the protests of the two bishops, who worked in the last third of the nineteenth century.[36] A new factor had been added, however, which was changing the perspective of the churches on the demands of the workingmen: labor was implementing these demands with organizational and ideological weapons which were proving effective. The Catholic Church did not anticipate the secular labor movement, which itself arose only after decades of suffering in the new industrial society. It followed the movement by many years and sought to counter its secular effectiveness by outlining the "true Communism" and organizing "Catholic unions." Bishop Ketteler, who was outstanding, vigorously denounced the extremism, the atheism, the doctrine of class conflict, which were important in German socialism:

> Even if all the Utopian dreams of the Socialists were realized, and every one was fed to his heart's content in this universal labor State, yet should I for all that prefer to eat in peace the potatoes planted by my hand and be clothed with the skins of the animals I reared, and therewith *remain free,* than to fare sumptuously in the slavery of the labor State. This makes the collectivist theory utterly detestable. *Slavery come to life again; the State an assemblage of slaves without personal liberty*—that is Socialism![37]

Such invective would not be wasted on a weak opponent. The church must have seen in socialism, and the labor movement generally, a strong competitor for the allegiance of the workingman. It is not surprising that the hierarchy should sanction and promote a few leaders who were "stealing the thunder" of the movement. (There is no question here of the sincerity of men like Bishop Ketteler.) Ketteler gave tentative support to some government ownership (the railroads in Germany) and strong support to organized labor:

> Whoever works for another and is forced to do so all his life, has a moral right to demand security for a permanent livelihood. All the other classes of society enjoy such security. Why should the working-classes alone be deprived of it? . . .
>
> The fundamental characteristic of the labor movements of our day, that which gives them their importance and significance and really constitutes their essence, is the tendency, everywhere rife among the workingmen, to organize for the purpose of gaining a hearing for

their just claims by united action. To this tendency, which is not only justified but necessary under existing economic conditions, the Church cannot but gladly give her sanction and support.

It would be a great folly on our part if we kept aloof from this movement merely because it happens at the present time to be promoted chiefly by men who are hostile to Christianity.[38]

The most significant attempt of Catholicism to adjust to the problems of modern industrialism and to a new balance of power is the famous encyclical of Pope Leo XIII, *Rerum Novarum,* issued in 1891. This document is an outstanding attempt to maintain the church at the center of an organically unified society, by admitting the labor movement as part of the "relative natural law," yet admitting also the major claims of nonlabor and even antilabor groups, and meanwhile demanding the allegiance of all to its religious absolutes. That such a reconciliation cannot be carried out in concrete circumstances is almost axiomatic (cf. Chapter II), but even its theoretical formulation is a difficult task, and wherever Catholicism has remained vital this pronouncement has been a factor to take account of in capital-labor struggles.

The encyclical is harsh in its denunciation of the evils of modern industrialism: ". . . a small number of very rich men have been able to lay upon the teeming masses of the laboring poor a yoke that is little better than slavery." But it is no less severe in its condemnation of socialism as a remedy for those evils: ". . . it only injures those whom it would seem meant to benefit, is directly contrary to natural rights of mankind, and would introduce confusion and disorder into the commonwealth." Only in the church, says Pope Leo, can the solution to these problems be found.[39] He vigorously defends man's "natural right to private property" and denounces the socialist practice of setting class against class, emphasizing instead "the Christian interdependence of capital and labor." What is needed, he says, is not less private property but a wider distribution of property ownership. He reaffirms the "dignity of labor," the church's concern for the material welfare of the poor, the "employers' moral obligation to pay fair wages," and other long-established Catholic doctrines. Perhaps the most important new pronouncement in the encyclical is the recognition of the right of workmen to organize (on a Christian, and preferably a Catholic, basis) and to strike in a just cause:

> Associations of every kind, and especially those of working men, are now far more common than formerly . . . . many of these societies are in the hands of invisible leaders, and are managed on principles far from compatible with Christianity and the public well-being; and that they do their best to get into their hands the whole field of labor and to force workmen either to join them or to starve. Under these circumstances the Christian workmen must do one of two things: either join associations in which their religion will be exposed to peril, or form associations among themselves—unite their forces and courageously shake off the yoke of unjust and intolerable oppression. No one who does not wish to expose man's chief good to extreme danger will hesitate to say that the second alternative must by all means be adopted.[40]

One gets the impression from this statement that Catholic unions are permissible, not because of labor's right to a share in the control of the industrial process—which is the position of the unions—but because the only other alternative, the industrial situation being what it is, is the loss of Catholic workmen to non-Christian unions.[41] The church-type reaction, as we have seen, is always *necessitous* in this sense. The church tries to keep the necessity from being a complete determinism by always demanding that the new development be carried on within the fold of the church: ". . . the church alone can solve the social problem."[42]

There have also been Catholic leaders in the United States, where a high percentage of the membership of the church is found among the urban proletariat, who have sought to find a place for the labor movement in official Catholic doctrine. Sixty years ago Cardinal Gibbons wrote a Memorial to the Holy See, requesting him not to condemn the Knights of Labor. He had the support of ten out of twelve American archbishops. If there are strikes, wrote the Cardinal, they are not invented by the Knights of Labor but are outbursts of anger against "obstinate monopoly." The leaders of the Knights do not promote the violence of the strikes but help to prevent it. If the Church takes sides against this group, it would lose, in popular estimation, the right to be called the friend of the people and would lose "the love of her children"—pushing them into an attitude of resistance against her teachings.

> . . . great numbers of Ecclesiastics were alarmed at the revolutionary principles which undoubtedly disgraced some members of the trade unions; the more so, as many of them were at least nominally secret societies. So great was this alarm in Canada that the Canadian bishops obtained from the Holy See, a condemnation of the Knights of Labor for Canada. But if many Bishops were alarmed at what they considered the revolutionary tendencies of these associations, many other Bishops, including Cardinal Manning and myself, were equally alarmed at the prospect of the Church being presented before our age as the friend of the powerful rich and the enemy of the helpless poor . . . . to us it seemed that such a thing could never take place. The one body in the world which had been the protector of the poor and the weak for nearly 1800 years, could not possibly desert these same classes in their hour of need.[43]

Cardinal Manning was also a staunch friend of labor. The most ardent trade-unionist could not hope for a stronger statement of his position than that given by Manning:

> If for a just cause, a strike is right and inevitable; it is a healthful constraint imposed upon the despotism of capital. It is the only power in the hands of working men. We have been for years blinded or dazed by the phrases of "free contract," "the independence of adult labor," "free labor," and the like. The meaning is this: Let working men maintain their independence of one another, and of all associations, and of all unions, and of all united action, and of all intervention of law in their behalf. The more perfectly they are isolated, the more independent of all defenders, the more dependent they are on capitalists. Starving men may be locked out with impunity. The hunger of their wives, the cries of their children, their own want of food will compel them to come in. It is evident that between a cap-

italist and a working man there can be no true freedom of contract. The capitalist is invulnerable in his wealth. The working man without bread has no choice but either to agree or to hunger in his hungry home.[44]

Fully in the Catholic tradition of reconciliation of society's diverse elements is the "program of social reconstruction" advocated by four American bishops (Muldoon, Schrembs, Hayes, and Russell) after the first World War. These men were the administrative committee of the National Catholic War Council and spoke, therefore, with some authority. They advocated no radical changes, but they demonstrated the concern of some parts of the church for the workingman. They called, among other things, for a United States employment service, the continuation of the War Labor Board, the maintenance of present wage levels, the improvement of housing conditions among the workers (without continuing, however, government building), a legal minimum wage, social insurance, labor participation in industrial management, the elimination of child labor. The whole labor movement was in accord with these demands. In a longer view the committee envisaged a more equitable distribution of income and better control of monopolies. On the other hand, however, the bishops made it clear that they were reformers, not revolutionaries; they were trying to soften the harshness of the American economic system, but they allayed any fears of the ruling powers that they might be trying to change that system: ". . . Socialism would mean bureaucracy, political tyranny, the helplessness of the individual as a factor in the ordering of his own life, and in general social inefficiency and decadence."[45] The most important thing altogether, the bishops declare, is the development of a new spirit, based on the principles of justice and charity; thus all things merely relative can be unified and controlled in the perspective of the absolute.[46]

We must not conclude, however, from this brief and incomplete discussion of some of the work of Catholics interested in the cause of labor, that the church as a whole has a liberal outlook.

On the basis of our typology, we should expect that if there are powerful antiliberal tendencies in society there will be elements of Catholicism that seek to encompass those tendencies and exploit them for a religious end. That this is indeed the case can be demonstrated amply by two well-known examples. In the United States, the most widely read and heard Catholic until the outbreak of the war was, not a high official, but the priest of a small parish in Michigan, Charles Coughlin. With his magazine, *Social Justice,* his network broadcasts, his immense correspondence, which required the services of two hundred full-time clerks, he has come to the attention of millions of people and has been an important factor in the formation of public opinion. There can be no other explanation of the reluctance of the hierarchy to silence his antidemocratic invective than that they believed he was serving the cause of the church as well as is the Catholic liberal. He who would encompass society cannot respect consistency.

Another example of "rightist" elements in the Catholic Church is the recent history of Spain. The sympathy of the church during the Spanish Civil War is not a matter for dispute; even the more liberal Catholic publications in the United States called for a Franco victory.[47] After the war the Vatican was not long in coming to terms with the new regime: "In Spain, a land that never applied *Rerum Novarum,* the Roman Catholic Church . . . accommodated itself to somewhat different necessities"—different from the necessary prolabor attitude in America, where most of its members are laborers, and where most of its priests come from the working class. "Reports from Rome and Madrid indicated that the Vatican had finally agreed to let Franco recover Alfonso XIII's power to nominate Spain's bishops, subject to papal ratification."[48] In the final agreement this process was reversed, for Franco was allowed only to choose the one of three men nominated by the Vatican that he preferred. This has proved to be a sufficient control for Franco: in the spring of 1943 the first four bishops to be nominated under the agreement took an oath of fealty to the Spanish state, an action long unknown. His regime was further associated with Catholicism by the restoration of millions of dollars worth of church property confiscated by the Republic and by the promise to pay $6,200,000 annually in salaries for the clergy. Recently Archbishop Spellman has re-emphasized the cordiality existing between Spain and the Catholic hierarchy by his endorsement of Franco as a fine Christian gentleman.[49]

One must not forget, however, that many Catholics were among the important centers of resistance against the later developments of Nazism. All over Europe, Catholics as well as other churchmen have shown that their acceptance of the established powers is qualified by the demand that certain minimum Christian standards be followed. Any one-sided explanation of the role of the Catholic Church today is almost certain to be wrong. That the Vatican made a concordat with Hitler in 1933 should not be allowed to obscure the strength of Catholic opposition—not so much from the hierarchy as from local Catholic leaders—to Nazism today. The governments of Great Britain and France, after all, also made something of a concordat with Hitler in 1938—and for reasons not notably different from those of the Vatican. While recognizing the general friendliness of Catholicism for the "corporate state," we must also remember its demands upon that state. These demands are based in part upon the church's own struggle for power, but also upon the vitality of its Christian beliefs.

Thus the Catholic Church continues to pursue the Thomist policy of reconciliation, attempting to maintain society in an organic unit for a religious end. The total effect of its policy and of its reaction to the dilemma of the churches is probably to enable it to adjust more easily to a relatively friendly corporate state (Franco's Spain or Mussolini's Italy) than to either democratic liberalism or communism. The ideas of freedom of thought and belief that characterize democratic liberalism are not readily accepted by the Catholic Church because such ideas allow freedom not to be Catholic, and even to oppose the church. The conflict with communism is not centered primarily in the atheism of communism—in the opinion of the present writer the church could adjust to that fairly easily—but in the emphasis given by communism to class conflict, i.e., disunity, thus denying the premise of unity which is basic in the teachings of Catholicism (and to a lesser degree in the teachings of all churches). Yet today, with the Comintern dissolved, we are beginning to see some kind of reconciliation between the Vatican and Moscow, for it now seems evident that the Catholic Church is going to have to live in Europe with a very powerful Soviet Union.[50]

Conservative Elements in the Churches

In the discussion above we have analyzed some aspects of the responses of the churches to modern industrialism. The effect of that analysis may have been to overemphasize the liberalism of the churches, because we have focused primarily on an important, but relatively small, part of the total religious situation. We have seen that the combined effect of a minority religious sectarianism and a liberalizing secular power (centered in the labor movement for the most part) has been to force the churches to pay some attention to the problems of modern industrialism. The dilemma of the churches has not disappeared, however, and denominationalism still has a secular as well as a purely religious significance. We should be surprised, therefore, if contemporary churches—in their total pattern—contradicted the prevailing balance of power. There is ample evidence to testify that such is not the case.

It is important to note, first of all, the wealth and membership of churches in the United States. In 1936 there were 55,807,366 church members, belonging to 256 different denominations. This is an incomplete list, estimated by the census to be several hundred thousand short. Since there are fewer children on church rolls than in the general population, the percentage of adults who are church members is higher than the above figure would indicate. Fry found that 55 per cent of the adult population of the United States were church members in 1926.[51] If the churches were a random sample of the population, their economic ethics would correspond to that of the country as a whole. While no definitive study has been made of the class distribution of church membership, the consensus of expert opinion is that the rolls are weighted in favor of the middle and upper classes and the nonurban lower classes in most of the large denominations, the Catholic Church being the chief exception.[52] When one takes into account the class position of church officials and the clergy (see below), the class perspective of the churches becomes even more apparent.

The wealth of the churches also reaches very large proportions. In 1936 church edifices in the United States were valued at $3,411,875,467 (compared with $3,839,500,610 in 1926). If the value of religious schools, hospitals, homes for children and the aged, printing establishments, parsonages, and other property is added, the value of church property in this country reaches a total of seven billion dollars. The annual expenditure is large. In 1936 American churches spent $518,955,571 (compared with $817,214,528 in 1926), or approximately one per cent of the national income.[53]

What is the correlation between the wealth of the churches in America and their economic ethics? Although there is great variation in the economic stand taken by religious groups, we are interested here in the net effect of religious teachings on economic attitudes. An occasional wealthy layman will raise a protest against radical tendencies within the church (see below), but there is general agreement among other persons and groups that on the whole the churches pronounce the present economic system "good" and alternative systems "bad." Swift, a liberal churchman, writes:

> It is, I believe, beyond question that organized religion in the United States by virtue of its vastly increased wealth is so closely interrelated with the whole capitalistic system, so committed to the sacredness of private property and to the notion that financial success is in some vague way an indication of divine favor, that it cannot help

but consider any real attack upon capitalism as a threat to its own security.[54]

In a series of statements by labor leaders, giving their opinions of the influence of the churches, there are a few extreme antireligious attitudes on the part of those far to the left and some enthusiastic praise of the churches from a few conservative trade unionists, but by far the greatest number of the statements, while not antireligious, condemn the heaven-centeredness, the conservatism, the failure to attack social and economic problems which they feel are characteristic of the churches in general.[55]

Protestantism appeared, as we have seen in Chapter IV, as part of the same movement which produced capitalism, and it is not surprising, therefore, that its ethic is a capitalist ethic. The recurrent sect movements—Quaker, Methodist, Salvation Army, the Holiness sects, and others—have continually demonstrated the inability of Protestantism to satisfy the needs of those who share least in the distribution of income under capitalism. Churchmen who would contradict the prevailing economic ethic find their influence waning. A story from *Time* is a good illustration of the process:

> Most Southern churchmen are theological, economic and political hard-shells. Eleven years ago one of the oldest and richest churches in Chattanooga, Tenn., Third Presbyterian, called a Scottish-born-and-burred clergyman who was anything but shellbacked—Rev. Thomas B. Cowan. In 1934 Pastor Cowan held a meeting of a new radical organization, the Fellowship of Southern Churchmen, later became its president. Thereupon 22 Chattanoogans seceded from Third Church. More left when Mr. Cowan helped organize labor unions, worked among sharecroppers, invited a Negro to a church dinner. Of late the chief listeners to Pastor Cowan's Sunday sermons have been newcomers and strangers in town.[56]

This is not simply a Southern or a Presbyterian situation; it is indicative of the dilemma of the churches. In the summer of 1935 a group of Methodist laymen—bankers, industrialists, utility men—who were worried over what they considered leftist tendencies among some of the clergymen, organized the Conference of Methodist Laymen. They expressed their protest at the substitution of "economic and social systems for *the Christian ideal of individual responsibility and freedom of choice.*"[57] Liberal church magazines such as *Zion's Herald* and the *Christian Century* raised a strong protest. Thereupon Burt Denman, a utility company official, left the Methodist Church, which, he said, had meant much to him, for he could not support "in my small way, either financially or spiritually" the leftest tendencies. He was literally right: no ruling class can support a religious ethic which challenges its right to rule. The dilemma of the churches is sharply outlined by his behavior.

Trott and Sanderson in *What Church People Think about Social and Economic Issues* have made a rather careful study of the opinions of white Protestant adults (over sixteen years of age) who are active church members in Baltimore. Of more than twenty-five hundred questionnaires sent out, only 41 per cent (1,087) were returned, but by use of a combination random and purposive sample the authors feel that they have greatly reduced the error that may have resulted from the failure to achieve a random sample.[58] While this is not a definitive study that can be generalized beyond its universe to interpret the economic ethics of American church people as a whole, it is indicative of a pattern that other evidence, both empirical and theoretical, seems to validate.

By a modified Thurstone-Chave technique, Trott and Sanderson arranged a series of statements in order from most radical to most conservative. They did this for three general questions: the church and the social order, property, and labor. Although the average opinion was slightly more liberal with regard to abstract principles (the church and the social order) than concrete situations (property), the total result was that church people are definitely "middle of the road" in their opinions on economic matters. In the seventeen statements on the church and the social order, number one, which was the most radical, was checked by 4 per cent of the 1,087 who returned the questionnaire. This statement read, "The church should help to establish world-wide communism." The most conservative statement, number seventeen, "Ministers who teach socialism should be run out of the church," was checked by 20 per cent. Statement number nine, checked by 89 per cent, was both median and mode; it is a thoroughly church-type expression: "The church should stand for equal rights and complete justice for all men in all stations of life."

In the series of questions on property, the opinions of church people in Baltimore are more conservative. Statements one to eight (the liberal half) were checked 2,357 times, while statements nine to sixteen (the conservative half) were checked 3,951 times. This indicates a more conservative opinion with reference to the questions relating to property than was shown in the general problem of the relation of the church to the social order. The data show clearly "that idealistically we hold to one position, practically we hold to another, and that our ideals are more liberal than our actions. The material shows sharply this gap between ideals and action, between the general and the specific."[59] This discrepancy was also revealed in a study by the present writer in which it was found that 45 per cent of the ministers canvassed checked such a liberal statement as "Socialism is a necessary economic system for the continued working out of Christian teachings on earth"; but in a later statement 61 per cent opposed what is generally regarded as the first and most important step toward socialism by stating that they considered the private banking system "essential to the best interests of a democratic society."[60]

With regard to the third series of questions given by Trott and Sanderson, concerning the rights of labor, the average opinion of Baltimore church people was more liberal than opinions on property. There was a strong minority group that expressed a definitely prolabor attitude. The total result, however, was still "middle-of-the-road." One may compare the responses to the three series of questions by preparing an index number in which "0" represents the most radical position and "100" represents the most conservative. On this basis, the average position of the sample of Baltimore church people was 49.0 on "The Church and the Social Order," 60.5 on "Property," and 49.0 on "Labor." The average for the total was 52.8, or slightly right of center.

> The church is pulled and hauled in opposite directions by the idealism and the practical interests of its members. The net result of its conflicting attitudes is that the church's average position is "middle-of-the-road." . . . By and large, the church is all-of-a piece with the society of which it constitutes so large a part. It is stronger at denouncing injustice than it is in implementing justice. . . . The church has its feet firmly on the ground of contemporary society. . . .[61]

The sharpest contrasts in economic attitudes were not found among the various denominations but between clergy and laity. "Ministerial scores are furthest to the left, whereas church officers' scores are somewhat more conservative than those whose church *connection* is less intimate. Non-members who are church attendants are less conservative than members."[62] Unfortunately, the authors did not calculate the significance of these differences nor include sufficient data to make it possible for the reader to work it out; but a simple appraisal makes it seem certain that the differences are too large to be due to chance. There has been no adequate explanation of why clergymen should be more liberal than their congregations, but we may offer two very tentative hypotheses, which will have to be tested by later research. Operating on the assumption that the religious "interest" is stronger in ministers, we may perhaps reasonably suppose that they are sensitive to deprivations of their parishioners and alert, therefore, to movements which claim to be able to reduce the deprivations. Secondly, the fact that clergymen find themselves in a low income bracket may give some of them cause to question the legitimacy of the economic system. Their average salary is less than $1,500,[63] which is at the bottom of professional groups and well below the income of many artisan groups.

One should not exaggerate, however, any tendency that clergymen may have to be somewhat more liberal than the average laymen on economic matters, nor suppose that their income is the only factor in determining their class and status position. Important influences tend to align them with the middle and upper classes: they are generally regarded to be of professional standing; they are given a place of prestige if not of power; they are invited to invoke God's blessing on political, business, and educational enterprises. Swift observes:

> . . . it is significant that in many Protestant churches the minister is financially dependent upon those men in his community who are least likely to approve any criticism of the existing economic order. Likewise it is significant for the spiritual and ethical pilgrimage of the average minister that he and his family are brought into most intimate and continuous contact with the more "influential" families of the church.[64]

Thus most clergymen are regarded and regard themselves as part of the "respectable" community, and the tendency toward greater liberalism which Trott and Sanderson found may largely be explained as an attempt to reduce hardships within the established system by teaching all their people that they are part of an essential unity. The dilemma which they face allows them to do no more, and often they do less. Liberal churchmen may be depressed by the fact that the churches are supported "largely by the upper and middle classes, by people who believe that God is a capitalist," but they cannot disregard it, and others accept the fact as a normal situation. "Although many churchmen have accustomed their congregations to socially radical words from the pulpit, most parsons pipe the tunes which businessmen call."[65] A meeting in a Chicago suburb (Barrington, Illinois) illustrated the relationship between churches and ruling economic interests. The occasion was a "town-warming" sponsored by the Jewel Tea Company, which is the big business of the town. The principal churches (Methodist, Catholic, Christian Scientist) all co-operated in the program. *Time* wryly remarked: ". . . Channing Pollock labeled his address: 'I am a Reactionary.' The others did not need to."

Of significance equal to the economic ethics of clergymen is the class position of the influential layman and church officers. On this subject there is very general agreement. Trott and Sanderson wrote: "In general, the church . . . elects its conservatives to office; and, unless one is the minister, the farther one gets into the administration of local church affairs, the more conservative one is likely to be."[66] Davis reached a similar conclusion:

> A study of 387 church boards of the leading Protestant denominations shows that there is a class control of the Protestant churches at present. . . . Fifty-five per cent of them [the board members] are either proprietors, managers, or in some professional service. Omitting towns under 5,000, the merchants are by far the most numerous class on the boards, with the clerks and bankers ranking on the average next.
>
> On all church boards, including those in towns under 5,000, in proportion to their numbers the bankers are most often elected chairmen, while manufacturers follow.[67]

This is not a surprising conclusion, but it is a significant factor in helping to account for the economic ethics of contemporary churches.

We are struck very forcibly, in a survey of the contemporary religious situation, with the continuing effects of the dualism which has been involved in Christian teachings from the beginning. On the one hand there are a group of churchmen who declare that religion must become increasingly liberal if it is to maintain its influence in the modern world. They claim that the churches, if they are not to be annihilated by "the secularized religion of Marxism" and its derivatives, must revise their doctrines to include what they consider to be ethical insights in socialism.[68] On the other hand are those who believe that the churches should concern themselves with personal salvation and purely religious matters. It seems probable, says Lord Stamp, that the preoccupation of the church with economic affairs "weakens the spiritual power of the Church, allows cults of all kinds to take its place as agencies for solving spiritual problems, and through not being expert, serves to confuse the economic issues themselves by ethical heat without economic enlightenment."[69] Stamp quotes with approval a statement by C. F. Adams:

> Suppose the United States Chamber of Commerce or the National Association of Manufacturers should take a vigorous stand on such matters as infant baptism, papal infallibility, the literal inspiration of the scriptures, vicarious atonement and the immaculate conception. Would the clergy accept these views as "competent, material or relevant"? Scarcely. Pulpits would thunder against laymen who presumed to speak with authority on an esoteric speciality. Yet the clergy is pursuing a course as rash and ridiculous with respect to economic issues.[70]

Few clergymen would submit to this drastic reduction of their field of competence, for most of them consider economic ethics to be one of their specialties. To claim that religion should "keep out of secular affairs" is obviously to limit its ability to judge the secular life. There is often involved in this claim a piece of fallacious logic which, entirely apart from any judgments of value, should be pointed out. The limitation of churches to a religious sphere is usually based on the assumption—which is doubtless true—that there is no one absolute Christian economic system or political form. It does not follow from that, however, that *at a given time* there is not a choice among the available alternatives which harmonizes with the Christian ethic better than the others.[71] The statement that Christianity demands no particular economic system has been used to rationalize church acceptance of the *status quo,* whatever it has been, from the beginning.

This confusion emphasizes again the dilemma of the churches to which we have so often referred and also illustrates the social correlates of religious doctrine. It is not by accident that religion is so often limited in its applicability to "an esoteric specialty." Those who profit most from the existing arrangement of society are loath to see their religion too much concerned over the justice of that society. They prefer, for the most part without conscious thought, that religion remain an esoteric specialty. There are other religious persons who would like to use religion as a force in secular affairs, but they run into sharp opposition. If they use the religious power to compete with the power of the secular ruling classes, they find the rulers withdrawing from the churches (see the examples given above) and giving their support to a more congenial religion. Swift writes:

> Truly the minister is deserving of sympathy for he can hardly escape the dilemma of his office. . . . Does he serve the church by antagonizing its more influenital members? Does he serve it by accomplishing his own expulsion from its pulpit? However urgent the issue, be it race or war or labor strike, is it not his task to offer to both sides the consolations of religion? Must he not so conduct himself as to maintain his influence and prestige in the community? By finding the easy answers to these questions, many continue to hold their pulpits but have surrendered all they have to preach about in order to keep the privilege of preaching. Others, finding the hard answers have been forced out of the church and out of its ministry. The majority find answers which neither force them from the church nor entirely rob them of their message.[72]

Few ministers, indeed, are forced out of the church because of their radical ideas. In Swift's experience, the vast majority become adjusted to the standards of their constituencies within the first five years, "thereafter making only minor efforts to rouse a divine discontent with the established order, but instead strongly attacking those personal sins in general frowned upon and offering the consolations and assurances of faith and love to offset the sufferings, the difficulties, the bereavements and disillusionments which are in some degree the lot of all men."[73] Stability, not prophecy, is the end which the churches usually fill.

Contemporary Religious "Prophecy"

We must note again, however, that there is a prophetic note within the total religious picture, manifesting itself in sect or sectarianism, which contributes to the breaking up of tradition. It is in time of crisis that this prophetic or "radical" element is likely to come to the fore. One might expect, therefore, that the contemporary religious situation would be full of "prophecy." And that is indeed the case. We shall concern ourselves here with one phase of that sectarianism: the pronouncements of churchmen on Christian standards for the postwar world. We cannot hope to study all the relevant data on this topic, and therefore we run the risk of falling into the errors of the old illustrative method. That danger can be minimized, however, by keeping constantly in mind the question of the representative nature of the illustrations.

One of the most important proofs of the existence of a "prophetic" note in religious thought today is the series of church conferences which have given testimony that a liberal element in the churches supports the war partly because it may furnish an opportunity for bringing about some rather drastic social changes. In the prewar years there were signs of an increasingly liberal tendency among many churchmen (as, indeed, there were among secular groups): the ecumenical tendency was developed in the much publicized Oxford Conference and in the early stages of development of a world church federation; there was a growing liberal temper in the Federal Council of Churches; and many churchmen were calling for an implemented League of Nations. In a study by the present writer in May, 1941 (a study which did not secure a representative sample, but may be somewhat indicative), twice as many clergymen checked the statement, "Municipal and national ownership and control of industry need to be pushed farther and farther, as rapidly as justice allows, into the domain of private business," as checked the statement, "America will not escape from depression and unemployment until private enterprise is freed from the present oppressive governmental measures, and given a free hand once again." Of two intermediary questions, the more liberal was also checked twice as often as the conservative.

After the start of war, many churchmen were in the forefront of those demanding the declaration of explicit war aims.

Disappointed with Churchill's failure to outline precise aims, the Church of England, which traditionally has little to do with Nonconformists and Catholics, took significant action when the Archbishops of Canterbury and York jointly signed a letter to the London *Times* with the late Arthur Cardinal Hinsley, Roman Catholic Archbishop of Westminster, and Dr. Walter H. Armstrong, Joint Secretary of the Federal Council of Free Churches. They set up five standards to guide statesmen: the abolition of extreme inequalities of wealth; the establishment of equal educational opportunities for all children, according to each one's capacity; the safeguarding of the family unit; the restoration of a divine sense of vocation in daily work; and the use of the natural resources of the earth as God's gift to all.[74] These were not radical demands, but they exceeded official pronouncements of the government.

A new but important American religious journal, *Christianity and Crisis,* although it was actively supporting full aid to Great Britain, expressed rather keen disappointment in Anthony Eden's "Mansion House" speech. It regretted the intimation that the old concept of exclusive German war guilt was being revived: ". . . what he said was ill-designed to keep alive the consciousness, so gratifyingly evident in other British utterances, of common responsibility for the international anarchy which led to this war."[75] They suggested their own hopes for the postwar world in a further statement:

> Mr. Eden said not a word about the abandonment of the principle of unlimited national sovereignty and the creation of a truly international government. He said nothing about the necessity of fundamental economic reconstruction such as the pronouncements of the Labor Party and of British churchmen have clearly implied. There is no hint—or at most, no more than a hint—of the requirement that the victors shall impose limitations upon themselves corresponding to those which are to be imposed on Germany.[76]

Most publicized of the gatherings to develop plans for the new society which is "quite evidently emerging" was the famed

Malvern Conference, in which the Church of England liberals formulated their war aims. These were quite startling pronouncements for the traditionally conservative Establishment. The conference declared that the war was not an isolated evil but a symptom of a widespread disease in the social order. One of the crucial factors in this disease, they held, is the supremacy of profit motivation, which has led to waste of resources, to production for profit, and has been a contributing factor in unemployment and war: "This method of ordering industry, which tends to treat human work and human satisfaction alike as means to a false and—namely, monetary gain—becomes a source of unemployment at home and dangerous competition for markets abroad. . . . The system under which we have lived has been a predisposing cause of war, even though those who direct and profit by it have desired peace."[77] The churchmen demanded that the rights of labor be equal to the rights of capital in control of industry; they called for freedom of international commerce and for conservation; they held that adequate educational opportunities for all children were a prime necessity. The conference accepted a statement of the Madras Conference which represents an approach the church does not generally make to social change:

> It is not enough to say that if we change the individual we will of necessity change the social order. That is a half truth. For the social order is not entirely made up of individuals now living. It is made up of inherited attitudes which have come down from generation to generation through customs, laws, institutions, and these exist in large measure independently of individuals now living. Change those individuals and you do not necessarily change the social order unless you organize those changed individuals into collective action in a wide-scale frontal attack upon those corporate evils.[78]

Other statements bore out the conference's desire to attack social problems directly, rather than by the means of personal religion alone. These criticisms were directed at the church as well as at other aspects of society. In a statement under the heading "Propositions Accepted," the conference declared:

It is a traditional doctrine of Christendom that property is necessary to fulness of personal life; all citizens should be enabled to hold such property as contributes to moral independence and spiritual freedom without impairing that of others; but where the rights of property conflict with the establishment of social justice or the general social welfare, those rights should be over-ridden, modified, or, if need be, abolished.

Among its "practical recommendations" the Malvern Conference stated:

Human status ought not to depend upon the changing demands of the economic process; no one should be deprived of the support necessary for "the good life" by the fact that there is at some time no demand for his labor. . . . There is urgent need that the Church of England should radically reorganize its own economic and administrative system, and so reconstruct this as to make it an expression of unity of purpose and especially of brotherhood in the ministry.[79]

While these statements represent a very liberal point of view, we must note that certain articles which were adopted by the Malvern Conference and reported in the press at the time were changed or left out of the official conference report which appeared a few months later. Two changes are perhaps most significant. The original statement contained this declaration: "Whatever may be the necessities of the period immediately following the war, our aim must be the unification of Europe as a cooperative commonwealth, first in common effort for the satisfaction of general need and secondly in such political institutions as express the common purpose and facilitate its development."[80] This statement did not appear in the final publication. Its deletion is perhaps of no great significance, since the final version was still of very liberal tone; but it represents a tendency toward greater caution and is at least symbolic of the forces operating on religious judgments. Another statement was modified in an important way. The conference adopted the declaration that "the ownership of the great resources of our community . . . [by] private individuals is a stumbling block" in the way of Christian living. The official published version read: ". . . In our present situation we believe that the maintenance of that part of the structure of our society, by which the ultimate ownership of the principal industrial resources of the community can be vested in the hands of private owners, *may be* such a stumbling block,"[81] making it "harder for men to live Christian lives." It is not possible to know the significance of these changes without knowing the reasons for them, but they may furnish a hint of the direction in which the church doctrine tends to go (see below).

The Malvern Conference did not have the support of Archbishop Lang (then Primate of all England); but it was dominated by the late William Temple, Archbishop of York (who became Archbishop of Canterbury and successor to Lang as Primate), and it had the active support of twenty-three out of ninety-eight bishops, fourteen deans, and two hundred other clergymen. Sir Stafford Cripps endorsed it later.

In June, 1941, the first North American Ecumenical Conference was held in Toronto, representing every major Protestant denomination in the Western Hemisphere—thirty-five in all. While problems of war were not formally a part of the agenda, they claimed a good deal of attention. In the United States delegation, pacifist and nonpacifist found common ground in their demand for a just peace. The conference stressed the need for fighting Hitler's New Order by demonstrating to the world a better order, one drastically different from the prewar world. The church must, they declared, work for a more constructive and more lasting peace than Versailles.[82] *Time* wrote, somewhat paradoxically, that the "Church's idea . . . seems, as interpreted, to have some sort of resemblance to the doctrine of Karl Marx—some sort of new Christian materialism for the underdog."[83]

Perhaps the most important American church conference on war aims was sponsored by the Federal Council of Churches through its Commission for the Study of the Bases of a Just and Durable Peace. This conference met in Delaware, Ohio, in March, 1942, and has been said by many to be the most distinguished gathering of churchmen in this country in the last quarter of a century: fifteen bishops (of five denominations), eight college and university presidents, the heads of seven seminaries, most of the important officials of the Federal Council of Churches, and many prominent laymen (Harvey B. Firestone, Jr., President H. W. Dodds of Princeton, Irving Fisher, and others) were among the 375 delegates. During the three-day session the group was addressed by six leaders in the study of international problems: Hu Shih, then Ambassador from China; John Foster Dulles, international lawyer, and head of the Commission; Bishop Francis J. McConnell, Methodist liberal; Leo Pasvolsky, special assistant to Secretary of State Cordell Hull; John Hambro, former Premier of Norway and former President of the League of Nations; and the late William Paton, General Secretary of the emerging World Council of Churches.[84] While these addresses were not an official part of the proceedings of the conference (only two of the speakers sat as delegates), they were fully in accord with the temper and quality of the leadership.

For its discussion of the Bases of a Just and Durable Peace, the conference divided itself into four sections, to study the social, political, economic, and religious factors involved. The statements which emerged, after revision and acceptance in plenary session, were sharply critical of contemporary economic and political arrangements. The conference strongly supported labor's demand for a larger share in industrial management as "fundamental to successful political democracy." It contended "that a new ordering of economic life is both imminent and imperative, and that it will come either through voluntary co-operation within the framework of democracy or through explosive political revolution."[85] The delegates insisted upon complete abandonment of United States isolationism; they favored worldwide freedom of immigration; international control of armies and navies; and, perhaps most important of all, the limitation of national sovereignty and the ultimate development of a supranational government. Resolved to avoid the errors of Versailles, the conference demanded that there be "no punitive reparations, no humiliating decrees of war guilt, and no arbitrary dismemberment of nations."[86]

It should be noted, however, that the pronouncements of the conference were not greatly influenced by the advice of E. R. Bowen, consultant of the economic section, that the "conclusions of the Committee be worded more specifically than is common with church pronouncements" (from a mimeographed list of suggestions). Bowen pointed out the ineffectiveness of abstract doctrines in concrete situations: "We might as well try to teach piano by lecture." The conference did declare that the profit system "has in recent years developed grave defects. There have occurred mass unemployment, widespread dispossession from homes and farms, destitution, lack of opportunity for youth and of security for old age."[87] And it recommended such specific economic changes as "a universal system of money . . . so planned as to prevent inflation and deflation . . ."; "the progressive elimination of restrictions on world trade"; "the fullest collaboration between all nations in the economic field with the object of securing *for all* improved labor standards, economic advancement and social security" (quoting the language of the Atlantic Charter); and "the establishment of a democratically controlled international bank or banks to make development capital available in all parts of the world without the predatory or imperialistic aftermath so characteristic of large-scale private or governmental loans."[88]

None of these statements has particularly radical implications, however, except "a democratically controlled international bank," and that recommendation is far from precise in its meaning. Moreover, the traditional religious *modus operandi* is revealed in the attempt to secure a balance between collectivist and individualist economic systems:

> We do not believe that we are limited to a choice between these two alternatives. If this seems the only choice it is largely because the churches have failed generally to inculcate Christian motivation. Willingness to strive and to produce and to render services should not be dependent either wholly upon profit motivation or wholly upon com-

pulsion. We urge upon the churches that they have the great opportunity and responsibility to make possible a generally acceptable solution *by bringing people to a different and more Christian motivation*.[89]

The importance of this conference lies in the field of public opinion. Hundreds of thousands of copies of the report have been distributed to Protestants throughout the country. It has been, and will continue to be, the topic of church study groups, of sermons, of articles. The Commission to Study the Bases of a Just and Durable Peace, which sponsored the conference, has sought to make the findings of the group more politically significant by relating them to six "political propositions." They have given wide publicity to the "Six Pillars of Peace," which they consider essential for a Christian postwar world: a world-government, with provisions for bringing neutral and enemy lands into the United Nations; use of this authority for development of international trade; provision for changing international agreements as conditions change; active work toward the goal of freedom for all colonial peoples as soon as possible; provision for international military control; world-wide freedom of religion and thought.[90] Fourteen religious leaders in Great Britain, including the Archbishops of Canterbury and York, the Moderator of the Church of Scotland, and spokesmen for nonconformist groups have given their approval to the "six pillars." The Methodist bishops of America have reduced them to a series of compact slogans, which became the topics for a series of meetings in which the slogans were interpreted by clergymen and laymen. These meetings were held between October, 1943, and January, 1944, after which the participating members took the discussion into the local churches.

It is difficult to evaluate the significance of this kind of activity on the part of churchmen. The *Christian Century* declares that the "Six Pillars of Peace" are a considerably weaker formulation of aims than the statements which came out of the original conference of the Commission to Study the Bases of a Just and Durable Peace. The editors point specifically to the absence of any statement concerning the rejection of revenge and retaliation, a weakening of the assertion that the control of peoples "not yet capable of self-government" be in the hands of an international authority, the absence of any specific reference to the need for basic changes in the national policies of the United States, and a less specific assertion of the need for reduction of national sovereignty.[91] Certainly the "six pillars" give a more conservative impression than the longer original statement of the findings of the Commission. This is perhaps due both to the growth of pressures against the tone of the original statement (note that the pronouncements of the Malvern Conference underwent a similar modification) and also to the need for developing a more immediately practicable campaign, for which the "six pillars" are slogans. The whole development of the work of the Commission is an interesting example of the growth of the conference method of influencing public action. Religious leaders are attempting to gather up the unorganized and diffused religious sentiments with regard to the postwar world and to form them into an effective political weapon. By means of wide publicity given to the explicit formulation of aims, expressing the unified voice of Christian thought, they hope to make a more effective use of religious feelings for influencing political action. They will not bring about a revolution; they cannot basically change the balance of power. They may, however, prepare those who have a religious interest to accept more readily any changes that are imminent and may modify the nature of the process by which those changes take place.

One could illustrate at much greater length the attempts of religious leaders to formulate the Christian standards for the postwar world and to make them effective in public action. In the spring of 1943 the Methodist Church sponsored a conference for the study of postwar problems. A few months later, religious representatives from fourteen nations, the International Round Table of Christian Leaders, assembled at Princeton with the aim of outlining the Christian approach to world order. The Central

Conference of American Rabbis, in a meeting in Cincinnati, expounded these principles:

1. The extension of democracy to all peoples including those residing in colonial possessions. 2. The creation of an international organization to adjust differences and to provide for co-operative enterprises. 3. Universal disarmament and the establishment of an international police force to be used to restrain aggressor or outlaw nations. 4. The removal of social injustices which lead to war. 5. The recogntion that the resources of the world belong to all the children of men and should be made available to all irrespective of national allegiances.[92]

Christianity and Crisis carries frequent articles on postwar adjustment, most of them of very liberal character. Between February 4 and June 3, 1942, the *Christian Century* published an important series of articles on "How Shall the Christian Church Prepare for the New World Order?" The almost unanimous import of the seventeen articles was that there must be a "new world order." Not only did they stress the need for a renewed religious emphasis and a restoration of prophecy, but also spoke in favor of a world police force, the limitation of national sovereignty, the establishment of a world government of some strength, and the modification of the profit motive. Some of the most influential clergymen in the country were among the contributors to the series.

The strength of this religious interest in the problem of world order is also shown in the Interfaith Declaration on World Peace, which has been issued by a large group of Catholic, Jewish, and Protestant leaders. The statement is the distillation of many official pronouncements from religious groups and is therefore quite representative, a least common denominator (in no derogatory sense), of active religious thought on the problem. It was sponsored by the Synagogue Council of America, the Federal Council of Churches of Christ in America, and the Social Action Department of the National Catholic Welfare Conference. The declaration does not deal with specific problems nor is it revolutionary, but it represents an active and organized interest on the part of religious leaders to have a voice in social policy. They declare: The moral law must govern world order; the rights of the individual must be assured; the rights of oppressed, weak or colonial peoples must be protected; the rights of minorities must be secured; international institutions to maintain peace with justice must be organized; international economic cooperation must be developed; a just social order within each state must be achieved. Forty-seven Catholic, forty-seven Jewish, and fifty Protestant leaders signed the declaration.[93]

In January, 1945, the National Study Conference on the Churches and a Just and Durable Peace, established by the Federal Council of Churches, came out strongly for the support of the Dumbarton Oaks plan. Bishop G. Bromley Oxnam, President of the Council, made several proposals for the improvement of the plan—it is part of the "relative natural law"—but asked for its unconditional support. Christians must strive, he said, not only for ultimate goals, but for attainable steps on the way to such goals.[94] John Foster Dulles, Chairman of the National Study Conference, also called for unconditional support of the Dumbarton Oaks plan, while striving for its improvement.

Summary

This discussion of the manifestation of the interest of churches in plans for the future could be greatly expanded; but perhaps enough has been said to illustrate the development, in this period of crisis, of tradition-breaking "prophecy" in the churches. It is essential, however, that we avoid misinterpreting the significance of these developments. Unless our conceptual scheme is an inadequate guide to the situation, there are many other factors involved that must be taken into account. A brief statement will demonstrate this to be the case. We must note first of all that the liberal element in the churches is not large; it is an important group, but it is a minority. The late William Temple, Archbishop of Canterbury, was an outstanding liberal, but seventy-five out of ninety-eight bishops did not support the Malvern Conference. In the discussion above we have given numerous illustrations of the basically conservative point of view of the churches.

Secondly, it is important to recall that churchmen are not alone in their demands for basic social changes. There has been a shift in the "productive forces," and just as specialization and intercity trade made necessary the enlargement of the feudal political unity, so corporation economy and world-wide trade are furnishing strong pressures toward the modification of the nation-state system and (theoretically) free enterprise. What the alignment of forces will be on this issue after the war is not yet clear, but it is clear that for some groups—namely, those that are suffering from the orientation around scarcity that typifies some aspects of the present economic system—*sheer economic expediency* is demanding some of the very things that liberal churchmen are now acclaiming in the name of justice and charity. That is not to say that the spiritual reinforcement which they give to these tendencies may not be important in their development. But the aims were not discovered by the church: contemporary economic conditions have been in the process of development for a good many decades; and Karl Marx wrote, after all, nearly a century ago. Mankind is forced to reflect upon the adequacy of its social arrangements by years of depression and war, and there are a great many today who contend that they have plans superior to the existing structure. In view of the function and tactics of the church, it is not surprising that these plans should be given some religious sanction.[95] Nor is it surprising, on the other hand, that a large proportion of churchmen should continue to hold that the larger element of "justice" depends upon the present (and past) economic and political system. Most people think traditionally; this is especially true of that important group which is in a "sheltered" position which protects them from the shock of an inadequate system of productive relations. Life has satisfied their needs, comparatively, and therefore they "know"—in the chief, if not the only, way that mankind can "know" anything—that the present system is "good," that alternative systems are "bad," and that therefore those who sponsor such systems are bad people.

The liberal minority of churchmen, on the other hand, is furnishing religious and ethical justification for a group who "know" —in the same way that the conservatives know the opposite— that collectivism is good and imperfect competition bad. One must not forget that there is a secular counterpart in this division: we have a Byrnes in our government, but also a Wallace; and Britain has replaced a Churchill with an Attlee. Contemporary religious "prophecy" is thus paralleled in political circles. A sociology of religion which does not give careful attention to this fact cannot hope to be adequate.

We must note, thirdly, the crucial distinction between the prevalence of liberal and even radical belief during a time of crisis and its realization in the struggle for power. Idealism ran high in many quarters during the Civil War, but it did not free the Negro. Only gradually, if at all, has the situation changed. In 1918 Wilson's Fourteen Points were hailed by the whole liberal world—but the United States did not join the League and the countries that did join used it for national interests for the most part. It may be that idealism runs high in times of crisis precisely to justify and rationalize the brutalities of that crisis. Men have to make deferent gestures to their own humanitarianism. Much of the idealism of a crisis may be a confessional that does not change the objective situation, but relieves the sense of guilt. One ought not, therefore, to rely too heavily on the pronouncements of churchmen during the war. This is not a question of sincerity but one of power.

This leads to a fourth point, to which we have already referred from time to time, namely, the weakness of religion in formulating precise and effective methods for realizing its aims in the concrete situation. This is an inherent weakness, based on the fact that religion is only one of man's interests, and in most people not a dominant one. It must continually fight a battle against the demands of man's other interests. If churchmen constantly appeal to "character" and "Christian motivation," this is not wholly out of a failure to understand what lies behind the behavior of men, but a recognition of the dilemma that they face: if they try to appeal to anything but character, they do not get even that. It is therefore perhaps inevitable that the conferences which we have discussed above were weak at precisely the point where strength was needed—the development of a *modus operandi.*[96] The editors of *Time* once wrote that it is as safe for the churchmen to be in favor of an economy of abundance as it is safe for them to be in favor of heaven. The question is, how to achieve it! The limitations in method, moreover, are likely to be accompanied by lack of precision in aim: There was a continual struggle in the Delaware Conference over the role of the churches, and it was almost always decided that they should lay down moral principles and not specific solutions to problems. It was left to experts to decide what was the most efficient way to realize the moral principle, and left to character to carry it out. Needless to say, the experts usually have a different means-end schema in mind, and factors other than character enter into its realization.[97]

We repeat, nevertheless, that many of the churchmen at these conferences were very able strategists and were deploying their power in the most effective way possible. Religion is only one of man's interests, and not a dominating one in the lives of most people; pronouncements on the postwar world cannot upset the balance of power which will give our society its basic characteristics. They can, however, so prepare public opinion that it will be easier to break down traditional barriers; they can give the new order an ethical justification; and they can keep the churches in a position where they can reduce the harshness of a given society even if they cannot determine it completely. Thus religious prophecy, however caused, is today a factor in the field of interaction in which new economic and political forms are being worked out.

Chapter VI

THE CHURCHES AND WAR

The relationship of religious groups to the society in which they are found is sharply revealed against the background of war. If one can preserve a vision unclouded by the powerful emotions that surround our thinking about military conflict, in peacetime as well as in war, he can go a long way toward understanding the conduct of religious groups in their relation to secular problems. Our task in this chapter is to attempt to interpret, from a sociological point of view, the significance of the contradictions and shifts in attitudes toward war that are characteristic of religious groups. We believe that these can best be understood by relating them to the concepts we have already used in earlier chapters—the concept of the "dilemma of the churches," a recognition of "the social sources of denominationalism," and a knowledge of the types of religious bodies.

The data with which we are concerned are not new, and there is very general agreement on the facts of the case. Students of organized religion have frequently pointed out the ease with which most church leaders shift, at the outbreak of war, from an explicit antiwar position to a vigorous prowar policy. Only seldom, however, has there been an awareness of the sociological significance of this shift in demonstrating the role that organized religion plays in society. Many critics have been antireligious and pointed to the "hypocrisy" of the church groups; others have been extremely, and often ascetically, religious and have lamented the demise of Christian belief. Neither extreme has contributed to an understanding of the problem.

Our analysis will be focused, for the most part, on the behavior of American churches during the two World Wars; but this requires a few words of background. We need not attempt to discover whether or not the founder of Christianity was a pacifist. This much is certain: churches and individuals have been able to find support in the teachings of Jesus for a great variety of different attitudes toward war, ranging from the holy zeal of the crusade to penitent and reluctant participation in war to complete pacifism. During the years when Christianity was a small and persecuted sect, pacifism was its dominant attitude. This is not surprising, for the sect did not command the resources necessary to give it any advantage in coercion. As Christianity grew in power and scope, however, the pacifist position was gradually given up. By the time of St. Augustine the small religious group had become a powerful secular as well as religious force, intimately connected with problems of coercion and conflict. St. Augustine was able to draw on a developing doctrine of justification for Christian participation in war to outline what continue to be the essential principles of the Catholic, and in large part the Lutheran and Anglican, doctrine of war: the Church can give its support to a war only if the cause of one side is manifestly just and only if it is fought without vindictiveness.[1]

Thus from the day that Christianity became the dominant religion of Western society down to the present time, churches have been involved in war. A study of churches in this country from its earliest beginnings will not reveal a different pattern. Yet that is not the whole story. Running through as a continuous part of the relationship between Christianity and war have been important elements of protest. These have typically been focused in the minority sects, but have been taken up, especially during the last century, by secular movements and in activities of the churches. Merle Curti in *Peace or War: The American*

Struggle has given us a careful account of the growth of the peace movement in this country. The first peace society was formed in 1814, although there had been agitation for peace from the beginning, and in the years before the Civil War a number of organizations and many influential persons sought to break the war pattern. The predominance of churchmen in the movement testifies to the religious basis of much of the activity.

Those who worked actively in the peace movement, however, were in a small minority. Moreover, there were very few who held to their antiwar position when conflict actually broke out. If in some wars, notably the Mexican, peace advocates in the churches continued their opposition to war in fairly large numbers, they were supported by peace sentiment throughout the country.[2] During the Civil War most of the leaders of the peace movement gave their wholehearted support to the government. The American Peace Society defended the position that this was not a war but a rebellion which must be suppressed by the police power of the government. Its treasurer, who refused to support the war, found that of eighty who signed a pledge against all war, only three adhered to the pledge.[3] A few of the leaders in the peace movement, to be sure, and many of the members of the traditionally pacifist sects continued to oppose war. But most churchmen and churches not only sanctioned the war but actively supported it.

In the half century between 1865 and 1915 there was an unprecedented growth of peace societies and peace sentiment. During this period there was a more realistic approach to the problem, manifest particularly in the attempts to extend the use of arbitration of international disputes. In contrast to the strongly secular opposition to war that developed in Europe, religious motivation was uppermost in America. Benjamin Trueblood, secretary of the American Peace Society, estimated that in 1909, on the Sunday designated as Peace Sunday, fifty thousand sermons were preached to observe the day.[4] The peace movement gradually obtained large financial support, particularly from

Andrew Carnegie. And it received what seemed to be a culminating support from the public when Woodrow Wilson, a member of the American Peace Society, came to the presidency of the country. He appointed as his Secretary of State, William Jennings Bryan, a Christian pacifist. It is not surprising that many people were convinced that war had been outlawed.

Then came the reversal. The activities of the churches during 1917 and 1918 seem to be an abrupt about-face from the peace work of the previous decades.[5] Any adequate theory of religious group behavior must make this shift meaningful. The facts of the case are widely known: once again the churches gave almost unanimous support to the government in the prosecution of the war. It is not enough simply to say that most people "lost their religion," or that they had not been sincere in their opposition to war. There were basic sociological reasons why the churches during the first World War, as in the earlier days, gave their support to the struggle. Some of these reasons are part of the immediate situation; others are the result of the nature of the relationship between religion and society in general and would operate in any war. Perhaps the most important influence was the earnest conviction that the war involved a struggle for many of the values that the churches represented. There were other factors which reinforced this conviction. In August, 1914, the British cut the one cable connecting the United States and Germany and thereby secured virtual control of information to this country. Add to that the language barrier and the general inexpertness of German propagandists in this country, and one can understand part of the British advantage in winning the support of Americans, churchmen and nonchurchmen alike. The two-billon-dollar financial stake of the United States in Allied victory, as compared with the twenty-seven millions loaned to Germany, was also operative as a cause of war sentiment on the part of church members as well as on the rest of the populace. Shortly after the start of the war, the American Defense Society and the National Security League were formed. They flooded the country with appeals for preparedness, discredited the pacifists, allied themselves with Britain. The American Legion was organized early in 1915 and pursued the same tactics. These groups were not uninfluential in shaping the attitude of the country toward the war.

Of more immediate influence on the opinions of churchmen was the conversion, by liberals (led perhaps by H. G. Wells), of the fight into a "holy war." The press became saturated with this point of view. The "holy war" campaign was convincing to churchmen, clergy and laymen alike, not so much because of its intrinsic quality (which we need not try to evaluate) as because it resolved a conflict in religious thinking. Churchmen supported the war for many reasons; but in so far as Christian doctrine was actually a part of the set of attitudes of an individual, he could participate in the war only by reconciling the fight with his religious beliefs.[6] In slightly different language, liberals and humanitarians reconciled their beliefs with the actualities of the war by seeing the war as a fight for democracy or civilization.

The national origin of churches and of their ministers was important in conditioning their position on the war. Bishop Manning and S. Parkes Cadman, for instance, who were strongly pro-British, were born in England. In regard to church groups, Scotch-Presbyterians, Wesleyan Methodists, Congregationalists, Baptists, Universalists, all with British origins, strongly favored the mother country even before the United States entered the war. Lutheran groups, especially before 1916, showed German sympathies. Irish Catholics were not active in the support of Britain.[7]

The sinking of the *Lusitania* in May, 1915, was a specific incident around which war sentiment could crystallize. After the sinking, the pronouncements of most clergymen moved closer to war, although the German Lutherans defended the sinking because of the munitions said to be aboard. Thus step by step the clergy, like the other citizens, under the influence of strong convictions, economic interests linked with the "defense" societies, propaganda, the sinking of the *Lusitania* and submarine warfare, and the prestige of national leaders such as Roosevelt, Root, and Taft, moved toward support of the war. In January, 1915, a questionnaire sent to ten thousand clergymen by the Church Peace Union showed that 95 per cent were opposed to an increase in armaments. But by March 11, 1917, 158 out of 210 New York clergymen who answered an inquiry from the Federation of Churches favored going to war.[8]

That most of the churches were thoroughly behind the government in its prosecution of the war is a matter of record. They acted as recruiting stations, urging the men to support the government and to defend Christianity. They sold liberty bonds, aided by nationally prepared sermon topics, and advertised them in their papers. The *Christian Work* wrote: "Kill the Hun, Kill his Hope"—buy bonds. In the food-saving campaign the churches led the war, for here was an activity in which self-sacrifice, generosity, and thrift—virtues highly esteemed by the churches—could aid in the war. The churches contributed to the war excitement, for many of them were most energetic in telling atrocity stories;[9] in many cases they drew brutal pictures of the Kaiser and the German people.[10] We need not give a cynical explanation of this fact, however, when we realize the *raison d'être* of atrocity stories: they are an attempt to offset the inhibitions against hate and killing that have been established by Christianity and democracy. These inhibitions are overcome only by proving that the group—which up until now has been accepted as part of "God's family"—is almost subhuman, at best an agent of the devil, and hence not deserving of good treatment. This is the reverse side of the coin which bears "Holy War" stamped on its face. Only thus can Christianity (or humanism or democracy) and war live together. If many of the clergymen were most vehement in relating atrocity stories, was it not because they had a deeper-rooted religious antiwar feeling to overcome?

Many churchmen were leaders in ferreting out the "plot" of Germany to undermine our morals and conquer the country. "Once aroused to the realities and dangers of the situation, the pastors exposed details of the vast plot, seeing evidences of its machinations in the German museum at Harvard, the German names of towns, and the use of Wagner's Wedding March."[11] Many preachers encouraged and engaged in the uncovering of "spies."[12]

"The first casualty of war is free speech," and many clergymen in the United States officiated at the obsequies. Some members of the Federal Council of Churches saw the approach of suppression and declared that "the abuse of free speech is not as dangerous as its suppression." But there was little opposition from religious forces to the passage of the Espionage Act in 1917 and the Sedition Act in 1918, although "both of these acts affected the right of conscience, the interpretation of the Scripture, even its distribution, and fundamentally all talk in favor of peace."[13] The *Churchman* wrote on September 22, 1917: "Democracy is not going to suffer from this temporary restriction [of free speech] and a little rest will prove wholesome to the tongue."[14] It became easy to say: Free speech is not license.

Clergymen in general co-operated with the government in abjuring rather than encouraging conscientious objectors (for whom, indeed, the teachings of the church were largely responsible). Often they were more critical of the conscientious objectors, less willing to take action to protect them, than the War Department itself. Chaplains and employees of the Young Men's Christian Association in the army camps were among the sharpest opponents of conscientious objectors. John R. Mott, head of the Y.M.C.A., resigned from the pacifist Fellowship of Reconciliation, which he had helped to establish in this country, when the United States entered the war. Religious groups, in their response to the position of the conscientious objector, were following the pattern of the law, which set very narrow limits to the rights of the objector, and of the Army, which attempted, for the most part successfully, to prevent the growth of any large group of pacifists.

Of nearly thirty thousand conscientious objectors who were found physically fit (out of fifty-seven thousand claims recognized by local boards) fewer than four thousand persisted in their claims to exemption from military service. These four thousand were sent to regular army camps, where treatment ranged from sympathetic understanding of their position to brutal and illegal punishment.[15] None of the churches made a systematic attempt to protect the pacifists nor to protest against the harsh sentences that many received. Nearly five hundred were sent to prison, and seventeen were sentenced to death (but none of these was executed). The maximum sentence in Great Britain was two years, subject to another two years if a person whose conscientious objection had not been accepted persisted in his claim.

It is not surprising that churchmen who were supporting the war should share the prevailing attitude toward pacifists. It is perhaps somewhat surprising that some of them should have been so vigorous in their opposition to the conscientious objectors. There may be a good deal of truth in Abrams's statement that this vehemence against "unchristian pacifists" can partly be accounted for by projection: criticism which applies most aptly to one's self being leveled at some innocent person or scapegoat instead of being endured in a conflict situation. In their condemnation of the attitudes of the pacifists, some clergymen "were actually denouncing as unpatriotic ideas with which they themselves frequently sympathized in secret. The unconscious motivation leading to the loud protests was not to squelch objectors but to suppress their own doubts, misgivings, and lack of patriotism."[16]

One of the chief aids to the government from church circles was the Federal Council of Churches, in many respects the most important religious organization in the country. It represented twenty-two Protestant denominations; it was in a good position to sense the trend of religious thought and to mold opinion. On declaration of war, the Council declared its loyalty to the government. The church, it stated, abhorred war, but war being a fact, it was behind the government in defeating the enemy.[17] The Federal Council measured the response of the ministers to the war by asking a representative clergyman in each city to report on the "prevailing opinion of the clergy" in his city. The result showed that the Protestant clergy were almost unanimous in urging the "vigorous prosecution of the war."[18] The Federal Council actively encouraged enlistment and the sale of liberty bonds. It issued formal statements in behalf of conscientious objectors but took no active part in the campaign to eliminate cruelty in their treatment. "There is no instance of a public protest from the organization."[19] The *Federal Council Bulletin* devoted a great deal of its space to activities in regard to the war. It was a veritable propaganda department for the government, continually urging war contributions, patriotism, support of the Red Cross.[20] The Council co-operated fully in the speaking division of the Committee of Public Information. Throughout the country hundreds of addresses and sermons were delivered, many of them full of vigorous attacks on the Germans.

In April, 1918, and again after the Armistice, the Federal Council of Churches refused an invitation to join a conference organized by Swedish churches to stress the need for reconciliation and elimination of hate. The administrative committee of the Council doubted the wisdom of the proposal "at just this time," because of the repercussion it might have on the official peace conference being held.[21]

By 1917 most of the thirty-five peace societies in the United States had disappeared. The *Advocate of Peace,* journal of the American Peace Society, which for several years had received its major support from the Carnegie Endowment, swung immediately into line when war was declared. Its editor became a leader in the prosecution of the war. The Delaware Society, largely Quaker, withdrew from the Peace Federation when its war aims were declared, but all of the other members co-operated. In 1915 the League to Enforce Peace was organized with William Howard Taft, strong advocate of preparedness, as president. It backed "going to war to enforce peace," and claimed to be the common ground where pacifists and advocates of preparation could meet. The League won widespread approval because it satisfied the need of the hour for channelizing the peace sentiment gracefully into war aims. Old-line peace societies after 1914 continually faced the difficulty of proving to a skeptical public that they were not pro-German (since their aim—to keep America out of the war—was the same as the German aim). This difficulty persistently undermined their influence.[22]

Despite the active support given to the war program by the main body of churchmen, however, there remained a kernel of antiwar activity, the religious sectarian element, which was not eliminated. The People's Council, formed in 1917, was perhaps the most influential peace group. Its aims were the upholding of the rights of labor, defense of the first amendment, repeal of conscription, an early peace, declaration of explicit war aims, formation of an international organization to prevent war. Among the members of the Council were many liberal clergymen, but the churches and the religious press generally fought it. Only *Unity,* among church papers, supported the Council. In Boston, in 1915, C. F. Dole, a retired Unitarian minister, founded the Association to Abolish War—an attempt to bridge the gap left by the extinction of the major peace societies. The Association took an active interest in the rights of conscientious objectors and political prisoners. But it had few members, clerical or lay.

The Fellowship of Reconciliation carried on throughout the war, working particularly to aid conscientious objectors. This group had a large proportion of clerical members, including such well-known men as J. N. Sayre, Richard Roberts, A. J. Muste, J. H. Holmes, Sidney Strong, Harry F. Ward, and Norman Thomas. The Friends, Mennonites, and Brethren (Dunkards) were also among the irreconcilables during the war. They all worked in behalf of conscientious objectors, of whom the Mennonites furnished more than any other religious group in the country. Even these traditionally pacifist groups, however, found themselves split on the war issue, and many members supported the government. Other small groups (the Russellites, the Civil

Liberties Bureau, the Chicago American Liberty Defense League) consistently opposed the war and the limitation of rights. Among their members was a large proportion of clergymen.[23]

Altogether there were probably several hundred ministers in the country with various shades of pacifism. Abrams was able to find accounts of ninety, mostly in the Northeast and in New York, not one in the South. Unitarians, Congregationalists, and Universalists furnished thirty-seven of the seventy with whom he was able to communicate. Some of these continued their pastorates through the war—preaching to reduced and changed congregations. Others felt the heavy hand of church discipline: the American Unitarian Association, which supplied funds for forty-nine ministers in 1918 (and which was of liberal character) declared that no funds would be available for churches with ministers not supporting the war. Bishop T. S. Henderson (Methodist), of Detroit, guaranteed either to regenerate or eliminate all recalcitrant ministers from his conference. In any event, the influence of pacifist ministers was small, because they were not heard.[24] The case of John Haynes Holmes, veteran liberal and pacifist, is instructive. He was in the Church of the Messiah (Unitarian) in New York. His board of trustees (a Wall Street financier, a Supreme Court judge, a vice-president of the New York Central, and others) allowed him to remain in his pulpit, according to Unitarian tradition, but his pacifism was alarming to his congregation. "They quietly departed, never to return. In their place came a strange assemblage . . . Germans and Americans, Mohammendans and Hindus, Greeks and Jews and Gentiles, Believers and Infidels—all drawn to the Church of the Messiah because they hated war."[25]

In that story is sketched the dilemma of the churches:[26] if their leaders try to pursue unwaveringly the Christian ethic, as Holmes tried to do, they lose their congregations; if they do not pursue such a course, they must give up the attempt to mold society directly after the religious pattern, and thereby reduce their influence to the point where they can only soften the harshness of the existing arrangements.[27] Most of the clergymen, like the rest of the populace, supported the war not only wholeheartedly, but uncritically. They made, in other words, an almost purely church-type response, with very few radical sectarian elements either opposing or attempting to modify the secular powers.[28]

Thus the paths taken by the churches of this country during the first World War followed the "expected" pattern quite closely. Most churchmen accepted and even sponsored the war, although in many instances this required a rather sudden change of belief. We shall postpone any further interpretation of this change until we have seen how far the contemporary scene reveals a parallel course.

Postwar Pacifism

After the war came the reaction. Preachers by the hundreds renounced their earlier war postion; resolutions denouncing war were passed by all the major denominations. Reinhold Neibuhr wrote: "Every soldier fighting for his country in simplicity of heart without asking many questions, was superior to those of us who served no better purpose than to increase or perpetuate the moral obfuscation of nations. . . . I am done with this business."[29] Harry Emerson Fosdick declared: "I do not propose to bless war again, or support it, or expect from it any valuable thing."[30] Stephen S. Wise pledged his word to his congregation never again to favor war. Charles Clayton Morrison, editor of the *Christian Century,* has for years been calling upon the churches to renounce war forever. Leavenworth will have to be enlarged for the new apostolic succession, he wrote, in event of another war.[31] The *World Tomorrow,* canvassing 53,000 clergymen, found that (out of 19,372 replies) 54 per cent of the ministers stated it to be their present purpose to sanction no future war. More than ever before, pacifism became the creed of American churches; prosperity and isolationism made it quite acceptable to the laymen as the Sermon on the Mount made it acceptable to the religious. By 1934 the *World Tomorrow* found that 62 per cent of the 20,870 clergymen (Protestant and Jewish) who answered its questionnaire stated it to be their present purpose "not to sanction any future war or participate as an armed combatant." Twenty-five per cent explained that they were not prepared to make such a statement. Sixty-seven per cent thought that the churches should go on record "as refusing to sanction or support any future war." Twenty-two per cent opposed this action.[32]

Numerous peace organizations flourished in the years after the armistice.[33] By 1934 the Fellowship of Reconciliation, with a basically religious orientation, had eight thousand members, many of them very active in the peace movement. Other groups of less specifically religious outlook won a great deal of public support. The Committee on the Cause and Cure of War was formed by nine women's organizations with which one fifth of the adult women of the country were affiliated. The National Council for the Prevention of War, the clearinghouse for seventeen national organizations, received widespread attention and influence. In 1935 the American League against War and Fascism claimed more than two million members. World Peaceways secured the signatures of over a million persons, in 1933, in support of a Peace Department in the government, the reduction of armaments, and measures to take profits out of the munitions industry. Its weekly broadcast, analyzing international problems, was sponsored by the Squibb Company and had an audience of millions. ". . . the fact that it had a commercial sponsor is striking evidence of the depth of the reaction against war."[34] The mobilization of opinion was strong enough to wield a vital influence in demanding arbitration of the 1927 dispute with Mexico over oil interests. The same pressures were doubtless involved in the activities of the government during the early thirties. In an era of disarmament conferences, peace treaties, and international pacts, the churches were given ample precedent for their behavior: the religious pacifism was an aspect of a more widespread denial of war.

But the disarmament conferences failed, the peace treaties were broken, and bit by bit the world began to remilitarize. Pacifism was rooted deep in American religious thought by the middle 1930's. How did it respond to its changing world? That is a story which in this first year of peace is not yet complete, but we can analyze lines of development. Our typology of religious group behavior can be of great help in this analysis if we keep it flexible enough to include the unique elements in the present situation.

The Catholic Church and World War II

Catholic response to war is never the same as Protestant and must, therefore, be treated separately. Official Catholicism has never adopted the position of absolute pacifism. War, it holds, is evil; it contradicts the Christian ethic; nevertheless, it is a fact in society which must be recognized. War is part of the "relative natural law" which the church cannot ignore but must try to bring under the control of Christian teachings. This may require compromises in order that Christ's Church may remain intact and influential. Catholicism has built up a series of precedents in regard to war which help to define the "legality" of the church's participation in any given conflict. Eminent Catholic moralists, the popes, and other high churchmen are the source of the "constitutionality" and "legality" of a position. Like lawyers, Catholic churchmen appeal to a body of precedent; and they, too, are able, generally, to find adequate precedent for any given decision—this decision usually being made in answer to the questions: Is this a "holy war?" Is there a clear case of right and wrong? Have all other methods of settlement been tried and failed? War, therefore, is not condemned *in toto*. The Catholic hierarchy—generally acting as a unit—makes a political decision: Is the victory of one side or the other in this war essential to the power and influence of the Church? That is not to

impute unworthy motives to the church hierarchy, which of course operates from the premise that the continued power of the Catholic Church is necessary to the furthering of the Christian teachings. They take this stand even though the continuation of that power may require the compromises with human frailty that appear in the "relative natural law." Moreover, the decision to participate in a war is made only when it appears to Catholic authorities that there actually is a case of right versus wrong.[35]

What, then, has been the response of American Catholicism to the present war? Without referring to all of the dozens of Catholic publications in this country and sampling clerical opinion, one may speak only tentatively; but the very great importance of the hierarchical source of opinion in Catholicism makes for a large degree of official agreement on any particular issue (if not for consistency on different issues). We shall speak with special reference to the *Catholic World, America,* and *Commonweal,* which are among the most influential of American Catholic journals. Before the United States entered the war, one finds an almost purely Catholic, as opposed to a national, interpretation of the war in the Catholic press: these publications seek to discover whether or not this can be considered a "holy war," which, therefore, merits support. Through 1940 this decision was practically unanimous: this is not a war in which the Catholic Church would find itself defending the right against the wrong; it is not a "holy war"; the church, therefore, must oppose it, and America should stay out. The *Catholic World* makes an appeal to "surrender the religion of nationalism and return to authentic Catholicism." "Governments are founded on pride, rapine, perfidy, murder."[36]

In general, the Catholic press, prior to 1941, attacked Communist Russia most vehemently. Before August, 1939, the date of the Russo-German Pact, radicals found an easy explanation for this fact in Catholicism's profascist tendencies. Later developments, however, proved this to be far too simple an explanation (see below); and when the Soviets signed the nonaggression pact with Hitler, the radicals discovered a certain irony in their condemnation of Catholic "opportunism." Even before the summer of 1939, there had been strong protests in the Catholic press against Hitler's "Aryan madness" and against the "essential atheism and materialism" of both fascism and communism. Despite a lesson in war guilt well learned in 1914-1918, writes the *Catholic World,* ". . . I venture the apodictic declaration that if world war breaks out again at this time, the one person responsible above all other men . . . the one chief villain in the tragedy, is Adolf Hitler."[37]

When war broke out, in September, 1939, there were factors which operated to encourage the isolationism of the Catholic press and others which tended to break it down. With reference to the latter, the pact between Stalin and Hitler produced a solid front of "atheism and materialism" against Britain. There were incontrovertible accounts from Poland of the persecution of priests—and many American Catholics are Polish. On the other hand, Italy, while not in the war, was Hitler's ally; and Irish influences in Catholicism carry many anti-British elements. There was also a strong desire, partially purely religious, among Catholics to preserve peace. In this they were doubtless at one with the majority of Americans at the time. The total result of these factors was, for the time being, to preserve the isolationism of the Catholic press after the outbreak of war in Europe. The *Catholic World,* in fact, seemed to modify its condemnation of Hitler slightly. The editor pointed to the genuine grievances included in Germany's statements; he preferred a British victory, but emphasized strongly that Britain was not free from war guilt (see, however, the statement quoted above).

> The *status quo* is not sacrosanct. In fact it is unjust. To fight for the maintenance of injustice would be immoral. If England voluntarily changes the *status quo,* declares that she will in the interests of peace pledge herself now to an equitable redistribution of the surface of the globe, and after that offer Adolf Hitler refuses an armistice, I

can conceive that we Americans might perhaps conclude that now at last and really the battle is on for world civilization. In that case we could in good conscience go in. In that case perhaps it would be sinful to stay out. But only *in that case*.[38] . . . Hitler may be a madman, but sometimes men go mad brooding over genuine wrongs. . . . We must, if we meddle at all, find out what made him mad—and correct it. . . . The evil is not totalitarianism, but the conditions and circumstances that created totalitarianism.[39] . . . we Americans are not persuaded that the present war is holy. If we were once convinced that Hitler's actions were entirely Satanic and England's innocence entirely angelic, we would not hesitate.[40] . . . It is not a holy war. It is at best a very dubious war. I will even venture to say that it is a war unjustifiable in the light of the rules laid down by eminent Catholic moralists.[41]

In January, 1940, Cardinal Hlond of Poland sent to the Pope a "detailed, verified report of Nazi atrocities in Poland." Brutality, obscenity, and sacrilege were rampant; priests were systematically persecuted and hundreds murdered; churches were destroyed. Although the editor of the *Catholic World* believed this to be a true report, although he was repelled by Nazi atrocities, he remained neutral, because, he wrote, it is difficult to see Britain and France as crusaders for Christianity. They fight for money and privilege; Britain did her land-grabbing earlier than Germany; she would have allied with atheist Russia had she been able. ". . . we do not consider the British Empire a democracy."[42]

After these strong statements had been made, two other factors entered the situation which were calculated to increase the tendency toward isolationism of American Catholicism: Italy entered the war actively, and Russia became a British ally. To support Britain now meant not only fighting against the mother country of Catholicism, but fighting on the side of atheist communism. The international papacy is of the utmost importance to Catholicism; and the American branch, loyal to the hierarchy, sought to take the stand which would put the Pope in the least awkward position that was possible. For the months immediately following Italy's entrance into the war, the Catholic press continued to insist that this was not a "holy war" (i.e., that Italy was not on an obviously evil side).[43]

In the long run, however, there were even more decisive factors on the other side. The first was the reaction of the papacy itself. It was not at once clear how Pope Pius XII would deal with the war. He had been an especially vigorous opponent of communism, but the situation did not allow him an unambiguous position. Italian Catholics were rivaling the British in preaching a "holy war." In the summer of 1940 the Pope was hunting for some kind of a working agreement with Germany. On August 19 *Time* reported: ". . . last week the Vatican let it be known that negotiations for a new concordat were 'progressing satisfactorily' with Germany, thanks to Nazi approval of the patriotic loyalty of German Catholics since World War II began." The Pope maintained careful neutrality, but *Time* observed that *Osservatore Romano,* the official Vatican newspaper, "has lately found a good word for the totalitarian way of life, in marked contrast to its pro-ally attitude in the months before Italy entered the war."

The Vatican, indeed, was in a grave dilemma. Roosevelt tried to have a voice in the solution of that dilemma by sending a special envoy to Rome (against the vigorous protests of American Protestantism). It took Hitler, however, to solve the problem—to his own grave disadvantage. We have noted the ability of Catholicism to come to terms with a great variety of regimes by use of the concept of "relative natural law"; there were beginnings of its application to Nazi Germany; there were continual reports in this country of the overtures that German Catholics were making to Hitler. But these attempts were thwarted. An absolute cannot swallow an absolute; and Hitler's unwillingness to come to terms, not only in Poland, but in Germany, crystallized Catholic opposition. Soviet Russia proved itself more politic in this regard: it re-established the seven-day week, practically cut out antireligious propaganda (because of a "paper shortage"), and appealed to the conquered peoples to rise against godless Germany. Stalin was at least partially successful in this strategy, for the Patriarch of the Russian Orthodox Church, despite the years of persecution, sent a letter to the faithful at the outbreak of war: "The Orthodox Church has always shared the nation's fate and we will not desert the nation now. . . . Christ's Church blesses all Orthodox members defending the fatherland's sacred borders. God will grant victory."[44]

In Germany, however, there has been a continuous struggle between the New Order and an element in the church.[45] It has been estimated[46] that 80 per cent of the occupants of German concentration camps are not Jews, but Christians. Einstein, a Jew and agnostic, writes:

> Being a lover of freedom, when the revolution came in Germany, I looked to the universities to defend it, knowing that they had always boasted of their devotion to the cause of truth; but, no, the universities immediately were silenced. Then I looked to the great editors of the newspapers whose flaming editorials in days gone by had proclaimed their love of freedom; but they, like the universities, were silenced in a few short weeks. . . .
>
> Only the Church stood squarely across the path of Hitler's campaign for suppressing truth. I never had any special interest in the Church before, but now I feel a great affection and admiration because the Church alone has had the courage and persistence to stand for intellectual truth and moral freedom. I am forced thus to confess that what I once despised I now praise unreservedly.[47]

The conflict between church and state in Germany was more than enough to offset the Pope's opposition to communism. While in the summer of 1940 the Pope was attempting to establish a new concordat with Hitler, on December 2, *Time* reported that the Vatican radio "condemned Nazism in the strongest terms the Vatican had used since Poland." When, six months later, Germany attacked Russia, Pius's important broadcast of June 29 maintained his neutrality and did not proclaim a "holy war" against atheist communism.

How did American Catholics react to these developments?

The continuous record of Hitler's persecution of recalcitrant churchmen did not, of course, make communists out of Catholics. It was not, to paraphrase, that they loved Stalin more, but Hitler less. The *Catholic World* wrote in May, 1941: "To defend democracy with the help of Stalin would be like calling Jesse James or John Dillinger to maintain law and order." But in the same month, Bishop Hurley became the first Catholic prelate to declare that nazism had replaced communism as the church's number one enemy. When Russia came into the war, and attempts were made in this country to reduce the objections to the Soviet regime (notably Roosevelt's statement that the Soviet constitution allows freedom of religion), *America* declared: We must distinguish between military necessity and truth; let us not cover the former with sanctity. This publication, being less thoroughly isolationist than other Catholic journals, reconciled itself to the necessity of choosing between Hitler and Stalin by saying: "There is a world of difference between aid to the Russian people, and aid to the thieves and murderers who make up the Communist party now in control in Russia."[48] Although Pius XI had strongly condemned atheistic Russia, *America* agreed with Archbishop Nicolas that

> . . . the Holy Father was not "laying down a course of action governing our country and all other countries regarding every future circumstance whatsoever, especially in a war of defense. . . . we must not forget that the suffering and persecuted people of Russia, deprived of freedom and put in bondage, have still some rights."
>
> All of us will readily join in the Archbishop's prayer that "God may guide the officials of our country so that they may do what is best for our citizens and for the peace and restoration of a shattered and war-mad world."[49]

Thus denying the applicability of Pius XI's anticommunist pronouncements to this situation, *America* was in a position to give at least guarded support to aid to Russia and other so-called interventionist measures. Catholicism, however, still had a strong isolationist bloc. In commenting on Hitler's attack on Russia, the *Catholic World* stated that he was forced to make the attack, because he "didn't dare go west for fear of being attacked from the east," and then added: "He would have been a fool to do what he didn't have to do. We shall be greater fools than he if we get into this war when we don't have to."[50] This was the dominant Catholic opinion until the very outbreak of war. The Catholic Laymen's Committee for Peace sent double postcards to every priest in the United States (34,616) between September 20 and October 1. This was a layman, nonofficial poll, and the sampling was not good (40 per cent—13,155—returned their answers), but the results are well worth noting: In answer to the question, "Do you favor the United States engaging in a shooting war outside the Western Hemisphere?" 12,038 answered no, 885 yes, with 232 void or not voting. In response to the question, "Are you in favor of the United States aiding the Communist Russian Government?" 11,860 answered no, 967 yes, with 328 void or not voting.[51] The comment of *America* is perhaps a just appraisal: "It is our opinion that the majority of the clergy would confirm the negative vote, but with clear distinctions as to the exact sense, and with a reduced percentage."[52]

Two months after this poll the United States was at war. Only the most liberal branch of Catholicism had deserted isolationism, but there was no question what the official pronouncements would be. The two cardinals who make the official statements in this country immediately proclaimed the loyalty of the Catholic Church to the government. Cardinal O'Connell of Boston, through the *Pilot,* stated: "Wars can be just. Violence may be used against the unjust aggressor." And Cardinal Dougherty of Philadelphia declared: "Like our fellow American citizens we will do our utmost to protect our country by winning the war, and . . . to that end we place at the disposal of our Government everything in our possession."[53]

Thus despite the fact that Italy was the enemy of the United States and Soviet Russia our ally, the Catholic Church in America gave her support to the war. This was a thoroughly churchlike decision. It does not mean that the support was without religious and political qualifications: war is always part of the *relative* natural law. Moreover, the international aspects of Catholicism continued to exert a powerful influence. The tight-rope neutrality of the Vatican was not unbalanced. In April, 1942, the Vatican accepted a minister from Japan, thus to enable the Holy See to keep in touch with Japanese Catholicism. There continued to be cordial relations between Rome and pro-Axis Franco; and only recently Archbishop Spellman has come out with warm words of praise for the Franco regime. Relations with Germany continued to be ambiguous, but not entirely antagonistic, for the Pope had to envisage the fact that the Church might have to live in a Nazi-dominated Europe. As Hitler's star began to set, however, the Vatican began to make overtures to Moscow, for it then appeared that the interests of the Church would be better served by having Russia as a friend than by conciliating Nazi Germany. On the fourth anniversary of the invasion of Poland, the Pope issued a sharp rebuke to Hitler. At the same time he sought to preserve some semblance of "organic unity" by calling for a negotiated peace. The Vatican sent special radio programs to Russia and offered prayers for the suffering Russian armies and people. A spokesman has said that an accord with Moscow would not be difficult if the Soviets would change their policy towards religious education. Anti-Catholics will interpret all of this as hypocrisy: it is hypocritical only in the sense that all political action, which must accommodate itself to inevitables, is hypocritical. The wiser student will be concerned, not with the policy of expediency, but with the ends in whose service the accommodation was made. There is no chance that the Catholic Church will soon begin to act like a sect.

The Protestant Churches and World War II

Protestantism's reaction to the war is in one sense more complicated and in another sense less complicated than the Catholic position. It is less complicated, because international political considerations are involved in Protestant behavior to a far smaller degree than in Catholicism. On the other hand, the traditional importance of between-war pacifism is and has been an important factor, particularly since 1919, in conditioning Protestant response to a war situation. We have noted above how widely pacifism had spread through the churches in the twenty years following the first World War. The growing power of Hitler in Europe at first only crystallized that attitude. One of the focal points of American Protestant pacifism was the nondenominational, but influential, *Christian Century,* which consecutively and vigorously opposed the "steps short of war" that characterized American action from 1938 to 1941. The editor, Charles Clayton Morrison, recognized the dilemma of the Christian in regard to war: he condemned war on one hand, but felt a moral responsibility in aiding China, for example, on the other. "Churchmen who still vie with one another in expressing their abhorrence of war are divided sharply—just as churchmen divided sharply before April, 1917—over their moral responsibility in the face of Japan's lawless assault on China."[54] One group says: Collective punishment of treaty-breaking nations; another: Keep out of war. This is a real dilemma, asserts the *Christian Century,* ". . . the Christian conscience finds it hard to sit by in impotence while an international brigand is at the throat of his victim."[55] The editor did not try to resolve this dilemma; he stressed the need for continued thought of what is to follow the crisis, and came again to the pacifist position:

> We have reached the point where the illusions of war are all gone. The pacifist case has been made. . . . Governments can no longer rely on the volunteer; they put their trust in conscription. . . . No one can believe that this universal regimentation, militarization and state control of all civil activities, necessitated by modern war, will, in the event of victory, revert to the democratic order of liberty as we have known it for a hundred and fifty years. Victory will spell fascism for such a victor. And defeat will spell either communism or fascism, if indeed it does not spell slavery or anarchy.[56]

In each of the minor skirmishes that preceded the outbreak of war the *Christian Century* took a pacifist stand. It criticized the President's handling of the "Panay" incident: his "bristling threats," his spy scares, his readiness to engage in "parallel action" with Britain, his demand for more navy money, his demand for immunity for United States citizens in China, were all, the editor wrote, dangerous demands. America should face the reality of the liquidation of its (relatively small) interests in China.

On the positive side, the *Christian Century,* even before the war, continually emphasized the need for churchmen to think in terms of a just and effective postwar settlement, involving the extension of democracy and equitable distribution of economic resources.[57]

When war comes, the editor wrote, beware of propaganda, atrocity stories, "sole responsibility" tales; remember 1914. He warned against propagandistic movies from Hollywood. The outbreak of war in September, 1939, did not change his position:

> . . . America's natural sympathies are overwhelmingly with the Allies. It is therefore necessary to guard the American mind at the point of its sentimental prompting to go to their aid. This can be done only by keeping the American public aware of the Allies' own share of responsibility for the war, by analyzing and displaying the real motives which actuate them, by constantly emphasizing the remoteness of these motives from America's national interest, and by insisting upon the illusory nature of the hope that the war will achieve any of the idealistic aims under which its real aims are hidden.[58]

This war, wrote the editor, is simply a continuation of the last; the causes must be rooted out—by enlarging democracy at home, encouraging its growth abroad by genuine economic and cultural measures, and demanding a peace that does not breed war. On July 24, 1940, a vigorous editorial denounced Professor H. P. Van Dusen's go-to-war stand. No just peace could follow even a victory; war is the supreme example of "escapism." "It is a confession that the nations are unwilling to solve their problems with intelligence and justice and voluntary sacrifice; rather than do so, they are willing to consign civilization to destruction."[59] Repeal of the arms embargo, conscription, and the exchange of destroyers for air bases were all vigorously opposed by the *Christian Century*. And in the autumn of 1940 the journal took a surprising (considering its exceedingly liberal position in economic matters) pro-Willkie stand, almost entirely because of its extreme opposition to Roosevelt's foreign policy (although a good deal was said of the third-term issue), which, it was convinced, was leading straight to an unnecessary war.

Although the *Christian Century* was an important center of Christian pacifism, it was by no means a lone voice. Perhaps the most important official stand was that taken by the Methodist Church, largest Protestant denomination in the country. The General Conference Commission on World Peace, in its annual session, September 19-20, 1939, prepared a vigorous peace platform. It declared:

> We believe that war . . . cannot achieve any good end but can only accentuate every evil it aims to correct. . . . Hence, in this present crisis we unhesitatingly declare that the great concern of the Church should be the ending of the war as speedily as possible, without a decisive military victory on either side, and the creation, by unforced negotiation, of a just and lasting peace.[60]

The maintenance of civil liberties, the promotion of the democratic process, the counteraction of war propaganda, and elimination of war trade with belligerents were held to be essential. Some of the most influential Methodist clergymen were members of this Commission. Moreover, their position merely reaffirmed the official position of the General Conference of the whole church, which, in the spring of 1939, declared: "We believe that war is utterly destructive and is our greatest collective social sin and a denial of the ideals of Christ. We stand upon this ground, that the Methodist Church as an institution cannot endorse war nor support or participate in it."[61]

The *New York Times,* in its weekly account of sermons preached in New York, is a good source from which to obtain the positions of many influential clergymen. Pacifism was not lacking in the accounts it gives. Before the outbreak of war, New York churchmen seemed to exhibit a traditional religious approach for maintaining peace. Their appeal was to character and right living: "Kindness is urged for better world," "God's way, not man's to recovery urged," "Right living held the price of peace," "Character and faith held needs of today," "Return to worship urged," "Key to amity found in yielding to God," "Urges childhood graces, wonder, cheer and trust." These topic headlines from the summer of 1939 illustrate a widespread point of view.

By the summer of 1940 pacifism, as registered in New York sermons, was losing ground. (We cannot tell how much of this was due to a policy of the *Times* in its selection of sermons to report. Other evidence would seem to indicate that selection must have operated rather strongly.) There were still, however, important pacifist voices. Harry Emerson Fosdick, perhaps the most influential Protestant minister in New York City, if not in the country, insisted—and still insists—that the church cannot support war. "It is not the special function of the Church of Christ to help win a war, . . . [but] to keep vivid . . . the higher world that war obscures."[62] There is implicit in his position the idea that war may be inevitable and even necessary for a nation, but the church's function, even during a war, is to keep before the people the truth of the Sermon on the Mount. He has stated the belief that the dictators will not be a total loss in solving the problems of the world, for they have at least caused a shake-up that may produce by force some of the necessary adjustments that the democracies failed to make peacefully.[63]

In the spring of 1941, the Reverend Allen Knight Chalmers, New York Congregationalist, obtained a thousand signatures to an affirmation of pacifism: "As a Christian, I see no possibility of reconciliation between the central teachings of Jesus and the necessary operations of war. . . ."[64] The signers were only one half of one per cent of American Protestant clergymen, but the survey was by no means exhaustive, and among the signers were some of the most prominent minsters in the country.[65] Two months later, the Fellowship of Reconciliation, a pacifist organization, announced that over two thousand ministers from every state in the Union had signed a statement that voiced "unalterable opposition" to America's threatened belligerency, and pledged themselves never to use their ministry to "bless, sanction or support war."[66]

In May, 1941, the present writer gave a questionnaire to ninety-three clergymen to discover, among other things, their attitudes regarding the war. Because the sample is inadequate, the results are not conclusive, but they merit some mention.[67] The ministers were asked to check the one of four statements which most nearly expressed their opinions regarding various questions. One set of statements, with the percentage checking each position, was as follows:

When the United States adopted peacetime conscription, it took a long step toward the destruction of democracy. 44%

Our army needed enlargement, but the conscription bill took in too many men, was too arbitrary, and has elements of danger for democracy. 16%

In view of the crisis, but not as a permanent policy, conscription was necessary and a wise move. 33%

We should have adopted conscription earlier, and must learn to think, even after the war, in terms of universal military training for our young men, for the defense of democracy. 7%

In another series of statements, the question of pacifism was raised more directly:

In the face of Hitler's menace to Christianity, it is impossible today to be both a Christian and a pacifist. 1%

It is possible to see how one could believe that a Christian should be a pacifist, but a deeper understanding of the present situation requires an acceptance of the necessity for resisting the march of evil. 19%

The Christian may find it necessary to recognize that the nation is faced with a crisis it must meet; but his task still remains to preach forgiveness and love. 56%

"Resist not evil, but overcome evil with good" is a phrase meant to be practiced, and requires that the Christian refuse to support or take part in any war. 24%

The response to these questions is evidence of a strong pacifism among the clergymen represented. It should be noted that the statement which was most frequently checked, although it tends toward pacifism, is sufficiently ambiguous to allow some reconciliation between religious belief and national policy. Even the relatively absolutist fourth statement, however, was checked more frequently than the two "interventionist" statements combined.

That the government has been worried over the strength of pacifist sentiment is shown by its more solicitous regard for church support than was shown in the last war. President Roosevelt not only sent a special representative to the Vatican, but he asked important Protestant clergymen, primarily the president of the Federal Council of Churches, to serve him in advisory capacity. The Senate has re-established the practice of having a daily invocation, although for years they had opened with prayer only after some extended absence. Chaplains are treated with more deference today than in 1917-1918, when many of them complained of their semi-errand-boy position. They are allowed to devote all of their energies to religious work; and each army post (of which some camps have as many as twenty-three) has, or is to have, a $21,220 chapel.[68] In August, 1941, 224 British Peers and Members of Parliament asked the government to place religious instructors in the schools, to make religion an optional subject in teachers' colleges, to begin daily services in schools, to arrange for textbooks on religion, and to appoint government inspectors of religion. Thus they sought to buttress the social order against the ideological attacks of Nazi doctrine, and to establish the foundation for "that new and better order."[69]

This tendency to align religion with the struggle was not lost on the pacifists. With reference to a speech by Roosevelt, the *Christian Century* pointed out that in fifteen minutes the President used six phrases "calculated to enlist the support of the Churches":

> The war was presented as a struggle for "the whole future of Christian civilization." There was a reminder that "freedom of worship" is at stake, and that Hitler has denied all rights "of the church," and has "persecuted religion." The President's own "devotion to our churches" was reaffirmed, and "American churchmen" were exhorted to join with him in his policies. The reasons which impel Mr. Roosevelt to impart this religious cast to the course he is following are fairly obvious, but we question whether this effort to make his policies appear to be indistinguishable from the interests of the churches will succeed. At least, there are still plenty of churchmen who view them with persistent misgiving. The rush for preachers to present arms has not yet started.[70]

The *Christian Century* was not entirely accurate in this last observation. We have shown above that pacifism was indeed widespread in American Protestantism, but it remains to trace the emergence of another line of thought which has gained steadily in importance during the last several years. No sooner had war broken out in 1939 than many influential clergymen joined the President in his demand for aid to the democracies. Episcopalians, with their strong English connections, were among the first. Of importance also were President H. S. Coffin, and Professors H. P. Van Dusen and Reinhold Niebuhr of Union Theological Seminary, one of the leading centers of Protestant thought in the country.

Among the sermons reported by the *New York Times,* a large majority, by the summer of 1940, voiced some shade of "interventionism." On September 8, which had been designated as the "Day of Prayer for Peace," there were numerous statements in New York City pulpits about the unchristianity of war and totalitarianism, and many pious hopes that war would be overcome by Christian teachings; but there were no demands that United States churches oppose this war. The attitudes from which church support of war might spring were readily apparent during this period. On June 30, 1940, the Reverend A. R. Kleps

(Lutheran) in dedicating a flag in the church, built his sermon around the recognition of "the demands of our country upon us" in return for protection. We must, he asserted, "give unto Caesar."[71] On September 22, 1940, W. W. Ayer (Baptist) declared that if democracy falls, Christianity falls with it. A week later the *Times* carried as a heading to its church page: "Sermons in Many Churches Voice British Cause." Bishops Tucker and Manning of the Protestant Episcopal Church appealed for aid to Britain. Rector Beekman of the American pro-Cathedral in Paris expressed his regret that the Pope had remained silent, especially since Italy's entrance, on the war. The Reverend Henry Darlington (Episcopal) declared that "pacifists are playing into the hands of the enemy."[72] The Reverend Mr. Priestly (Universalist) praised the Conscription Act because it recognized the necessity of being prepared to fight for freedom.[73]

By 1941 the interventionism of churchmen had reached very large proportions, with Lutherans and Catholics being least represented. One of the important developments was the appearance, on February 10, of the first issue of a small publication, *Christianity and Crisis,* which was to devote its energies to determining "the Christian's responsibility in the world conflict." The journal was the outgrowth, of course, of months of development and thought. It attempted to fill a need for adequate channels of expression for a point of view that the sponsors thought was insufficiently recognized in the Protestant press. (In many ways the periodical was a direct protest against the stand of the *Christian Century.*) The sponsors stated their principles in an introductory circular:

> In the conflicts in Europe and Asia, ethical issues are at stake which claim the sympathy and support of American Christians. By our Christian faith we are committed to the realization of a community of nations founded in justice. When men or nations must choose between two great evils, the choice of the lesser evil becomes their duty. We hold that the halting of totalitarian aggression is prerequisite to world peace and order.

Reinhold Niebuhr, the chairman of the editorial board, is assisted by C. C. Burlingham, R. E. McCulloch, J. A. Mackay, F. P. Miller, E. L. Parsons, and H. P. Van Dusen. Among the twenty-five other sponsors were many eminent churchmen, both clerical and lay.[74]

In April, 1941, a "Fight for Freedom Committee" was organized, under the chairmanship of Bishop Henry Hobson, with its object the immediate entry of America into the war. Four of the sponsors of *Christianity and Crisis* and many other important churchmen were members of the committee.[75]

In May, 1941, at least five official Protestant assemblies concerned themselves with the war. Northern Presbyterians took a middle ground. Henry Sloane Coffin, later elected moderator of the church, said of the resolution which they passed that it "takes back in the second half what it says in the first."

The original draft was strongly pacifist, but such words as "war is without capacity to accomplish righteous aims" were voted out and replaced by a plea to sustain the democracies "to the utmost in their brave struggle"—except that "much more still is to be gained by America remaining free from military participation."[76]

Southern Baptists adopted a ringing affirmation of the faith of the Church militant. "We declare our belief that some things are worth dying for . . . and worth defending to the death. . . . We are ready to oppose any tyrant. . . . England's heroic resistance . . . is one of the great sagas of the human spirit." They voted for all-out aid to Britain, speedier rearmament, an embargo on arms for Japan.[77]

Northern Baptists took a middle position that expressed sympathies with democratic peoples, commended the President for keeping us out of war, and yet sanctioned aid to the democracies. The Disciples of Christ voted two to one to request the President to do all in his power to keep us out of war. Southern Presbyterians did not discuss United States participation in the war, but they prayed for an Allied victory.[78]

Thus the churches, like the rest of the country, slowly adopted a war mentality. When the United States finally entered the conflict, many clergymen were ready to give it immediate support, and all of the large denominations pronounced their official loyalty. The bishops of the Methodist Church, which had renounced war in 1939 (see above), declared: "There can be no peace in the world until totalitarian threat against the liberties of all freedom-loving people is thoroughly eradicated. Our duty, as American citizens, is clear. . . . The Methodists of America will loyally support our President and our nation."[79] In reply to a questionnaire from *Time,* the official heads of all the major denominations declared that their churches stood solidly behind the government.

Thus once again the churches exhibited how thoroughly intertwined with the rest of society they are.[80] The dilemma that they face is made manifest by the inevitable retreat of the great majority from a position of pacifism. Once more they have had to accommodate themselves to an "inevitable," even though it may be far removed from their pure ethic. Even were their loyalties entirely religious, many thought that to stand aloof from the conflict was not to stop it, but only to lose much of the influence for good that the churches might have in the midst of it.

Religious Absolutes and War's Relative Justice

By tracing the process of accommodation of religious thought to war, however, one does not tell the whole story. In this war particularly there are complicating issues which cannot be disregarded. Not only do the pacifist sects maintain their traditional position (although not without internal conflicts), but there is also a very strong sectarianism within the churches—a very noticeable difference between the response of the churches to the present war and their response to World War I. We must refer both to the pacifists and to those who, while supporting the war, are demanding that it be an instrument of justice.

The pacifist group did not melt away nearly so rapidly as it did in 1917, and many churchmen gave the war only qualified support. Upon the declaration of war, the *Christian Century* wrote: "We, too, must accept the war. We see no other way at the moment but the bloody way of slaughter and immeasurable sacrifice. Our government has taken a stand. It is *our* government. It spoke for us as the voice of our national solidarity. It was *our* voice. The President is *our* President, and all his official acts, even those which we disapprove, are our acts. . . ."[81] The same editorial, however, went on to say:

> The nation has chosen the hard way. It is the way of unimaginable cost and of doubtful morality. It has invited the attack upon itself by its adamantine assumption of responsibilities in the Pacific which were beyond our interests there, beyond our understanding of the situation which exists there and, if not beyond our power to discharge, will surely pile up a cost in suffering and sacrifice for ourselves and others which is incommensurable with any just ends we may hope a successful war will achieve.[82]

After the United States entered the war, the position of the *Christian Century* can perhaps best be characterized by this statement: The church as such is not at war; it does not obstruct the work of the government, but takes upon itself a different task—the reduction of hate, the exposure of atrocity stories, the defense of civil liberties, the improvement of race relations, and the development of war aims. This is the general line of thought of most of the other renowned pacifists within the church: they accept the war as inevitable, but try to minimize its dangers and focus it on some moral end. Among these may be mentioned Harry Emerson Fosdick, Ralph W. Sockman, Walter W. Van Kirk, Ernest Fremont Tittle, Georgia Harkness, John Haynes Holmes, Bishops Walter Mitchell and W. Appelton Lawrence (Episcopal), and Bishop Paul Kern (Methodist).[83] That this does not by any means exhaust the list of pacifists during the war is demonstrated by the 1942 meeting of the National Council of Congregational Churches. The Council issued two separate statements on the war. One read: "Many of us in obedience to Christian conscience support the present war effort of our country at whatever sacrifice of life and treasure. We do so because the aggressions of the Axis powers are so unspeakably cruel and ruthless and their ideologies so destructive of those freedoms which we hold dear." Four hundred and nine delegates voted for this statement. The second one read: "Others of us, convinced of the futility of war as a method to achieve the goals which should be sought, feel that we cannot, in loyalty to our Christian conscience, accept the way of violence and bloodshed. We are convinced that reconciliation, intelligent goodwill, Christian love and suffering are the most effective ways of meeting cruelty and wrong." One hundred and thirty-five delegates voted for this statement. Thirty-five persons took no stand.[84] One may not assume from this that 25 per cent of all ministers are pacifists today, nor even that 25 per cent of the Congregationalists are, but there is no doubt that a far more important group of ministers is maintaining the pacifist position today than during World War I.[85]

One must not, moreover, forget the sects which have been the chief pacifist element through many wars. These vary from the otherworldly and emotional Jehovah's Witnesses to the thoughtful Quakers, with their efficient organizations for carrying on nonmilitary, but important, public services. The most important new development of the sects in this war, perhaps, is the establishment, with the help and permission of the government, of Civilian Public Service Camps. Largely under the leadership of Rufus Jones, the Quakers, Mennonites, and Brethren secured the inclusion in the Selective Service Act of provision for conscientious objectors to war. Despite violent persecution of their members in many instances during the last war, the pacifist sects made valuable contributions to the reconstruction of Europe immediately after the armistice. Now their work has been given some kind of official status. The government has provided the camps, while religious groups—largely the three sects—finance administration and maintenance.[86] On March 1, 1945, there were 8,118 men in Civilian Public Service; 2,605 others had been released, for various reasons, during the preceding four years. On May 15, 1943, there were 4,612 men in the Civilian Public Service Camps and 1,566 on detached service. Mennonites constituted about one fourth of the total, with Friends and Brethren furnishing many more; but there are also many pacifists from the larger denominations. It is impossible to state how many conscientious objectors have been assigned noncombatant duty in the Army. The War Department estimates have not run over 5,000; but some well-informed observers think that 50,000 is a more accurate figure.[87]

The Civilian Public Service Camps have by no means solved all the problems associated with the treatment of conscientious objectors in wartime. Present difficulties are concerned with the narrow interpretation of what constitutes "public service,"[88] with a stricter interpretation of the law as it applies to conscientious objectors than was followed in 1917-18—although the present law is itself more liberal—and with the denial of basic Army pay to the objectors. The objectors are required, in fact, to pay thirty dollars a month, two dollars and a half of which is returned for incidental expenses. One of the purposes of this last requirement has been to induce objectors to take noncombatant service. A result of the strict interpretation of the present draft act has been, according to the figures given by the Department of Justice, December 15, 1944, to send 4,872 men to prison for various violations, compared with fewer than five hundred during the last war. Over two thirds of the prisoners are Jehovah's Witnesses, most of whom have claimed exemption as ministers, although not thus engaged full-time, and thus not coming within the statement of the law. Most of them have refused to participate in the program of the Civilian Public Service Camps.[89] A recent Supreme Court decision has upheld an Illinois court ruling which barred a conscientious objector from practicing law in Illinois. There is a growing opposition among conscientious objectors to the dominance of the military over the service camps. Many of them are coming to believe that pacifists have made a mistake in accepting a place within the draft system rather than demanding unconditional release from military service for all who have established sincere religious objections to war.

Despite these and other problems it seems evident that there have been substantial changes in the treatment of conscientious objectors since the last war. In 1917 one had to be a member of one of thirteen recognized "peace churches" to obtain classification as a conscientious objector. Under the present law men of all faiths may obtain such a classification. In general the public has taken a more tolerant attitude toward them. There has been fairly widespread favorable comment in the press. The Princeton Office of Public Opinion Research has found that large majorities favor granting them pay, giving them permission to work abroad, and to work at tasks commensurate with their skills. They have not been sent to army camps, and control of their activities has at least partly been taken out of the hands of the military. And what is perhaps most interesting to us, many of the major churches have agencies that are actively affiliated with the National Service Board for Religious Objectors, through which the Civilian Public Service Camps are operated. This is in contrast to the almost complete disregard of conscientious objectors which characterized the major religious groups during the last war.

It is interesting to note the treatment of conscientious objectors in Great Britain, where the law is distinguished from the United States' statute chiefly by the provision for unconditional release of some of the objectors. Draft records indicate that pacifism is more widespread in Great Britain than in this country. Of 6,700,000 registrations for service in Great Britain, 61,000 registered as conscientious objectors—slightly less than one per cent. Of these, 56,900 had appeared before tribunals by June 30, 1943: 2,760 (4.9 per cent) were given unconditional exemption; 21,423 (37.6 per cent) were given conditional exemption, i.e., work of national importance; 16,194 (28.5 per cent) were placed at noncombantant duty in the army; and 16,525 (29 per cent) were rejected as conscientious objectors.[90] Thirty-seven were reported to be in prison (as compared with 816 during the last war).[91]

Pacifism is a word that covers a variety of opinions.[92] It is sometimes associated in the public mind with political isolationism. In its most complete sect form—represented by Jehovah's Witnesses in the last few years—it means not only refusal to participate in war, but is also associated with a more far-reaching withdrawal from the "world of sin." This has led, during recent months, to refusal even to register in the draft, for which several hundred persons have been sentenced to prison in this country. In contrast with this position, the Quaker concept of "vocational Christian pacifism" has very few elements of withdrawal. Among some of its adherents it includes the recognition that the nation, as a nation, may be forced to go to war. Pacifists become, under this interpretation, a small minority whose role it is to keep before the majority in the midst of conflict a different conception of how the world may be ordered. Elton Trueblood, editor of *The Friend,* writes:

> The pacifist who keeps alive this different conception is contributing to the future welfare of his people by providing a balance to the extremes of hatred which arise, and by holding aloft the principles of ultimate peace which might otherwise be forgotten. He is keeping a humble fire burning, to light the new fires which must burn again after the storm is over. If he understands his position rightly he accords his government the same courtesies which he expects. That is, the government grants him a measure of recognition of his conscientious objection and he, in turn, does not try to embarrass the government. It is for this reason that some of the recognized leaders of English Quakerdom have refused to sign a petition asking the government to sue for peace now.[93]

Pacifists of this type are very much disturbed by some of their isolationist bedfellows. Before the United States entered the war, Trueblood wrote: "The prospect of those who call themselves Christian pacifists uniting in public meetings with Hearst and Wheeler and their kind is most discouraging. . . . Our task is to keep alive in a world that needs it sorely a minority based on convictions about which we do not waver, but convictions which do not hinder the conscientious efforts of others who are as eager as we are to do their Christian duty. . . . Our task is to bear witness, but not to obstruct."[94] We must not assume that this conception of the role of the pacifist is accepted by all, or even most, Quakers. Some pacifists contend that it involves so much compromise that the essential sectarian condemnation of war is lost; others have called it a return to monasticism—where a small group maintained the religious principles in relatively pure form and lived them vicariously for the whole society. From the point of view of our study, the concept of the "vocational pacifist" is interesting primarily as an attempt to maintain the sectarian protest against war while at the same time participating in the larger society. In other words, it is an attempt to avoid the limitations on power that are imposed by the tendency of the sect to withdraw from the "world."

This is a very incomplete sketch of the activities and doctrines of pacifist groups and individuals, but it is perhaps enough to show their importance in the present religious situation. Moreover, when we return to the study of the majority of churchmen who are supporting the war, we must note an important difference between their behavior today and in 1917-18. We have already discussed in Chapter V the attention that is being given, by liberal churchmen, to plans for postwar reconstruction. It is readily apparent from a survey of the religious literature during the two periods that clergymen today are far more careful about making this a "holy war," are much more concerned with America's share of the responsibility and more desirous of making the war an instrument of justice, than they were in the last war. It is necessary to point out, of course, that this is probably also true of the government: there is a minority group in both church and state who have memories that go back twenty-five years. *Christianity and Crisis,* despite the fact that it was organized, in the last analysis, to insure American participation in the war, has not become an ideological spearhead for the War Department. It stated as its aims for 1942: (1) to recognize responsibilities as citizens of a belligerent nation, (2) to "resist tyranny and help to establish justice without hatred or bitterness. This can only be done if we avoid self-righteousness . . . ," (3) to develop the resources of the church for service to both civilians and men in the armed forces, (4) to keep the consciousness of the universal church alive, (5) to deal at length with the problems of postwar reconstruction.[95]

Three weeks after the United States entered the war, the executive committee of the Federal Council of Churches met to draft a message to their constituents. Among the eighty members, opinions ranged from pacifism to "holy war" advocates; but they reached unanimity on the statement which they ordered sent to 150,000 churches. It condemned "the calculated treachery of recent aggressions," but made a very different interpretation of the place of the church than was made in 1917. The committee declared:

> We do not disclaim our own share in the events, economic, political and moral, which made it possible for these evil forces to be released. . . . As members of the church in America we have responsibilities which only the church can discharge. It must ceaselessly bring to judgment those individual and social sins, at home and abroad, which are the cause of our disaster. . . . The church should minister in mercy to those on whom the cruelty of war most heavily falls, refugees and prisoners of war and all others caught in the appalling suffering of our world. The church must be in the vanguard of preparation for a just and durable peace. The great sacrifices of treasure and of life must not be in vain. We must build now the spiritual foundations for a better order of the world. This task is immediate and cannot be delayed. As members of the world-wide church which transcends all differences of race and nation, we have obligations which reach beyond our own country. We must preserve at all costs the world-wide Christian fellowship, without which no free world order of justice and peace can be achieved.[96]

In terms of our typology, these developments seem to show that there are some elements in the American churches today who are maintaining some kind of balance between church and sect tendencies; they are accepting the basic social fact—that is, the war—as part of the "relative natural law," but they are also reserving the right to keep war in proper perspective, to show its evils and dangers, by measuring it against their absolute values. In so far as they can maintain this balance, they will, if past experience is a guide, maximize their ability to influence the situation. The balance is precarious; it will become more difficult to maintain as the war is prolonged; and the influence of this group will not be great at best. But our previous analyses have seemed to show that religion makes most effective use of its power when it does not resort either to extreme sectarianism (withdrawal) or extreme church-type behavior (accommodation).

One of the most significant contemporary interpretations of this balance is that of Reinhold Niebuhr. He attributes the strength of pacifism today to the "uneasy consciences" that have resulted from the war hysteria of many churchmen in 1917-18. He holds that pacifists are not profound enough to see that abstaining from all judgment between contending forces is not the only alternative to proclaiming a "holy war." "It has become almost a universal dogma of American Christianity that any kind of peace is better than war. This always means in the end that tyranny is preferred to war; for submission to the foe is the only certain alternative to resistance against the foe."[97] Niebuhr holds that pacifism *as a political strategy* is not the position of classical Christianity. The kind of pacifism which is not a Christian heresy is a part of ascetic attempts to achieve a standard of perfect love in individual life. "This perfectionism did not give itself to the illusion that it had discovered a method for eliminating the element of conflict from political strategies."[98] This kind of pacifism, Niebuhr observes, is a valuable asset to Christianity: "It is a reminder to the Christian community that the relative norms of social justice, which justify both coercion and resistance to coercion, are not final norms, and that Christians are in constant peril of forgetting their relative and tentative character and of making them too completely normative."[99]

Most men, however, he says, must resist aggression and injustice with force. Society may be largely responsible for the development of criminal tendencies in some of its members, but it must, despite its own involvement, restrain their actions.

It is perfectly true that national societies have more impartial instruments of justice than international society possesses to date. Nevertheless, no impartial court is as impartial as it pretends to be, and there is no judicial process which is completely free of vindictiveness. Yet we cannot dispense with it; and we will have to continue to put criminals into jail. There is a point where the final cause of the criminal's anti-social conduct becomes a fairly irrelevant issue in comparison with the task of preventing his conduct from injuring innocent fellows.[100]

The task is not to eliminate the spirit of vengeance—that is impossible—but to check its brutalities:

The moral logic of history is never pure and dispassionate precisely because judgment upon evil cannot be executed without stiffening the spirit of justice with an alloy of the spirit of vengeance. If the life of collective man were completely rational those who commit evil would repent of it and those who suffer from evil would temper their vindictive passions with the spirit of forgiveness. Unfortunately only a small proportion of those who commit social evil are capable of repentence and likewise only a few among those who suffer from it are able to develop a corresponding spirit of objective justice. The stubbornness with which social evil is maintained requires that the force which is to dislodge it be propelled by the impulses of nature as well as the ideals of the spirit, by vengeance as well as by justice. The executors of judgment in history are always driven by both hunger and dreams, by both the passions of warfare and the hope for a city of God.[101]

The spirit of justice is to become a part of the conflict by the influence of the Christian doctrine that *all* men are sinners. Political controversies are not between righteous men and sinners, but between sinners. The crucial need, says Niebuhr, is for a spirit of contrition, the complete avoidance of self-righteousness: "If it is powerful enough it may be able to restrain the impulse of vengeance sufficiently to allow a decent justice to emerge.[102]

Thus Niebuhr supports the present war but is fully resolved that it must, in part, be an instrument of justice. In this he is upheld by an important group of churchmen. They have made a church-type acceptance of the evils of society, but they also have included some of the sectarian element of radical challenge to the *status quo*. If this is preserved throughout the crisis, the churchmen will have made an effective response, in terms of their religious interest, to the dilemma they face. Not the "all-out" church of 1918 (nor the "all-out" element in the churches today), but the "contrite" church makes the most efficient use of its power.[103] And, conversely, not the self-isolating Jehovah's Witnesses, but the Quakers who are willing to work in an "evil" society, while trying to avoid direct participation in its evil, are the sect elements which exert the most influence. Thus in a sense we have a double dilemma: In a war situation there is a strong tendency for the pacifist to be forced into the camp of the thoroughgoing isolationist, and for the religious interventionist to be forced into the camp of the militarist. Today there seems to be an important minority element in both groups which recognizes this difficulty and is trying to avoid it. In many respects the religious pacifist and religious nonpacifist are standing on common ground today. Men like Niebuhr, Van Dusen, Hough, and McConnell, on the one hand, and Fosdick, Sockman, Tittle, and Morrison, on the other, have not allowed a difference in method to obscure, to nearly so great a degree as it did in the last war, the fundamental similarity in purpose. In other words, church and sect tendencies are fairly well blended in the work of leading churchmen in the present crisis. If our analysis is correct, this will increase the power of religion to influence the present situation.[104]

To summarize this interpretation of the relation between religious groups and war, we can refer again to our typology. The main body of church people can no more disentangle themselves from society during a war than they can contradict the basic economic structure. Sects which for both religious and socioeconomic reasons feel themselves to be outside the structure (and hence the loyalties) of the main body of society can contradict its pattern of behavior. Most church people, however, have a political, economic, emotional, and professional, as well as a religious stake in a society: these command loyalties. If these loyalties outweigh religious sentiments, and a war situation puts the two into more than usually distinct conflict, churchmen will have to modify or eliminate the lesser. Moreover, a person motivated by purely religious loyalty, when faced with the dilemma which is an inevitable result of the struggle for power, must make a choice between losing a major share of his influence or accommodating his ethic to the existing situation. Thus out of purely religious loyalty one may accept and even support the war. Those who feel themselves outside the dominant group, because of a sectarian religious orientation (this can be due to other than religious causes), feel no such conflict when the dominant group fights a war, and hence are able to retain their religious position unmodified. In doing so they relinquish the possibility of participating in and modifying the situation to any great extent. There are some few, however, who are able to arrive at a balance between accommodation and radical challenge. We have seen that this is one of the unique elements in the present situation: although there is an exceptionally high proportion of pacifists among the clergy, they are not withdrawing from society; and although the large majority of churchmen are, as usual, supporting the war, there seem to be more qualifications in their support, a more sophisticated understanding of its meaning and dangers. One may perhaps account for these facts by reference to the nearness of the last war, and by the emergence, in a time of great crisis, of a genuine tradition-breaking "prophecy."

Chapter VII

SUMMARY AND CONCLUSION

Semper idem is the appropriate motto of the Catholic Church. In many lands through many centuries she has paid all necessary homage to the powers that be, particularly those that have courted her favor, but never has she relinquished her absolutes nor peacefully given up the privilege of teaching them. And yet *semper idem* does not tell the whole story: the very ability of the church to remain the same in some of its aspects depends upon its ability to change in others. This is true not only of the Catholic Church, but of all churches—of all groups, in fact—that seek to mold the behavior of men according to a pattern that is not willingly nor easily followed. The investigation of this factor of variety within unity has led us to the study of the relation between religion and social change. We have attempted in this volume to develop a group of concepts that would contribute to the sociological interpretation of the conduct of religious groups. We have been concerned with the general problems: How has the interactional process within which the religious interest is pursued affected religious doctrine and conditioned the structure of religious groups? And how, in turn, has the religious interest been a factor in social changes?

Three major concepts have informed the discussion. The phrase "the dilemma of the churches" refers to the struggle between a religious interest and loyalty (which we have very briefly defined as an attempt to give man a perspective larger than his own immediate interests and personal desires) and other powerful interests of men which often contradict the religious teachings. Religious groups face the dilemma either of asking more than they can get from often recalcitrant constituents (motivated in large measure by other than religious interests) or of so modifying their demands that the concrete realization of their ideal in history is largely given up. In the former case, the group can hold the allegiance of only a small number; in the latter case, it can hold, in the concrete, to only a small part of its ideal.

Our second concept refers to the typical responses of religious groups to this dilemma. There are two fundamental types. The members of some religious groups refuse to compromise their ideal in any thoroughgoing fashion and are forced by this decision to withdraw from normal participation in the dominant social structure. They prefer to maintain their ideal, to the extent of human ability, in a small, intimate community, rather than have it sharply reduced in the competition with secular powers that it would face to a much larger degree if they tried to control the whole society. Being outside, in a sense, the dominant social structure, the sects (as we have called these groups) are in a position to make a radical challenge, either directly (as in the case of sixteenth-century Anabaptists) or implicitly (as in the case of medieval monastics), to those aspects of society which contradict their ideal. Other religious groups, however, refuse to accept this limitation in scope; they take the steps necessary to win a place of power. This is the church type. It gains more formal influence than the sect because it compromises its ideal, accepts the basic pattern of the *status quo* despite its failure to come up to the religious ideal, and thereby establishes itself alongside the ruling powers. By this means the church maintains a good deal of influence. Most of it, however, is not religious influence—that is, the power to attain the purely religious ends—but is simply secular power clothed in religious garb. The church no more escapes the dilemma than does the sect; it wins a place of greater importance in society, but only at the expense of compromise and the sacrifice of ability to challenge directly basic social patterns (slavery, inequality, war, etc.) which contradict its ideal. The thorough accommodation of the church, as a type, to the *status quo* is demonstrated by the fact that only when a new secular power is already beginning to win a place for itself will some elements of the church find a place for it. Thus when the middle classes began to gain power, religious ethics found room for their peculiar qualities; when the labor movement began to implement its demands and workmen were withdrawing from the churches where their case was not heard, religion discovered the justice of labor's demands. Pacifism swept the churches in an era of isolationism and peace conferences, but fared poorly in time of war.

The compromise of the churches, however, is seldom complete, for there is a sectarian element in religion which defies institutionalization. Not all of this element is located in the sects. It seems apparent, in fact, that religion maximizes its power as an agent in social change when the church and sect tendencies are combined by some kind of organizational principle.

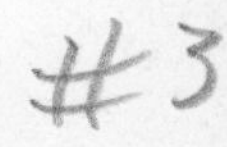

The third concept which we have employed is concerned with the reasons why some religious groups should choose the way of compromise and others the way of radical challenge and withdrawal. This is at least partially explained by the concept of the social sources of denominationalism. The religious interest is thoroughly entwined with secular interests and needs; it is not by accident that the radical sectarian reaction to the dilemma of religion is usually chosen by the poor and disinherited;[1] nor is it an accident that the way of prestige and compromise is the choice of religions which appeal to the ruling classes. Were the religious interest alone involved in the choice of method, the wealthy religious would be sectarian as often as the religious poor. The best proof that that is not the case is the transition which sects go through when their members gain wealth: they turn from radical challenge to acceptance of the social structure. This is as true of medieval monasteries as of Protestant sects. It is not surprising that those groups which share most largely in the income and prestige of a society should find it easy to accept that society as basically good, and that, therefore, accommodation of their religious ideals should be relatively easy. On the other hand, one would expect the disinherited groups to find religious compromise with a society which has treated them so poorly to be especially obnoxious. These are among the social sources of religious divisions.

These three concepts have grown out of a study of the behavior of religious groups and persons, and they in turn inform the investigation of religious data. We have been concerned primarily with the application of these concepts to three historical circumstances. Our study of the relationship of Protestantism to capitalism has been focused on a problem somewhat different from that of Weber, but it is in part a criticism of his thesis. By recognizing the dilemma of religious groups, we have attempted to show that a religious ethic favorable to capitalism could scarcely have prospered within a society where the ruling classes were anti- or non-capitalistic. The origin of Protestantism can be partially explained by a purely religious dialectic. But few people have as strong a religious interest as the founders of a new religious movement. If that movement is to achieve significant proportions, as Protestantism did, it cannot contradict the secular powers but must rather harmonize with them. Thus we have interpreted the rise of Protestant churches and Protestant ethics as, in rather large measure, the religious expression of the rise of the middle classes. The Protestant sects, on the other hand, have been, from one point of view, the successive attempts of the poor to gain religious sanctification for their demands for a greater share in the world's inheritance. They have largely failed in this attempt, either because of the transformation of the sects into churches, or by failure to win the support of the ruling classes and being denounced as heretical.

In the survey of the economic ethics of contemporary churchmen, we found that the prevailing economic system is generally blessed by the churches. There has been a gradual adjustment, however, to the emergence of organized labor, and there is also a small sectarian element that sharply criticizes modern economic society. Under the influence of a crisis situation, this last group is especially important today. We have tried to avoid exaggerating its importance, however, by stressing the difference between a crisis ideology and the more brutal struggle for power that is even now going on apace and will be intensified after the war. If history is a guide, and if present tendencies continue, the power of the group against whom the liberal churchmen are working, far from being reduced after the war, will be greatly increased. The necessities of the war production program have put many industrialists in a position favorable to the increase of their patent, technical, market, and raw material monopolies. The battle between nations is not the same as the struggle within a society for shares of the social product: the one, in fact, confuses the other. On the one hand, the continual struggle for profits and wages retards the war production program; on the other hand, the war is realigning the power element within our society, in favor, for the most part, of the large-scale industrialist.

Nevertheless, one must not forget the ideological element. The liberal churchmen, if their programs are given sufficient publicity, may strongly influence public expectancy and public opinion. These are important factors in the choice of leaders and will not be unimportant in postwar reconstruction. Needless to say, those groups that disagree with the liberal churchmen will not be inactive—and are not—in the formation of a public opinion better suited to their needs.

In our study of the relation of the churches to war, the concept of the dilemma of the churches has allowed us to avoid a cynical interpretation of religious behavior during war. The dilemma is especially sharp during war, and the attempts to resolve it lead to many extremes—from atrocity stories to complete withdrawal from civil participation (refusal to register). During a war it is particularly difficult to maintain the balance between church compromise and the radical challenge of sects. In World War I, the American religious groups failed almost completely in maintaining that balance. They seem to be dealing with the problem with more success today, however, for the pacifist withdrawal from the "world of sin" is far from complete, and interventionists are giving only qualified support to the war.[2] Many elements in both groups are interested in wringing from the present crisis a society that is nearer to their ideal.

It may be well to try to summarize our conclusions regarding the influence of religion on the secular life: Churches, when they have not lost all sectarian elements, can soften the harshness of an existing order; they can, for instance, develop in the employer a paternalistic regard for his workers, a measure of generosity, a greater willingness to listen to the grievances of his employees, a reduced opposition to ameliorative legislation. To be sure, churches cannot persuade the ruling classes to step down and cede their power to a new elite. But their ability to reduce hardships within the existing structure should not be disdained. Not only is this a gain for the present, but it may well reduce future difficulties. If, as many people contend, the present distribution of power among classes is undergoing or will undergo crucial changes, it is important that the harshness of the old society be kept at a minimum, because the justice of the old is of great signficance in conditioning the nature of the process by which the new society emerges. Reinhold Niebuhr observes:

> The cruelties of Czardom are avenged by the furor of a communism which so mixes creative and moral elements in its enterprise with so many primeval passions and so many of the old cruelties inverted that only a very objective and sympathetic observer can discern what is good in the welter of what is evil. It must therefore always be the purpose of those who try, in a measure, to guide the course of history to check the desperate brutalities of a dying civilization in order that the new which emerges may not be too completely corrupted and blinded by the spirit of vengeance.[3]

In so far as the churches are able to contribute to the reduction of injustice and brutality in an old order, they are contributing to the new. That stands regardless of one's values concerning what the future should be.

On the other hand, by the sanctity which they throw around the *status quo,* the churches help to preserve a social structure, whether it be just or not, and thus they add to the very brutalities they are trying to soften. Most eulogists of religion, even those who hold that innovation is its minor role, point to its significance as a "conserver of attested social values." This is doubtless true; but by the same token it is also true that religion, by the use of powerful emotional sanctions, can strongly inhibit necessary changes. Religions vary greatly, of course, in the degree of their congeniality for "prophecy." Taking as objective a position as is possible for those immersed in the Christian tradition, we may say that Christianity is more able to adopt innovations than are the other major religions.[4] To an Occidental, the restrictions of the Hindu caste system preserve far more than "attested social values": they are an enormous barrier to the appearance of what he considers a more adequate life view. Christianity, however, is by no means free from this same difficulty. Its restrictiveness becomes most dominant when the church fails to incorporate within its central doctrines and practices many sectarian tendencies, when it succumbs almost completely to the secular powers, as, for example, in Russia and Mexico. Under these conditions religion becomes primarily traditional. It describes the *status quo* in terms of the absolute, "so that devotion to God comes to mean loyalty to 'holy Russia' or obedience to the Jewish law, or acceptance of the prejudices of western civilization, or conformity to puritan moral standards or maintenance of a capitalistic civilization."[5] It sanctifies the relative with "the aura of the absolute." That is not the total picture, for a virile religion will accept the relative only with qualifications, and seek to change it, yet in large measure the secular powers refuse to accept the label of relative. The religious institution, having accommodated itself to the existing society, often comes under almost complete domi-

nance of the rulers of that society. An important measure of the predominance of the "opiate" element in a church is the loss of any ethical orientation. (That is not to imply, however, the opposite—that a church is most effective in social change when it centers around a purely ethical principle.)

While the church tends to lose its ability to influence social change by the sanctity that it puts upon the old, the sect often loses its influence by lack of an organizational principle and by its tendency toward otherworldliness and withdrawal. Since there is little chance of realizing its ideal on earth, the sect concentrates on its realization in heaven, preserving the ideal, meanwhile, in a small community of believers. By this withdrawal from the secular life of the whole community, the sect is able to maintain its ethic in a purer form but does so only at the expense of a sharply reduced breadth of influence.

We must say again, however, that despite these limitations on the power of a religious ideal, whether embodied in church or sect, there remains an explosive element in Christianity which seems never to be completely bottled up. Some religious groups are able to retain part of the radical implications of the Christian ethic and at the same time develop an effective organization. This is true of some of the less esoteric sects, and is also true of a small sectarian element within the churches themselves, who generally prevent the compromise with the *status quo* from being carried to the farthest extreme. In the last analysis, therefore, sect and sectarian preserve the radical element of the Christian ethic and implement it to a degree, while the churches, partly under this stimulation, seldom become so completely dominated by secular powers that they do not demand behavior of their members which, within the pattern of the existing social structure, approaches the religious ideal. In terms of the present study it would seem to be an error to discount completely the influence of the purely religious idea working in history, and equally an error to fail to see the limitations of its power and the frequency with which it is dominated by other interests. The limitations are partly intrinsic: the religious interest is dominant in only a small minority of persons. No matter how skilfully religious leaders use the power at their command, they cannot erase the influence of other powers and interests, particularly in the relations of groups—of classes and nations.[6] Part of the limitations of religion in controlling the behavior of men, however, are not intrinsic but are based on the inexpert use of the moral resources of religion, the failure to recognize the dilemma which religious groups face, and the consequent loss of power through excessive compromise or excessive withdrawal. These two limitations have often combined, with the result that the influence of religion over the relations of men has been minimized. In days of wiser leadership religion has used its resources more fully and has thus achieved a greater share of the goals for which it strives.

NOTES

Chapter I

1. R. H. Lowie, *Primitive Religion,* pp. xi-xii.

2. This is close to Reinhold Niebuhr's definition: "All profound religion is an effort to answer the challenge of pessimism. It seeks a center of meaning in life which is able to include the totality of existence, and which is able to interpret the chaos as something which only provisionally threatens its cosmos and can ultimately be brought under its dominion" (*Christianity and Power Politics,* p. 179).

3. See, for instance, in addition to the pioneer studies of Tylor, Spencer, Lang, Frazer, Marett, and others, such important works as Rudolph Otto, *The Idea of the Holy;* Emile Durkheim, *The Elementary Forms of the Religious Life;* George Simmel, "A Contribution to the Sociology of Religion"; Max Weber, *Gesammelte Aufsätze zur Religionssoziologie* and *Wirtschaft und Gesellschaft,* pp. 227-363; William James, *The Varieties of Religious Experience;* John Dewey, *Intelligence in the Modern World,* pp. 1003-1037; V. I. Lenin, *Religion;* Ernst Troeltsch, *The Social Teaching of the Christian Churches;* Reinhold Niebuhr, *Reflections on the End of an Era;* and for more general works: R. H. Lowie, *op. cit.;* Joseph Needham (ed.), *Science Religion and Reality;* and Paul Radin, *Primitive Religion: Its Nature and Origin.*

4. *Op. cit.,* pp. 1004-1005.

5. *Ibid.,* pp. 1003-1037; L. L. Bernard, "The Sociological Interpretation of Religion," *Journal of Religion,* XVIII, 1-18; H. E. Barnes, *The Twilight of Christianity;* Walter Lippmann, *A Preface to Morals;* J. H. Leuba, *The Belief in God and Immortality.*

6. This statement carries no judgment of value concerning the desirability or regrettableness of this fact.

7. *Op. cit.,* p. 427.

8. MacMurrary, in Lewis, Polanyi, and Kitchin, *Christianity and the Social Revolution,* pp. 508-509.

9. *Christianity and Power Politics,* p. 191.

10. Jacques Maritain, *True Humanism,* p. 28.

11. Cf., for instance, in addition to Reinhold Niebuhr and Maritain, Arnold J. Toynbee, *A Study of History,* V, 176 ff.; John MacMurray, *The Clue to History,* pp. 206-207; R. H. Tawney, *Religion and the Rise of Capitalism;* H. R. Niebuhr, *The Social Sources of Denominationalism,* pp. 72-76.

12. P. viii.

13. *Op. cit.,* p. 48.

14. *A Contribution to the Critique of Political Economy,* pp. 11-12.

15. *Op. cit.,* p. 38.

16. *Social Actions,* p. 9.

17. That sociology has fought a long battle against reductionism of another kind illustrates the same kind of error. It is based on the Spencerian formulation of Dar-

win's theory, which tends to reduce the explanation of one group of phenomena (e.g., the sociological influences on human behavior) to the next most "basic" science. Many writers have held, for instance, that cultural influences can best be explained in relation to man's "basic needs" or other biological influences; in other words, that the influence of group patterns is only a thin veneer over the fundamental "natural" impulses. Thus sociology is lost in psychology and psychology in biology, and so on, until one gets to what he considers the foundation. This type of reasoning is not so much false as it is scientifically meaningless. Reductionism destroys most of the *differentiating* factors which are absolutely crucial to prediction.

Reductionism may be on the social level: one may seek to explain the war with Japan, for example, as a result simply of "economic" factors, and describe all other factors as outgrowths of basically economic problems. Whatever the truth in the economic interpretation of war, and it is exceedingly difficult to test, it certainly oversimplifies the actual situation. Questions of national honor and the search for power of an ambitious group—*whatever their ultimate cause*—are involved. For some problems these are precisely the important factors, and must be treated as relatively autonomous causes of war.

18. Note again that one can consider the religious interest simply another expression of the world of "nature" one degree removed, if he so desires, without altering the argument of this volume. We are not attempting to explain the ultimate origin of religion.

Chapter II

1. Cf. Weber, *Wirtschaft und Gesellschaft,* Part II, chap. iv.

2. It is perhaps no longer necessary to say that an "ideal type" is not necessarily a "desirable type," but a conceptual tool, ideal only in the sense of not necessarily corresponding to empirical reality. See Weber, *op. cit.,* chap. i; Barnes, Becker, and Becker, *Contemporary Social Theory,* chapter on the constructed type; Talcott Parsons, *Structure of Social Action,* pp. 601-610.

3. Cf. "Supreme Values and the Sociologist," *American Sociological Review,* VI, esp. 159-162.

4. This dilemma is discussed at length below.

5. This point is treated more fully below.

6. On the limitations of typological constructs, see Howard Becker in Barnes, Becker, and Becker, *op. cit.,* pp. 39-42.

7. One must not stress this factor to the exclusion of others. Compare the section on "Religion and Social Change."

8. *Op. cit.,* p. 336. By permission of the Macmillan Company, publishers.

9. *Ibid.,* p. 337.

10. Not only do church and sect flow one into the other in terms of organization, but the sectarian idea also gets embodied, to some degree, in the doctrines of the church. We shall refer often to the radical sectarianism of a small minority of churchmen. Because of their position within the church—even if that position is unstable—they are usually able to exert a stronger influence than the sects, whose tendencies toward withdrawal often lead to extreme otherworldliness.

11. Cf. Troeltsch, *op. cit.,* pp. 331-349. Failure to recognize the presence of both church and sect has led to many errors in the interpretation of the role of religion. Marx and Nietzsche, for instance, made opposite critical attacks on religion, and thus failed to understand its total meaning. Without reference to their value judgments, which were very different, one may see that their interpretations led to half-truths. When Marx spoke of "the opiate of the people," he stressed the control that the ruling classes maintained by means of the *church.* Nietzsche, however, enlarged the *sect* tendencies into the total religious principle, for he thought of religion as the upsurgence of the "slave" against the men of talent. Nor does combining the two errors produce

an accurate view, for the interaction of church and sect is crucial in producing the total effect of religion, as we shall see.

12. A. L. Swift, Jr., *New Frontiers of Religion,* pp. 126-127.

13. This basic dichotomy with which we are dealing might prove to be valuable in the analysis of other attempts to gain a position of influence in the world. In a rough analogy one might, for instance, compare the American Federation of Labor on the one hand and radical workingmen's groups on the other with the church and the sect. The Federation stresses achievement as part of society, conservatism, compromise, recognition of the powers and traditions in the American environment that cannot be disregarded with impunity or success. Radical groups demand immediate change in the "relative natural law," that is, in the economic system, and do not accept compromise.

A similar dichotomy can be seen in the attempts to secure a more advantageous position for the Negro in this country. The dominant school of thought, following Booker T. Washington, says: Do not aggravate an already tense situation by continual struggle for "rights." That will only intensify the struggle for power, and the weaker side can only lose. Rather, accept your lot with equanimity, improve your talents, and gradually justice will be granted. Another group, however, impatient of inferior status, demands and fights for equal rights here and now.

The contrast between church and sect in religious behavior is perhaps most strikingly paralleled by political activity. Those who are familiar with Max Weber's terminology may, in fact, prefer to think of church and sect as types of "parties," as he has used that term, that is, as groups specifically concerned with the struggle for power. We have used the terms "church" and "sect" because of their more specifically religious meaning. It is not surprising that Mosca, in discussing political parties, should call Catholicism "political" nor that he should discuss churches and parties together, for there is a great deal of similarity in the tactics of groups in political and religious activity. A small minority party, for instance, can afford to speak out explicitly and directly on controversial issues; but a party aspiring to office must maintain "organic unity" (the Catholic phrase), must, to come back to political language, straddle the fence to encompass as many as possible of the conflicting powers. This is precisely the contrast between sect and church. The recent debate over the meaning of President Roosevelt's apparent shift to the right illustrates much of the contrast between church and sect ways of thinking. Leftist critics tended to say: We know what we want—repeal of poll taxes, higher income taxes, or whatever—why doesn't the President come out sharply and vigorously for these things! The more cautious and more "political" minded said: We have to make allowances for the opposition, else we'll be thrown out of power; we must compromise, not try to do more than is possible under the circumstances. (We are assuming here that there is agreement among those debating with respect to ends to be achieved.) There are weaknesses in both approaches, and also advantages: the sectarian may lose power, but he may prevent unnecessary compromises; the more flexible person, on the other hand, may be able to stay in power, but, as George Soule writes: "Every man who makes power a major criterion of action runs the risk of letting other values slip through his fingers" (*New Republic,* CIX, Sept. 6, 1943, 327). Power, in other words, may become an end in itself, with no concern for the ends for which the power was originally sought.

The "church-sect" dichotomy is also revealed when one studies the behavior of a nation's foreign office. The officers in charge, in attempting to get decisions favorable to the policy of their government, are faced with the powers and desires of other governments. In many instances these are "inevitables" that must be accepted by the foreign office, just as secular interests have to be accepted by the churches. Simply to ignore them can lead only to conflict and the failure to achieve one's objective. This was the dilemma, for instance, of the State Department of the United States in dealing with the situation in North Africa. Assuming for the moment that the only aim of our officials was to encourage democratic tendencies, within the limits set by military necessity (I have no quarrel here with those who think this is a false assumption), we must recognize that there were other powers at work besides those of American arms and diplomacy, powers which our officials could ignore only at the cost of American lives and perhaps of the battle. Hence compromises were necessary. That is not to say that the compromises may not have been carried too far (still assuming that the maximization of democratic elements was the prime objective). Indeed, the writer's own opinion is that either our officials did not want to sponsor what he defines as democracy or else they were poor tacticians. It is necessary to recognize, however, that failure to compromise with an "inevitable" is no service to one's cause. The sharpest critics of the decisions of our State Department were "sectarians"—they proclaimed that we were fighting for certain principles, that compromise with other principles was to betray our cause, that "expediency" was simply a cloak to cover undemocratic aims. That might well be the criticism leveled by a pacifist sect against a church supporting a war; it is the same struggle between the two basic reactions to the dilemma faced by any group struggling for power. In so far as our officials compromised more than the opposing power made necessary, of course, or in so far as they compromised because they did not favor democracy, the protests of the "sectarian" critics were entirely justified. We need not try to decide here how much these may be true. But the dilemma is certainly there: whether to compromise, and face the danger of being forced into continually more compromise; or whether openly to oppose other powers, and face the danger of being entirely defeated.

We cannot state here which is the more efficient of the two reactions. In a large measure the major problem of this study is to try to discover whether the church-type or the sect-type of behavior, or some combination of them, is most effective. But to anticipate briefly, we may say that complete victory of either of the approaches, whether it be in the activities of a foreign office, a trade union, or among groups interested in improving the lot of the Negro, seems to reduce greatly the effectiveness of the search for power. If the "church" type dominates completely, compromise leads to rigidity. If the "sect" type dominates, the energy of the group is likely to be wasted in futile attacks against superior forces. Maximum efficiency seems to be achieved by a balancing of the two tendencies. We shall see that this is also true of religious groups. An effective administrator, whether he is a churchman or an official of the State Department, is one who knows when to say, This is part of the "relative *natural law*," and when to say, This is part of the "*relative* natural law."

14. Wiese-Becker, *Systematic Sociology,* pp. 624-625. Published by John Wiley & Sons, Inc. Reprinted by permission.

15. All of the Reformation churches, however, shared with Catholicism the institutional principle of social organization; to none of them was the church a voluntary society. They also adopted the doctrinal emphasis; creed and ritual were stressed, ethics neglected, except in its individual phases. Cf. H. R. Niebuhr, *op. cit.,* pp. 124-134.

16. Becker's term "denomination" does not sufficiently clarify the two ways in which a sect may evolve. He describes a denomination thus: "Denominations are simply sects in an advanced stage of development and adjustment to each other and the secular world. The early fervor of the self-conscious sect has disappeared, as a general thing, by the second or third generation, and the problem of training the children of the believers almost inevitably causes some compromise to be made in the rigid requirements for membership characteristic of the early phases of sectarian development" (Wiese-Becker, *op. cit.,* p. 626). While this analysis is correct, we find it necessary to classify further by noting that a sect may evolve into a church, as we have used that term (Methodism), or it may develop into an established sect (Quakerism), depending upon the extent to which compromise is carried. This in turn involves both socio-economic and religious factors.

17. Cf. Preserved Smith, *The Age of the Reformation,* pp. 14-20.

18. Cf. John S. Curtiss, *Church and State in Russia.*

19. Further examples of the importance of political connections and class origin of the clergy will be given throughout the study. For other illustrations see W. J.

Warner, *The Wesleyan Movement in the Industrial Revolution,* pp. 248-267, on "the bias of Wesleyan leadership"; D. O. Wagner, *The Church of England and Social Reform Since 1854,* pp. 12-32.

20. Wiese-Becker, *op. cit.,* p. 617.

21. *Sermons,* I, 441. Quoted by K. W. MacArthur, *The Economic Ethics of John Wesley,* p. 97.

22. H. R. Niebuhr, *op. cit.,* p. 21.

23. Warner, *op. cit.,* p. 56.

24. Maritain, *op. cit.,* p. 202.

25. This is the title of the important book of H. Richard Niebuhr, already mentioned, to which we are greatly indebted in this section. His analysis is similar to Troeltsch's.

26. Niebuhr, *op. cit.,* pp. 16-17.

27. *Ibid.,* pp. 113-114.

28. *Ibid.,* pp. 118-124.

29. Toynbee uses the term "internal proletariat" to refer to an element in a society which does not share largely in the gains which the dominant minority monopolizes. The "internal proletariat" is an explosive element, and in many cases is part of a dynamic religious sectarianism. Cf. Toynbee, *op. cit.,* V, 160 ff.

30. R. B. Schlatter, *The Social Ideas of Religious Leaders, 1660-1688,* p. 186.

31. Cf. H. R. Niebuhr, *op. cit.;* Elizabeth K. Nottingham, *Methodism and the Frontier;* Gilbert Seldes, *The Stammering Century;* H. H. Maurer, "Studies in the Sociology of Religion," *American Journal of Sociology,* XXX and XXXI.

32. Niebuhr, *op. cit.,* p. 28.

33. *Ibid.,* p. 62.

34. Cf. *ibid.,* pp. 54-65.

35. Warner, *op. cit.,* p. 122.

36. *Ibid.,* p. 196.

37. Quoted by MacArthur, *op. cit.,* p. 140.

38. *Ibid.,* p. 137.

39. Hammond and Hammond, *The Town Labourer,* p. 281.

40. *Ibid.*

41. Cf. Warner, *op. cit.,* pp. 122-206; MacArthur, *op. cit.,* pp. 136-153.

42. We are interested here in religion as a power element in society, that is, in its ability to achieve its own peculiarly religious and ethical goals, which we have briefly described as an effort to give individuals a perspective larger than their own desires and needs of the moment. (For our purposes, but not of course for all purposes, these aims can be accounted for in any way suitable to the reader.)

43. Reinhold Niebuhr has developed a typology somewhat similar to the one given here, using, however, a different vocabulary. A profound religion, in his terms, is one which can face all the pessimism that man's continual egocentrism forces upon a religion which is trying to control that egocentrism, and still (by mastery of the meaning of God and other religious insights, as Niebuhr would say) not succumb to that pessimism. Few movements in history, secular or religious, have achieved, he believes, the profundity necessary to an adequate view of history. He directs sharp attacks against the shallow optimism of modern liberalism, with its faith in education and man's reasonableness. He holds that its failure to recognize the "evil" in nature, its failure, in other words, to be sufficiently pessimistic, leads it to an entirely inadequate world view. Most contemporary Protestantism, Niebuhr contends, has been very much influenced by his error. On the other hand, some religious movements have a sufficient grasp of the "evil" of the world; but they tend to fall into an opposite error: "In the main body of Christian orthodoxy the pessimism in regard to the political order was too thoroughgoing to allow for a strong insistence upon individual rights. It was recognized that whatever the moral and spiritual ideal might be, in a 'world of sin' individuals would always be claimed by societies and nations for the attain-

ment of their own ends, and would sacrifice both their liberty and their equality to the necessities of the communal order. But in the sight of God individuals were to be regarded as still free and equal. The basic assumptions of an individualistic morality were, in other words, transmuted from socio-moral principles to religio-moral ideals. Naturally this solution of the problem led the church into premature compromises with the injustices and inequalities of society, but it was in many respects superior to modern liberalism in its recognition of the actual realities of life; for the latter still gives itself to the simple faith that both the ideals and the needs of individuals can be fully realized in an ideal society" (*Reflections on the End of an Era,* pp. 108-109).

The "premature compromises," we suggest, are caused not so much by an overly strong spirit of pessimism as by power arrangements; but the analysis is certainly accurate. Niebuhr further parallels our interpretation by noting that there are elements in the church which protest against these compromises: "The ascetics of the mediaeval period and the sectaries of the Protestant church both have their chief significance in their effort to establish a purer ethic than the necessities of the political order permitted" (*ibid.,* p. 110). The ascetics withdrew to form a miniature society in which their law of love could prevail. The fact that they withdrew from society showed that they shared some of the pessimism of the church: they did not believe that a pure moral ideal could be established in a political society; thus they were oriented, explains Niebuhr, by a "pessimistic realism." The Protestant sects are similar in their demand for a society of love, equality, and liberty; and like the ascetics, they realize their ethic in a small religious community—they sacrifice a larger social responsibility. Their asceticism is not as rigorous as that of the monastics; it remains within the world. "But it refuses to be involved in the coercion and the inequalities of the political and economic order, and it is to that extent ascetic." For the most part the sects were apocalyptic in their interpretation of history. "This apocalypticism was the mark of their religious pessimism. In the case of the Mennonites it is unqualified. The Quakers, particularly under modern liberal influence, have a greater admixture of the rational liberal hope for the progressive establishment of an ideal social order through the gradual infiltration of pure moral ideals into the world of politics" (*ibid.,* p. 112).

Another development which shares some of the pessimism of classical Christianity is communism. It is partially pessimistic, because it sees present tendencies running counter to its ideal; but it has an ultimate historical optimism. It also shares with "classical religion" the belief that purely rational ethical activity is insufficient; it holds that there is a logic of self-destruction of evil in history: all things—even evil—work together for good. In communism this expresses itself in the affirmation that even capitalism is a necessary stage on the way to the highest development of communism.

Niebuhr is well aware of the dilemma that these varied responses signify. "The peril of classical religion is that its ultimate optimism tends to be supramoral because it has emerged from a pessimism so profound as to question the moral significance of every moral achievement" (*ibid.,* p. 204). It is inevitable that "social religion," which hopes to achieve relative goals in history, should conflict sharply with this "ultramundane optimism." Niebuhr's interpretation is well summarized in the following statement: "The Christian religion is thus an ethical religion in which the optimism, necessary for the ethical enterprise, and the pessimism, consequent upon profound religious insights, never achieve a perfect equilibrium or harmony. On the whole, however, the religious note triumphed over the purely ethical one. The purely ethical note never gained the ascendancy in classical Christianity, either primitive, mediaeval or protestant. It did triumph in modern liberal Protestantism. Its victory there was significantly due to influence of eighteenth-century rationalism and nineteenth-century liberalism and not to elements in Christianity itself. In classical Christianity the contrast between the moral ideal and the facts of history is too sharp to allow for a pure ethical optimism. Its insistence upon the transcendence of God and the fact of original sin is an authentic mythological expression of its understanding for the perennial conflict between the moral ideal and the impulses of nature" (*ibid.*, pp. 213-214).

One can recognize the brilliance of this analysis without subscribing to all the conclusions which Niebuhr draws (which are, in brief, the need for a more radical political orientation and a more conservative religious orientation. These have not been significantly altered in his latest volumes). One might only suggest that the causes of the various overoptimistic or overpessimistic fallacies rest not only on immanent religious developments, but also on class perspectives and secular needs. In other words, the failure to achieve a harmonious "religious insight" is due, at least in part, to the thorough intermixture of religious and secular interests.

It also ought to be pointed out that liberalism and optimism are not necessarily always conjoined. It is possible for one to be very pessimistic (although not completely pessimistic) about the chances of realizing in history those things which he most desires, and yet to believe also that what little chance there is depends upon the extension of rationality and other liberal attributes. There are many liberals today who feel that the swing toward classical religion, even on the part of many who are politically radical, is a sign of fatigue and disillusionment. In criticizing the unrealism of optimism, therefore, Niebuhr does not necessarily destroy liberalism. With reference to the historical expression of liberalism, however, his judgments seem to be sound. In the opinion of the present writer, one of the greatest intellectual tensions of the day is the inability to criticize contemporary liberalism—and its failure to recognize the importance of the selfish and the irrational as powers in society has been enormous—without going over to equally unsatisfactory apocalyptic Marxism or apocalyptic religion.

44. Troeltsch, *op. cit.*, p. 47. As Barnes and Becker put the same idea: "Christianity as a social and religious phenomenon arose out of a definite historical configuration; it did not spring suddenly from a vacuum, but was a natural product of hopes and fears prevalent in the Jewish and Greco-Roman world of the period" (*Social Thought from Lore to Science*, p. 216).

45. MacMurray describes the temptations—to turn stones into bread, to lead a popular revolt, etc.—as temptations to interpret life dualistically, in other words, to break down the synthesis between ethical and religious elements, the church and sect tendencies, which a great religious leader achieves, but which is impossible for most "laymen." See *The Clue to History*, pp. 43-48.

46. Troeltsch, *op. cit.*, p. 75.

47. *Ibid.*, p. 61.

48. It should be noted that a politico-economic system is also dualistic in a certain sense: it contains elements of dissatisfaction which contradict the orthodox views. How widespread this disaffection will be, and how influential it will be, depend upon the ability of the system to satisfy basic expectancies and upon power arrangements. This study is largely concerned with the relation between the appearance and survival of the "radical" aspects of the dualism in economic systems with their appearance in religious systems. That is, are they concomitant variations, or are they causally connected, or are they in no way related?

49. We have noted this above in connection with the sect-to-church transition. One should not, however, exaggerate the weakness of this sectarian tendency. It is a constant challenge to the existing power arrangement, and can never be completely disregarded. If it is given too little attention in the church—as in the eighteenth and nineteenth centuries—it expresses itself in secular movements.

50. Troeltsch, who emphasizes the nonrevolutionary aspects of Christianity, observes, however: "In our works on Church History, this necessary revolutionary effect of the universalistic-transcendental religious idea on the whole existing order in the State, in Society, and in civilization is not sufficiently stressed. . . . The State, religion, and civilization mutually condition each other. . . . That the radical opposition still exists . . . can be seen in the following ways: in the constant struggle of the Roman Catholic Church with the State and with modern civilization, which is not due merely

to reactionary motives or to the need for centralization; in the clash between religious cosmopolitanism and the Peace Movement with political interests, in the hostility of ethical policy and its 'humanitarianism' to the lack of principle which characterizes all politics which are simply moved by the desire for power, in the suspicion of revolutionary tendencies which is cherished by the conservatives whenever a Christian social policy is outlined, and, in Calvinistic countries, the frequent interference of congregations and ministers by inserting socio-ethical demands into political programmes" (*op. cit.*, p. 178). In other words, although Christianity is not a revolutionary movement, it carries within it the seeds of constant conflict with the existing order. Any purely materialistic explanation would have to resort to argument of the utmost subtlety to attempt to account for these factors that Troeltsch has mentioned.

51. *Ibid.*, p. 256.

52. There were, of course, factors which worked against the success of the Christian ethic in medieval society. Its connection with the warlike spirit of feudalism and its clear-cut class distinctions opposed some of the original elements.

53. Cf. J. J. Walsh, *The Thirteenth, Greatest of Centuries.*

54. The church may actually have intensified the problem of slavery; the Gnostic sects, however, which the church opposed, fought against slavery.

55. On the other hand, it can also be perverted to such an extent that the most glaring contradictions to the ethics of the church are accepted without protest. The history of the church, particularly in the fourteenth and fifteenth centuries, abounds with examples of this.

56. Troeltsch, *op. cit.*, p. 272.

57. Tawney, *op. cit.*, pp. 56-57.

58. On the importance and nature of the medieval orders, see G. G. Coulton, *Five Centuries of Religion,* particularly Vol. I. See also the *Cambridge Medieval History,* V, 658-696.

59. See Chapter III.

60. Tawney, "Religious Thought on Social and Economic Questions in the Sixteenth and Seventeenth Centuries," *Journal of Political Economy,* XXXI, 492. To put this idea in different terms: the church cannot keep out of power a group that holds the material advantage, nor put in power a group that holds no such advantage, but it can so modify the behavior of individuals within the given power arrangement that some of its harshness is softened.

Without undertaking a thorough analysis of the influence of the medieval church in this regard, we can state Troeltsch's conclusions regarding the extent to which "the Christian ideal determined the social development of the Middle Ages after it had itself been effectively and even decisively influenced in its development of a social philosophy by the actual conditions of the life of the day" (*op. cit.*, pp. 323-324):

(1) The church succeeded in basing society on the Christian conception of the family.

(2) In the transition from semianarchistic feudal states to the modern sovereign state, the example of the church was important.

(3) Absolute values of the church have influenced all thought. For instance, individualism: ". . . Liberalism perpetuates in a secular form an idea which had first been realized by the Church, and it is very doubtful how far this ideal can be maintained against naturalistic reactions without any religious support at all" (Troeltsch, *op. cit.*, p. 325). MacMurray makes the same point: ". . . the main evidence that Christianity is a real creative force in history is the pressure and the struggle to realize, by reform and revolution, a society based on the principles of freedom and equality" (*op. cit.*, p. 69).

(4) The modification of slavery, the weakening of serfdom, the tendency toward free industry of guilds "were at least partially conditioned by the religious ideal of personality and its practical realization in law" (Troeltsch, *op. cit.*, p. 326). This is somewhat in contradiction to other statements by Troeltsch; he must have envisaged

the influences of the church in the destruction of slavery as having been very indirect, for elsewhere he writes: "All the statements of theologians who claim that Christianity in the mediaeval period at least did away with slavery are based either upon crass ignorance or mendacious apologetics. Almost the very opposite is the truth" (*ibid.*, p. 431). Political and economic changes destroyed slavery. In South Europe, in the Middle Ages, slavery increased, "and the church was not merely implicated in the possession of slaves, but it also inflicted the penalty of enslavement for all kinds of offences" (*ibid.*).

(5) The unity of European civilization was due to the centralizing influence of the church and her victory over the territorial churches.

(6) On the other hand, the religious orders of the Middle Ages, encouraging education and reflection, were the strongest forces leading to the individualism of city civilization. MacMurray also stresses this point: The monastic system is the segregation of the radical elements in the Christian ethic; but these elements are not suppressed by segregation. "The two movements in which the modern world takes its rise—the Renaissance and the Reformation—came from monasteries" (*op. cit.*, p. 160). They stem, writes MacMurray, from St. Francis and Luther, both monks who had vowed self-suppression: out of this came symbolic expression: "The monasteries . . . provide a psychological laboratory for bringing the unconscious forces of Christianity to consciousness" (*ibid.*, p. 161). By encouraging continual self-examination, they also encouraged individualism—"the key to the spiritual character of the modern world." (It is necessary to remark here that the two movements which MacMurray discusses by no means completely account for the modern world. In many ways they are only symptoms.)

61. This remark, and the whole discussion of Catholicism, carries no value judgment. Those who support the church will say, What brilliant strategy; those who oppose it will say, What mendacious apologetics; we say only, What a fine example of the church-type reaction!

62. Joseph Van Vleck, *Our Changing Churches*, p. 170.

63. *Reason, Social Myths, and Democracy*, pp. 76-77.

64. We draw here from Earle K. James, "Church and State in Mexico," *Annals of the American Academy of Political and Social Science*, CCVIII, 112-120. See also Charles S. MacFarland, *Chaos in Mexico: The Conflict of Church and State.*

65. James, *op. cit.*, p. 115.

66. *Ibid.*

67. One should note that this process of accommodation did not go very far until the new regime had demonstrated its ability to remain in power despite the church. The church was one of the heartiest foes of the revolution in its early stages, and even now, of course, has accepted no more than is necessary for continued influence. It is interesting to speculate what the position of the church in Spain would have been in 1965 if the revolution had turned out in favor of the Loyalists. That the process of reconciliation continues in Mexico is illustrated by the fact that less than a month before his inauguration (Dec. 1, 1940) Avila Camacho declared: "I am a believer." Many officials followed his example. (Cf. *Time*, Nov. 11, 1940, pp. 62-63.) There is still a good deal of antagonism, of course. Moreover, one of Camacho's motives was probably to minimize the moral support that was being given to his conservative rival, Almazan. It is significant, nevertheless, that the state as well as the church is coming to the point where it is willing to make some overtures.

68. Maritain, *op. cit.*, pp. 81-82.

69. *Ibid.*, pp. 85-86. One may accept the truth of this analysis, of course, without agreeing with the author's remedy.

70. It cannot control the relative, because that is simply the term that the Catholic Church gives to the power arrangements of the *status quo*.

71. J. A. Ryan and Joseph Husslein, *The Church and Labor*, p. x. By permission of the Macmillan Company, publishers.

72. *Ibid.*, p. xv.

73. *Ibid.*, p. 2; quoting Count de Mun.

74. *Ibid.*, p. 7.

75. *Ibid.*, pp. 66-67. One of the chief reasons why the Catholics (and most church groups) attack communism so strongly is, of course, the emphasis that communism gives to the class struggle, in direct opposition to the idea of organic unity expressed here by Leo XIII. The program of the universal church is absolutely dependent upon maintaining the idea of organic unity.

76. Cf. Nathaniel Micklem, *National Socialism and the Roman Catholic Church;* C. S. MacFarland, *The New Church and the New Germany;* Paul B. Means, *Things That Are Caesar's: The Genesis of the German Church Conflict;* and the collection of "facts and documents," *The Persecution of the Catholic Church in the Third Reich.*

Chapter III

1. Cf. Troeltsch, *The Social Teaching of the Christian Churches,* pp. 349-354.

2. Quoted by H. B. Workman, *The Dawn of the Reformation,* I, 222.

3. *Ibid.*, p. 213.

4. *Ibid.*, p. 226.

5. Quoted, *ibid.*, p. 227.

6. Troeltsch, *op. cit.*, p. 366; cf. also pp. 354-369.

7. These were akin to, but not synonymous with, the sect movements. They were more radically political in their orientation. Witness the Peasants' Revolt in England, the Jacquerie in France, and repeated uprisings of peasants in Germany. The church had closed its eyes to serfdom. "It was not the Church, but revolting peasants in Germany and England, who appealed to the fact that 'Christ has made all men free'; and in Germany, at least, their ecclesiastical masters showed small mercy to them" (Tawney, *Religion and the Rise of Capitalism,* p. 59).

8. This was a direct challenge to the whole medieval idea of Christian unity of civilization as well as an attack on the church as a religious body. Marsiglio was expressive of the tendencies toward a secular government and a "reformed" church, both of which were highly important in the societal development of the time. Cf. Barnes and Becker, *op. cit.*, pp. 288-293.

9. Cf. Thomas N. Lindsay, *A History of the Reformation,* I, 79-113; Troeltsch, *op. cit.*, pp. 369-378.

10. Preserved Smith, *The Age of the Reformation,* pp. 15-16.

11. *Ibid.*, p. 21.

12. *Ibid.*, p. 24.

13. Quoted by Workman, *op. cit.*, pp. 36-37.

14. Smith, *op. cit.*, p. 24. For an extended treatment of the economic factors in the medieval church see G. G. Coulton, *Five Centuries of Religion,* Vol. III; see also Lindsay, *op. cit.*, I, 7-17.

15. Smith, *op. cit.*, pp. 46-47.

16. Troeltsch, *op. cit.*, pp. 465-466.

17. *Ibid.;* italics mine.

18. See, for instance, *ibid.*, p. 466: ". . . the theories proclaimed by the Nominalism of later Scholasticism and the mysticism of the pre-Reformation opposition parties, were doubtless to some extent connected with the social changes which took place during the later Middle Ages. The whole tendency to emphasize the value of personal religious experience which this movement expressed, and the severance of religious interest from the secular and political interest, was a result of the general situation, of the city-civilization, of the growing independence of national States, and of economic interests. Nevertheless, this influence was only indirect. It only cleared the ground for the new ideas which arose out of the intensely personal struggle and labours of the Monk of Erfurt and Wittenberg. . . ."

19. We shall attempt here no systematic and complete treatment of Luther's reli-

gious thought, except as it pertains to our problem. To mention briefly some of the theological and ethical elements which we do not discuss in greater detail below: Protestantism is a revival of Pauline and Augustinian religion of grace, in contrast to Catholic religion of law; or, more accurately, it is a reinterpretation of the law. Sacraments were reduced to two—baptism and the eucharist. Emphasis was on the inner miracle of faith, one's own personal relation to God, without elaborate priestly intermediation (this phase did not always stand in church-type Protestantism). Protestantism re-emphasized the importance of the family; it limited the sex life to procreation.

20. Cf. A. C. McGiffert, *Protestant Thought before Kant,* p. 41.

21. *Address to the Christian Nobility of the German Nation.*

22. McGiffert, *op. cit.,* p. 37.

23. *Ibid.,* p. 59.

24. Troeltsch, *op. cit.,* p. 509.

25. Smith, *op. cit.,* p. 111; cf. also pp. 95-115.

26. McGiffert, *op. cit.,* p. 20.

27. See Tawney, "Religion Thought on Social and Economic Questions in the Sixteenth and Seventeenth Centuries. II. The Collision of Standards," *Journal of Political Economy,* XXXI, 648.

28. *Address to the Christian Nobility.*

29. Cf. Tawney, *op. cit.,* "III. The Social Ethics of Puritanism," p. 805.

30. Cf. Tawney, *Religion and the Rise of Capitalism,* pp. 90-93.

31. Quoted by Troeltsch, *op. cit.,* pp. 871-872.

32. *Ibid.,* p. 510.

33. Cf. Howard Becker, "Sargasso Iceberg: A Study in Cultural Lag and Institutional Disintegration," *American Journal of Sociology,* XXXIV, 492-506; and Maurer, *op. cit.*

34. H. M. Robertson, *Aspects of the Rise of Economic Individualism,* p. 54. Cambridge University Press. By permission of the Macmillan Company, publishers.

35. Smith, *op. cit.,* pp. 516-517.

36. See, for instance, several of the early chapters of Barnes and Becker, *Social Thought from Lore to Science.*

37. That is not to suggest that these are the only elements in the spirit of capitalism, especially as understood by Weber. See below. Weber certainly would not deny the importance, and perhaps even the primacy, of these "material" factors.

38. Robertson, *op. cit.,* pp. 176-177.

39. Amintore Fanfani, *Catholicism, Protestantism, and Capitalism,* pp. 178-179.

40. *Ibid.,* pp. 172-176.

41. John R. Commons, *Labor and Administration,* pp. 219-266.

42. There may be an interesting connection here with Cooley's theory of the origin of "primary ideals." Rational pursuit of economic gain, unfettered by earlier restraints, may be a function of the extension of the market which brings in a new moral code for dealing with customers who are not members of one's own primary group. Calculation of one's personal responsibility toward a stranger differently from one's responsibility to a neighbor or kin is a commonplace of all times and places. Modern economic developments greatly increased the number of "strangers" who were involved with each other in economic and financial matters.

43. Some writers have pointed out that Protestantism encouraged the spread of capitalism by the migration of its persecuted followers. While this may well be true, the stimulation given to enterprise, as Fanfani points out, is not logically connected with their religious beliefs, but with their minority position and their place as foreigners. Industry and thrift are often characteristics of foreign groups in new countries, as many researches show. "It may be objected that none the less these exiles were such on account of their religion, but this argument, if it led anywhere, would lead to the absurdity of attributing the effects of such enforced exile, not indeed to the religion

of the persecuted, but to the measures taken by their persecutors" (Fanfani, *op. cit.*, pp. 185-186).

44. Cf. Troeltsch, *op. cit.*, pp. 617-625.

45. McGiffert, *op. cit.*, p. 87.

CHAPTER IV

1. Weber, *The Protestant Ethics and the Spirit of Capitalism*, p. 52. As Sombart puts the same idea: ". . . for business purposes the mere appearance of respectability is sufficient. As a matter of fact, it does not by any means suffice actually to be respectable. You must be regarded as such" (*The Quintessence of Capitalism*, p. 124).

2. Tawney, *Religion and the Rise of Capitalism*, p. 36.

3. Weber, *op. cit.*, p. 25. One must not assume, of course, that this statement of aims is always achieved in his treatment of the problem.

4. The significance of this point is referred to below. In this section we are simply outlining Weber's thesis. Fanfani points out the indirect and unintended ways in which Catholicism also contributed to the growth of capitalism. The Pope encouraged capitalism by entrusting tithes and other dues to laymen, which stimulated them to look for large profits and to travel in search of gain. "Through these emissaries, protected by apostolic authority, they facilitated the interrelation of markets and contributed to the cultural and spiritual formation of the great medieval merchant and banking class" (*op. cit.*, p. 154). Thus the area of faith became a vast and unified market. Despite an anticapitalistic ethos, according to Fanfani, Catholicism stimulated the growth of capitalism. Cf. *ibid.*, pp. 154-160.

5. Weber, *op. cit.*, p. 91.

6. *Ibid.*, pp. 26-27. Note the phrase "obstructed by spiritual obstacles." There is little disagreement with respect to the restrictive or conserving effects of religion. But we must not confuse that with initiating power. See n. 9, below.

7. As we shall see below, why continuous and systematic work came to be thought of as a proof of rebirth and genuine faith is of the utmost importance.

8. Weber, *op. cit.*, p. 172.

9. Weber, *General Economic History*, pp. 361-362. For the complete study of the effects of Hinduism on business ethics, see *Religionssoziologie*, II, Part I. This quotation concerning India brings to attention the studies with which Weber followed up his essay on the Protestant ethic, in which he developed further the relation between religious doctrines and business ethics. These essays are not part of our central concern but must be discussed briefly, particularly because of their methodological importance. By the investigation of Confucianism and Taoism, Hinduism and Buddhism, and Ancient Judaism, Weber sought to discover in what ways religious ideas blocked or encouraged the appearance of rational business enterprise. In each case, political, economic, and social factors were also taken into account (thus differing from the study of Protestantism, which took into account only one side of the causal chain). Confucianism, for instance, Weber found contained a good deal of the rationalism characteristic of Western business ethics; it was quite definitely utilitarian; it had a positive evaluation of wealth. Despite all this, however, Confucianism was limited by a fundamental traditionalism. The ideal of the Confucian gentleman was a traditional, static idea—the assimilation of the traditional body of literary culture expressed in the classics. Tradition was not only accepted but sanctified. Moreover, the specialization of Western bureaucratic structure was thoroughly opposed in the classical education of the Confucian gentleman, who was to become a well-rounded, harmonious work of art. Again, the Western ethic rests on universalism and far-reaching mutual confidence; Confucianism, on the contrary, was a "particularistic" structure of relationships. Finally, the basic metaphysical foundation of Confucianism, says Weber, the concept of Tao, the principle of Order, is in contrast to the evolutionism, the idea of development in

Judaeo-Christian thought, as shown in the prophets. Cf. Weber, *Religionssoziologie,* I, 373-536.

Without undertaking a thorough discussion of these essays, we must raise two fundamental problems (and here we anticipate much of our later discussion): Why is it that China continued to be bound by Confucian traditionalism, while Europe was gradually freed from the equally or more restrictive influence of the Christian traditionalism? If one answers, as Weber does, that Christianity was reinterpreted by the Protestant "prophecy," the question immediately arises: Why did the prophets appear in Europe? Why did Confucianism not have a Reformation? The natural congeniality of Christianity for prophecy is probably a legitimate part of the explanation. (The cause of this congeniality can be disregarded for Weber's immediate problem, although it is of the utmost importance for more general questions of causation in history.) That conditions in sixteenth-century Europe were ripe, however, for all kinds of prophecy is proved by the series of revolutions—commercial, legal, political—that was going on. This limits his conception of the immanence of the religious developments.

Related to this is a second problem: To demonstrate that a religious ethic can *restrict* the appearance of a new economic form and to claim that a religious ethic can *precipitate* a new economic form are two different things. All of Weber's essays, except *The Protestant Ethic,* seek to show how the appearance of capitalism was greatly restricted by a religious system. Very few will deny, except in points of detail, the thoroughness of his demonstration. The most rabid historical materialist is the one who insists that "religion is the opiate of the people"—an admission that it has a telling effect on their behavior. A religion *once established* (whatever the cause of its own doctrine) certainly becomes in its turn a "cause" (see below for a discussion of this term) of succeeding events. But in *The Protestant Ethic,* Weber argues precisely that the congeniality of Calvinism for capitalism preceded the major development of capitalism and was greatly responsible for its peculiar spirit. Moreover, he held that this Calvinistic doctrine emerged—although not entirely—out of a religious dialectic, and became conjoined with emerging capitalism only by a "historical accident." That this claim is on an entirely different level from that of the others is immediately apparent, and much of the discussion in this chapter seeks to investigate that claim.

With regard to Weber's conclusion that nonreligious factors were as conducive, if not more conducive, to capitalism in China than in Europe, the present writer is unable to judge. Consequently any validation that this study gives to Weber's thesis, and any criticism it makes of it, will have to be offered from the evidence in connection with the history of Calvinism itself. It should be stated, however, that the establishment of the adequacy of a theoretical formulation in one group of historical data is prima facie evidence, if not proof, of its usefulness in other similar contexts.

The comparative studies are found in *Religionssoziologie,* I, 237 ff., and Vols. II and III. The first part of Volume I contains the study of Protestantism. See also *Wirtschaft und Gesellschaft,* throughout Part II, chap. iv, particularly pp. 267 ff.; Parsons, *op. cit.,* pp. 539-578 (Parson's study is undoubtedly the best treatment of Weber's work available in English); L. L. Bennion, *Max Weber's Methodology,* pp. 85-120; Albert Salomon, "Max Weber's Sociology," *Social Research,* II, 60-73.

10. Asceticism, as Weber used the term, was one of two type reactions to the inevitable conflict between the religious values and the world of "nature." One reaction is to devalue this world—this is mysticism. The other is to control or overcome the world in the interest of the religious idea—that is asceticism. Cf. *Religionssoziologie,* I, 538-542.

11. See below for a fuller discussion of the doctrine of the calling.

12. *Op. cit.,* p. 112. Note that this quotation from Tawney suggests a different interpretation from that which Weber made. The significance of the doctrine will be discussed later.

13. Cf. Bennion, *op. cit.,* p. 84.

14. Bennion has a brief discussion of the Mormons which shows the relation between their religious ideas and the economic development of the territory in which they settled. Had the Mormons not migrated, "the development of Utah and much of the surrounding territory would have occurred later and exhibited a very different character" (*ibid.,* p. 133; cf. also pp. 128-135). One should note, however, that this effect may have had nothing to do with their religious ideas, but only with their place as newcomers. One must not attribute to religious beliefs all the effects on economic behavior brought about by religious groups. If the effect is due to their being a persecuted minority which has to go into business because other activities are closed to them, or if the effect is due to a necessity for migration, the religious belief is not the cause of the economic behavior, but only a concomitant variation. One must control all the factors. This is a point which Troeltsch does not always take into account; and Weber's essay is somewhat subject to a similar difficulty in certain places.

15. Weber, *The Protestant Ethic and the Spirit of Capitalism,* p. 43.

16. Parsons, *Journal of Political Economy,* XLIII, 691; italics mine.

17. The dichotomy "secular-religious" is not wholly satisfactory. The need is for a word that will exclude religion but include all other aspects of life. When used as the anonym of "sacred," "secular" excludes more than the religious, and since sacred-secular is a frequently used dichotomy, our use of the term "secular" can be misunderstood. There is no clear consensus, however, on other terms: "mundane" and "profane" have connotations which are difficult to overcome; "naturalistic," as contrasted with "supernaturalistic," implies a definition of religion that many would not accept; "lay" generally refers simply to nonclerical church people (as in "laymen"), and therefore the dichotomy "clerical-lay" does not serve our purpose. Under the circumstances, it seems best to use the word "secular" in the simply dictionary meaning: that which is not religious.

18. In other words, the appearance of a new power group in society will force changes on church doctrine, for only by changing can the church stay in a place of influence. Groeythuysen puts this problem in an interesting fashion: "The God of the Christians, in creating the world and in preparing the coming of his Church, does not appear to have foreseen that one day the bourgeois will claim his place and wish to play an important part there. . . . Yet . . . the Church . . . must now interpret in its own way the social phenomenon which the bourgeoisie represents in modern times. It must be able to tell the bourgeois why God has created him, and assign him his functions here below. But how will it set about securing this bourgeois of quite profane origin? How will it join the mind and the manner of life of the bourgeoisie to religious traditions, in order to give it its consecrations?" (quoted by Robertson, *op. cit.,* pp. 165-166). Certainly the church cannot do this by declaring at the start that his manner of life is evil, but by finding a place for it. This was a need of Catholicism as well as of Protestantism.

19. *Op. cit.,* p. 894 n.

20. Both Troeltsch and Parsons seem to exaggerate the care with which Weber took account of the differences between early and late Calvinism. In terms of general theory, Weber was well aware of the factors which influence religious ethics (e.g., the class of those who constitute its principle adherents); but this awareness was not sufficiently prominent, in the opinion of the present writer, in his treatment of Calvinism.

21. Reinhold Niebuhr points out that communism has as difficult a time as Calvinism in keeping a balance between voluntarism and determinism: "The idea that the downfall of capitalism is inevitable is as powerful an incentive to moral energy as was Calvinistic determinism in the heyday of Calvinistic faith. The belief that determinism inevitably leads to an inclination to take 'moral holidays' (William James) is a typical illusion of a rationalistic and individualistic age. On the contrary, men

develop the highest energy in the pursuit of a moral or social goal when they are most certain that they are affirming the preordained 'counsels of God.'

"Nevertheless there are perils of fatalism in every deterministic theory and they are revealed in Marxian as well as in Christian thought and practice. When the attainment of an historical goal is regarded as preordained it may nerve the early small flock of faith to tireless energy and yet tempt the later church to a sleepy fatalism. The German parliamentary-revolutionary socialism elaborated by Kautsky succumbed to this temptation; against it and similar tendencies Lenin insisted: 'Some revolutionists attempt to prove that there is absolutely no way out of a crisis. That is an error. There does not exist a position from which there is absolutely no way out.' Lenin's insistence that the objective forces of history must be consciously directed toward a revolutionary goal by a revolutionary class seeks to preserve a proper 'dialectic' balance between 'religious' determinism and the voluntarism of an adequate moral theory" (*Reflections on the End of an Era,* pp. 130-131).

We are interested here in discovering what it is that prevents a deterministic creed from becoming rigid, on the one hand, or causes it to swing toward fatalism on the other. Cf. Toynbee, *op. cit.,* V, 615-618.

22. H. R. Niebuhr, *op. cit.,* p. 86.

23. Troeltsch, *op. cit.,* p. 625.

24. Tawney, *op. cit.,* pp. 104-105.

25. Barnes and Becker, *op. cit.,* p. 324; italics mine. The word "quickly" is not entirely appropriate, since the full transition took two centuries. See below. Moreover, it is important to remember that the union of capitalism and religious doctrine was possible in the mind of Calvin partly because the capitalistic conditions in Geneva at the time were quite provincial. In this form, Calvin found capitalism suitable to the life of the city, and yet able to be combined with loyalty, seriousness, honesty, thrift, and consideration for one's neighbor. Under conditions of highly developed capitalism, the *rapprochement* is not so easily accomplished.

26. That is not to say that the compromise may not be so complete as effectively to cancel the power of the religious element in the church. Whether or not this is the case depends largely on the incorporation, or the failure to incorporate, of sect elements in the church synthesis.

27. See the section on usury, below.

28. *Institutes* (translated by John Allen), I, 639-642. Published by the Westminster Press. Used by permission.

29. This difference between Calvin and Calvinism, and the reasons for the difference, could be discussed at greater length, with regard to other factors. For instance, a theory of the unity of all Protestant churches resulted from religious conflict in the early years. This led to the duty of mutual support, and to the same obligations for the states which were united with the churches. From this came a justification of the religious wars, despite the fact that Calvin's position on war was like Luther's: religion had no part in it. After the religious struggles Calvinism regained its antiwar ethic. (Cf. Troeltsch, *op. cit.*, pp. 650-652.) Sovereign princes opposed Calvinism because it threatened their sovereign power; strong city republics opposed it because it threatened the traditional power of the great families. Thus in Geneva Calvinism took on a semidemocratic emphasis not altogether natural to it. John Knox's complete antimonarchism was due to the danger that the Queens of Scotland and England might marry Catholic foreign nobles and thus endanger the gospel. (See *ibid.,* pp. 625-641.) Niebuhr thus sums up this modification of Calvinism: "The modification of primitive Calvinism under this influence is marked in four particular areas: in the democratization of the originally autocratic and authoritative plan of government, in the abandonment of the essentially medieval social ethics, in the substitution of independency and tolerance for the conception of the church-state, and in the acceptance of doctrinal modifications under the influence of the humanism and rationalism which were prevalent in the middle classes" (*The Social Sources of Denominationalism,* p. 99).

30. It is not necessary here to discuss the many reasons why Great Britain developed so extensively and so rapidly into a capitalist country. We need only mention the political struggle which led to confiscation of church property, the reshifting of classes, the enclosures, favorable geographical position, fairly good transportation, a large, unified market.

31. Tawney, in the Introduction to Weber, p. 10.

32. *Ibid.*, p. 232. Weber uses the term "Puritan" in the sense in which he held that it was popularly understood in the seventeenth century: the ascetically inclined religious movements, especially in Britain and Holland. Cf. *op. cit.*, p. 217 n. 2. Others—for example, Woodhouse—give it a broader meaning.

33. See David W. Petegorsky, *Left-Wing Democracy in the English Civil War;* G. P. Gooch, *English Democratic Ideas in the Seventeenth Century;* A. S. P. Woodhouse, *Puritanism and Liberty.*

34. Petegorsky, *op. cit.*, p. 240.

35. Quoted, *ibid.*, p. 179.

36. Cf. Schlatter, *op. cit.*, and Hall, *op. cit.*

37. Tawney, *op. cit.*, p. 246.

38. *Ibid.*, p. 247.

39. *Ibid.*, p. 267.

40. Pp. 15-16.

41. That is not to say, of course, that the traditional element (in the sense of original Calvinism with its derivatives) was not strong throughout all of Calvinism, even those portions which were most emancipated from *economic* traditionalism. Ostentation, elaborate clothing, idle talk, excess sleep, pastimes, inordinate recreations, sports, plays, excess of worldly business and cares—those are among the things opposed. Cf. Baxter, *A Christian Directory*, Vol. III. Puritanism descended "like a frost on the fine arts." It attacked vehemently the *Book of Sports,* allowing sports on Sunday, which was put into law by James I and Charles I partly to fight the anti-authoritarianism of the Puritans. Science, however, it stimulated somewhat. Cf. Weber, *op. cit.*, pp. 155-169; R. K. Merton, *Science, Technology and Society,* and Troeltsch, *Protestantism and Progress.*

42. T. C. Hall, *The Religious Background of American Culture,* p. 217.

43. Cf. Richard Baxter, *op. cit.*, VI, 287-348.

44. *Ibid.*, p. 287.

45. *Ibid.*, IV, 379-384.

46. As Tawney explains, this is a charge always brought against those who call attention to the causes of class hatred. That is not to deny that there is some justice in the charge, in so far as leaders crystallize class antagonisms; but the bases for the hatred precede them.

47. Schlatter, *op. cit.*, p. 199.

48. E. S. Bates, *American Faith,* p. 70.

49. Tawney, *Religion and the Rise of Capitalism,* p. 238.

50. Bunyan, of course, was not a Calvinist, but in this matter his views were similar to Baxter's. He had been influenced by the same developments that affected Calvinism as well as by Calvinism itself.

51. Cf. Tawney, "Religious Thought on Social and Economic Questions in the Sixteenth and Seventeenth Centuries," *Journal of Political Economy,* XXXI, 813-814.

52. Pp. 226-227.

53. All the values and difficulties of the sociology of knowledge abound in this problem. Indirectly we are using this approach to interpret the thought of Calvin, and especially that of Calvinism. Calvin's ideas do not appear out of the blue, even his religious ideas. They have a definite connection with the existing society.

54. Cf. Weber, *Wirtschaft und Gesellschaft,* chap. iii, sec. 10.

55. Cf. Tawney, *op. cit.*, pp. 656-657.

56. Schlatter, *op. cit.*, p. 216.

57. Cf. Erich Roll, *A History of Economic Thought,* p. 51.

58. Cf. Robertson, *op. cit.,* p. 160.

59. Tawney, *op. cit.,* p. 657.

60. Lord Stamp writes: "The Jesuits made marvelous efforts to reconcile the old view with economics, or to escape the infamy of interest, e.g., 'where the borrower's payment is of his free will the lender may keep it,' or 'it is not usury to exact something in return for the danger and expense of regaining the principal.' . . . At last Rome bent so far as (a) to allow special circumstances in which an additional sum might be paid, without being very generous in stating what they were, and while reaffirming the sinfulness of usury; and (b) no longer putting books which advocated interest upon the Index. By 1830, without formal recantation of doctrine, priests were permitted to treat interest in practice as not a matter for condemnation. Clever priests still fought strange rearguard actions, but in 1872 the authoritative statement was made that those who take eight per cent. interest per annum are 'not to be disquieted'" (*Christianity and Economics,* pp. 46-47, by permission of the Macmillan Company, publishers; cf. also Weber, *General Economic History,* pp. 268-270).

61. Quoted by Robertson, *op. cit.,* p. 115.

62. *Ibid.,* pp. 111-117, and Tawney, *op. cit.,* p. 806.

63. Cf. Robertson, *op. cit.,* pp. 118-132.

64. Baxter, *op. cit.,* VI, 328.

65. Quoted by Robertson, *op. cit.,* p. 4.

66. Quoted by McGiffert, *op. cit.,* pp. 33-34; cf. also Troeltsch, *op. cit.,* pp. 128-131; Weber, *The Protestant Ethic,* pp. 79-89; and Hall, *op. cit.,* p. 216.

67. Maurer, *op. cit.,* pp. 276-277.

68. Robertson, *op. cit.,* p. 11.

69. Weber, *op. cit.,* p. 215 n.; italics mine.

70. Cf. Robertson, *op. cit.,* pp. 19-21.

71. *Op. cit.,* II, 333.

72. Cf. Robertson, *op. cit.,* pp. 1-32, and Fanfani, *op. cit.,* pp. 200-205.

73. Weber, *op. cit.,* pp. 74-75.

74. Cf. E. A. J. Johnson, *American Economic Thought in the Seventeenth Century;* T. C. Hall, *The Religious Background of American Culture;* and W. W. Sweet, *The Story of Religion in America.* It should be noted, however, that Pennsylvania was probably more completely Calvinistic than either New England or Virginia.

75. *Religion and the Rise of Capitalism,* p. 29.

76. Sombart, in fact, asserts that the capitalist spirit (not to be entirely equated, however, with Weber's use of the term) appeared first in Italy in the fourteenth century. There were the ideas of "holy economy"—thoughtfulness and thrift, which led even the wealthy to be thrifty, a thing unheard of before. It was no longer sufficient to spend no more than one earned; one must spend less than he earned. This change in the traditional view preceded Calvinism by two centuries. Cf. *The Quintessence of Capitalism,* pp. 50 ff.

77. Weber, *op. cit.,* pp. 55-56.

78. Religious doctrine itself was not an unambiguous stimulant to enterprise. Governor Bradford spoke harshly against that "notorious evil . . . whereby most men walked in all their commerce—to buy as cheap and sell as dear as they can . . ." (Tawney, "Religious Thought on Social and Economic Questions in the Sixteenth and Seventeenth Centuries," *op. cit.,* p. 809). And Governor Winthrop acted severely against profiteers. See *ibid.,* pp. 804-813.

79. Sweet, *op. cit.,* pp. 7-8.

80. Weber's conflict with the "materialist interpretation" is unnecessarily sharp at this point because he misinterprets the position given to ideas. Of course ideas and religious ideals are important in history—his observation is sound—but one must also raise the question of their origin before he can adequately understand that importance.

This does not mean that historical materialism is therefore an adequate explanation (see Chapter I).

81. Fanfani observes that Holland can scarcely be given as an example of the influence of the Reformation on the development of capitalism, because the Netherlands actually declined in the sixteenth century, "whereas in the fifteenth they had been acquainted with such a definitely capitalistic phenomenon as the migration of industries from the towns to the country in order to avoid guild restrictions, and at the same time had seen the cloth merchant assume the role of the modern capitalist employer. While the Flemish ports were of such importance that the Venetian galleys braved the ocean in order to call there" (Fanfani, *op. cit.*, p. 168).

82. Some regions in the Highlands remained Catholic for some time after Knox, but the question that Hall raises is: Why did the final acceptance of Calvinism not stimulate the capitalist spirit?

83. Hall, *op. cit.*, p. 211.

84. Pietism, especially of the German variety, vacillated among various doctrines. It combined emotional elements, Lutheran influence, and some aspects of Calvinism. Spener, Zinzendorf, and Franck were important leaders. Cf. Weber, *op. cit.*, pp. 128 ff.

85. *Ibid.*, p. 131.

86. *Ibid.*; cf. Troeltsch, *The Social Teaching of the Christian Churches*, pp. 644-650.

87. The dependence of Christian socialism on conditions is clear. Tawney writes: "Mankind does not reflect upon questions of economic and social organization until compelled to do so by the sharp pressure of some practical emergency" (*Religion and the Rise of Capitalism*, p. 66). Troeltsch makes the same point: the ideal of a radical sect is aroused only by general social development. Thus the influence of Christian socialism is always of a secondary nature, being exerted along with more general movements which it interprets, appropriates, and rectifies. Cf. Troeltsch, *op. cit.*, pp. 809-818. The idea of a socialist church, he adds, is nonsense (in a capitalist society): the church is on the side of law and order. "But a Christian socialism which is separate from the church in spirit can appeal to the Gospel" (*ibid.*, p. 805).

88. *Op. cit.*, p. 70.

89. *Ibid.*, p. 181.

90. This is strong inferential proof of its social source and function.

91. Cf. Coulton, *op. cit.*, II, esp. 174-194.

92. Weber, *op. cit.*, p. 175. Sombart has made this point very strongly in his distinction between the old and the new capitalist. The old, still under traditional sentiments and restraints, was concerned with the "weal or woe of the living, breathing human being." The new type seeks only profit. Cf. *op. cit.*, pp. 154 ff.

93. Our discussion in this chapter has been limited, for the most part, to the church-type reaction to the important changes that took place in the late medieval period. We have sought to describe the attempts of churchmen to control and moralize the powerful new elements in the economic structure of society. At the same time many religious persons and groups were thoroughly sectarian in their reaction, and a sociological analysis of the period cannot be complete without a careful study of the Protestant sects. Although we shall not attempt that study here, we must make a brief reference to the significance of the sects. Both Lutheranism and Calvinism, in their original opposition to Catholicism, involved sect elements. Sectarian development had been very important in setting the stage for the Reformation; we have record of at least four pre-Reformation movements that were preparing the ground for later revolt: the Cathars, Waldenses, Lollards, and Hussites. These were essentially lower-class protests which were attempting, by their interpretation of the gospel, to oppose the existing social structure and its religious foundations. The pre-Reformation leaders did not fail to achieve a thoroughgoing religious change because of personal inadequacy. They represent the continuous religious protest of the disinherited against their lot; and their failure is another testimony of the weakness of the religious weapon in winning out over the more mundane weapons of economic advantage.

Luther and Calvin succeeded where the others had failed, not because of enormously greater personal power, but because a new factor was added: to the sectarian protest was joined the desire of an emerging power group who needed a "reformation" to establish themselves. These two elements were not in essential harmony, however, and soon split apart. The sectarian expression of Christianity appeared again, even before the Reformation was well underway. Its first protest was against the Lutheran compromise with civil authority (justified on the grounds that the compromise would make possible the supremacy of the true faith) which reduced the distinction between the Christian ethic and the secular ethic of natural law. Continuously, from that day to this, there have been sectarian movements which opposed the compromises the church has made with the *status quo*. The inequalitarian aspects of capitalism, the stress on individual responsibility and adequacy, slavery, war—these have been among the important centers of conflict. We shall discuss some of them in later chapters, but at this point only mention some of the post-Reformation sects:

The Anabaptist movement broke out in Zurich in 1525, mainly among the masses. The wave spread over Central Europe. Its opposition to the idea of the Christian unified society, however, resulted in persecution at the hands of Catholics and Protestants alike. This may account for some of the fanatical revivalism among the Baptists. The Mennonites compromised with the church in Holland, and prospered. A movement in England called the "Diggers," led by Winstanley, propounded a radical Christian socialism. The Quakers and Owen were directly influenced by them. The Methodists were "an attempt to leaven the life of the National Church with the influence of smaller groups of genuine and vital Christians" (Troeltsch, *op. cit.*, p. 721). Though they sought no separation, their emphases demanded it. Eventually, like the Quakers and Moravians, they became an established group, through the inevitable association of children of members as part of the church community. As a sect, they emphasized franchise reform, liberation of slaves, philanthropy, and an opposition to modern culture. See H. R. Niebuhr, *op. cit.*, pp. 31-65, and Troeltsch, *op. cit.*, pp. 691-729.

In terms of Weber's thesis, many of these sects encouraged capitalism by their religious rationalism (although one must read Weber's account with the same caution that is necessary with reference to Calvinism). Among the Quakers, the sincere repudiation of the world, the silent waiting to overcome everything impulsive and irrational, were not even Lutheran, but rather Thomist terms in which the idea of the calling was held. One should do only what is necessary to live in the world. This naturally weakened, in the same way as Spener's Pietism, the tendency toward capitalism. On the other hand, the Quakers' repudiation of the world, like the Baptists', and their repudiation of political activity, forced them, says Weber, into nonpolitical callings. With their shrewd and conscientious rationality, this was a drive to capitalism. Thus Christian asceticism left the monasteries and strode into the market place. Cf. Weber, *op. cit.*, pp. 144-154.

Mysticism is another aspect of the tradition of dissent, more amorphous in form than the sects, but related to them in sociological meaning. Mysticism may also be discussed in terms of its derivations in the social and religious setting. But this cannot be done here. Suffice it to say that mysticism is a direct, personal, religious experience, often expressing itself in frenzy, ecstasy, visions, subjective religious experience. Like that of the church and the sects, its origin can be traced to primitive Christianity. Luther was influenced by mysticism, but Calvin scarcely at all. All Protestantism, however, with its emphasis on personal salvation, is congenial to mysticism. This "spiritual" tendency is clearly different from the sect; the spiritual reformer recognized no external body of believers. Mysticism is radical individualism; unlike the sect, it places no emphasis on the relation between individuals; there is no obligation to organize and evangelize. The mystic, however, also needs fellowship; hence small groups are often formed.

In its criticism of doctrine, mysticism establishes a close relation with rationalism, though in most respects it is in contrast with it. Spinoza, Edelmann, and some of the

Deists went easily from mysticism to rationalism. The tolerance of the mystics went far beyond Anabaptist tolerance. The ethic of mysticism is personal perfection and salvation. Problems of secular morality, of state and society, do not concern it. Mystics, in fact, often stay within the church, which they, unlike the sects, do not wish to replace with a new organization. We should note that in actual practice the sect and mysticism constantly merged: "The sect aspired to the inwardness of mysticism; mysticism strove to actualize the sacred fellowship of the sect" (Troeltsch, *op. cit.,* p. 753; cf. also pp. 729-790).

94. That does not mean, of course, that that portion of Calvinism is uncaused, but that the causes are independent of capitalism.

95. It is not necessary to say that our explanation is also causally inadequate as a complete explanation. We simply add it to others. One might ask the more general question why religious groups and leaders *want* to remain in a place of influence *as religious groups and leaders.* We have been somewhat concerned with this problem in Chapter I.

96. Not only must one explain the origin of Calvinism, of course, but also the process of its evolution, as we have seen, and why, out of the many new religious developments of the time, Calvinism prospered.

97. Cf., for instance, Sombart: "Think as you like of the genius of the founder of a religion, this much is clear—that before any religion can strike root certain conditions must exist. . . . However (and this is the important thing), once a religion (or a philosophical system) has become accepted, there can be no doubt that its teachings, surrounded with a divine halo as they often are, cannot but influence the whole of life, and therefore of economic activities" (*op. cit.,* pp. 268-270).

98. *Social Causation,* pp. 177-178.

99. This is not unrelated to Weber's idea that the reformulation, by means of prophecy, of religious doctrines during a time of unrest will be in terms of the problems and needs of the various classes and groups. Troeltsch makes something of this same point in trying to ascertain the precise influence of Protestantism on the modern world. Its chief influence, he writes, is in the religious domain itself. Only there has it had any "really revolutionary effects." Only in "the second or third place" is Protestantism a civilizing force outside the religious sphere. (Cf. *Protestantism and Progress,* pp. 174-176.)

100. McGiffert, *op. cit.,* p. 188; cf. also Troeltsch, *op. cit.,* pp. 150-154, on Calvinism and individualism.

101. Cf. P. C. Gordon-Walker, "Capitalism and the Reformation," *Economic History Review,* Vol. VIII, No. 1 (Nov., 1937).

102. Weber, *op. cit.,* p. 7 (Preface).

103. Quoted by Tawney, *ibid.,* p. 8.

104. We have not discussed Sombart's theory at length because it is somewhat outside the specific topic of this volume; nonetheless, it deserves brief mention. Sombart held that the capitalist spirit is peculiarly the Jewish spirit, that capitalism's development in Northern Europe is closely correlated with Jewish migrations to the North, that Puritanism's affinity for capitalism is due to its Jewish origin. "Puritanism *is* Judaism," he writes. "Whether the first was influenced by the second, and if so, how, are most difficult questions to answer. It is well known, of course, that in the Reformation period there was close intercourse between Jews and certain Christian sects, that the study of Hebrew and the Hebrew Scriptures became fashionable, and that the Jews in England in the 17th century were held in very high esteem by the Puritans. Leading men in England like Oliver Cromwell built up their religious views on the Old Testament, and Cromwell himself dreamed of a reconciliation between the Old and New Testaments, and of a confederation between the Chosen People of God and the Puritan English" (*The Jews and Modern Capitalism,* pp. 249-250). The reasons for Jewish success in capitalistic enterprise, according to Sombart, are their dis-

persion over a wide area, their treatment as strangers, their semicitizenship, and their wealth.

In evaluating this theory, one must note immediately that Judaism cannot be the crucial cause of the development of a capitalist spirit as the accepted pattern, for Judaism existed for many centuries without that spirit becoming dominant. And even though Sombart might succeed in showing the affinity of the Jews for capitalism, it is only with difficulty that he can show how the Puritans got hold of the same spirit. As Troeltsch points out, his virtual identification of Puritan and Jewish religion and economic ethics is far too simple. Even if this were accepted, however, Sombart would have to explain why Calvinism tended to move toward the Jewish religious type. Our whole discussion above serves to answer this question, but not in the way Sombart would have done. That Judaism sponsored certain aspects of the capitalistic spirit, and that in many respects the Calvinist and Jewish ethics are similar, are not denied. In fact, it is an interesting sociological question to ask why both should contain an ethic that favors worldly activity. What, in addition to common dependence on the Old Testament—which in itself is only a surface explanation—is there similar about the sociological conditions in which they grew which would explain their business ethics? While we do not directly answer this question, the discussion should throw some light upon it.

105. Parsons, *Journal of Political Economy,* XLIII, 693.

106. Cf. *Society: Its Structure and Changes,* p. 522.

107. Cf. Parsons, *Structure of Social Actions,* pp. 552-553.

108. Troeltsch, *The Social Teaching of the Christian Churches,* p. 1003.

Chapter V

1. Cf. Élie Halévy, *A History of England,* pp. 9-109, and D. C. Wagner, *The Church of England and Social Reform Since 1854,* pp. 12-173.

2. There are a great many studies of the Christian socialist movement. See, for instance, A. V. Woodworth, *Christian Socialism in England,* and the Fabian tracts *Christian Socialism,* by Stewart Headlam, and *Socialism and Christianity,* by Percy Dearmer.

3. C. H. Hopkins, *The Rise of the Social Gospel in American Protestantism 1865-1915,* pp. 79-80.

4. *Ibid.,* pp. 79-84.

5. *Christianizing the Social Order,* p. 108. By permission of the Macmillan Company, publishers.

6. Hopkins, *op. cit.,* p. 85.

7. *Ibid.*

8. Sweet, *The Story of Religion in America,* pp. 498-499.

9. Hopkins, *op. cit.,* p. 12.

10. Rauschenbusch, *op. cit.,* p. 44.

11. *Ibid.,* p. 92.

12. "The really effective religious ideas are more faithly mirrored by the hymns of a given time than by its theology and sermons, and a study of our hymnals, especially of the innumerable collections of Gospel hymns which are a really native expression of American Christian life, gives an overwhelming impression of the predominance of other-worldly desires. 'In the Christian's home in glory'; 'Shall we meet beyond the river?'; 'I will sing you a song of that beautiful land, the far-away home of the soul'; 'That will be glory for me'—what endless variations of the same . . . theme!" (*ibid.,* p. 75).

13. This dominance was perhaps due, first of all, to the necessity for organization in order to survive early persecutions; but as Rauschenbusch says: "The Church thus built up a State within the State, and its constructive ability was expended on that task. But in thus confining its political activity it limited its political outlook. When the Church emerged from the era of oppression, it had a powerful organization to be

maintained and the conviction that to maintain that organization was practically the whole social duty of Christianity" (*ibid.*, p. 78). Like other institutions, the church developed a kind of "corporate egotism" which fought for survival.

14. We have already noted Weber's discussion of the correlation between "prophecy" and social crises. See *Wirtschaft und Gesellschaft*, pp. 250-257. And Troeltsch shows with abundance of illustration that it is precisely in times of great unrest that the radical element in Christianity is most prominent.

15. Three things must be noted in connection with this statement, however: (1) we are speaking here of religion, not of the church: the church may have vast power as a secular institution; (2) even the maximum power of religion to give individuals a perspective larger than themselves is not great when compared with the influence of other powers; (3) this renewed religious influence usually soon becomes institutionalized and formalized, with the death of the prophets and the decline of the crisis that produced them.

16. Twenty-three million copies of this novel were sold in the English-speaking world; it was translated into twenty-one foreign languages, and made into a movie. Cf. Hopkins, *op. cit.*, p. 143.

17. *Ibid.*, p. 148.

18. Cf. *ibid.*, pp. 167 ff. It is interesting to note, however, that in the country's largest Presbyterian seminary no formal course in "social ethics" was offered as late as 1936. Note also that the Presbyterian Church has the highest per capita expenditure of all large denominations in the country; and that Presbyterians listed in *Who's Who* make the largest showing among businessmen, bankers, judges, and lawyers. Cf. C. D. Fry, "The Religious Affiliations of American Leaders," *Scientific Monthly*, XXXVI, 247.

19. In 1891 the Lutheran Church in Germany had organized The Supreme Evangelical Council with the express purpose of winning the workers away from socialism. This could be done, of course, only by incorporating into the teachings of the church the tenets of socialism which were attracting the workers, giving them only a religious hue. Powerful industrialists forced the suspension of the Council after four years, showing how few sectarian elements had been incorporated into Lutheranism at that time. But the attempt is an interesting illustration of the response of churches to a new secular power.

20. Cf. Charles Stelzle, *The Church and Labor*, and Hopkins, *op. cit.*, pp. 280-283.

21. Cf. *ibid.*, pp. 280-301; H. F. Ward, *The Social Creed of the Churches;* the Central Conference of American Rabbis, *Declaration on Social Justice;* C. S. MacFarland, *Christian Unity in Practice and Prophecy.*

22. On the function of religion in legitimizing the power arrangement, see Weber, *Gesammelte Aufsaetze zur Religionssoziologie*, I, 237 ff.

23. Hopkins, *op. cit.*, p. 291.

24. *Op. cit.*, p. 30.

25. See the *Report of the First Meeting*, Federal Council of Churches of Christ in America (1908).

26. See the *Report of the Commission on the Church and Social Service*, Federal Council of Churches (1912).

27. Cf. MacFarland, *op. cit.*, pp. 295-315, and *The Social Ideals of the Churches*, Federal Council of Churches (1932).

28. Note again that several levels of influence must be distinguished in evaluating the relation of religion to social change: (1) What religious opinions and doctrines are given most attention? (2) How many influential churchmen hold those opinions? (3) How many churchmen are actively working to realize those opinions? (4) What is the effectiveness of that work in the balance of power? It is too often assumed that an answer to one of the first three questions also answers the fourth. We try to avoid that confusion in our treatment of the problem by careful attention to the dilemma of the churches.

29. Refer again to Chapter II, where we have dealt briefly with Catholicism.

30. *Reason, Social Myths, and Democracy,* pp. 91-92.

31. In terms of the present writer's values, the Catholic Church is actually *too* skilful in accommodating itself, on the surface, to its environment. Not only does this skill cause it to adjust to situations that are generally considered non-Christian more easily than the less politic churches do; but Catholic adaptibility to the "relative" has been precisely the factor which has allowed it to preserve its so-called "absolutes," which are loaded with ancient and medieval elements which less flexible churches have been forced to drop or modify.

32. *Catholicism, Protestantism, and Capitalism,* p. 142.

33. Ryan and Husslein, *The Church and Labor,* p. xvi.

34. Many writers see in this situation a factor that makes Catholicism especially hospitable, under present circumstances, to fascism. To Maritain's claim that the Catholic Church greatly modified the totalitarian principle in Italy, Hook replies: "The simple fact is that in coming to terms with Mussolini the Catholic Church strengthened totalitarianism in Italy. 1931, the date of the papal agreement, marks the stabilization of Italian Fascism in the eyes of the world. It was the Catholic Church that affixed the certified seal of stabilization. Clericalist sentiment which was at a low ebb in democratic Italy has grown tremendously in Fascist Italy, aided and abetted by Mussolini for value received. Did the Church lift up its voice against the Ethiopian campaign or did it rather improve the opportunity to convert heretics? Is there any doubt that Mussolini's invasion of Spain was carried out with the active collaboration of the Papacy? True, the Church took exception to Mussolini's ideological adventure into 'racism,' not on scientific but organizational grounds. The ideology of Catholicism after all is indispensable for its proselytizing efforts outside of Italy. But it did not succeed in deflecting the course of Mussolini's policy one iota. Most eloquent of all, however, is the implication of the admission that it was with the Italian Fascist State and not the Italian democratic state that the Pope succeeded in coming to terms" (*op. cit.,* p. 91).

35. Ryan and Husslein, *op. cit.,* p. 2.

36. One should note, however, that earlier in the century Joseph von Görres (1776-1848), a vigorous exponent of Catholicism in his later life, had raised a liberal voice. See *Encyclopaedia Britannica,* Fourteenth ed., X, 553.

37. Ryan and Husslein, *op. cit.,* p. 34; cf. also the intense denunciation of socialism by six German bishops, pp. 251 ff.

38. *Ibid.,* p. 41.

39. *Ibid.,* pp. x-xi.

40. *Ibid.,* p. 88.

41. Note Harry F. Ward's statement: ". . . the Catholic view of the future organization of society looks backward for its pattern. . . . The Christian Socialism of its European radicals was used by its ecclesiastical diplomats to get church control of the workers, their unions and their cooperatives, and to block a democratic socialism of the people's power" (*Democracy and Social Change,* p. 206).

42. For the complete encyclical (Imprimatur and Nihil Obstat) see Ryan and Husslein, *op. cit.,* pp. 57-94.

43. Cardinal Gibbons, *ibid.,* pp. 146-147; cf. also pp. 145-158.

44. *Ibid.,* p. 172.

45. *Ibid.,* p. 237; cf. also pp. 220-239.

46. It should be noted that John Ryan and Joseph Husslein, the editors of the collection of documents from which we have drawn in the preceding pages, are themselves among the foremost American Catholics attempting to maintain a social unity centered in the church—which in the present situation means, for the most part, finding a place for the demands of labor without antagonizing nonlabor interests. See *ibid.,* pp. 240 ff.

47. Practically the only Catholic voice in the United States which did not acclaim the "holiness" of the Spanish Civil War was that of the Rev. Timothy Rowan, editor of

the Chicago *New World,* a liberal journal with a circulation of fifty-five thousand. In the summer of 1939 he had written strongly against the biased church accounts of Spain. In March, 1940, new Archbishop Stritch of Chicago, in his first appointment, sent Rowan from the editorship to a pastorate. Cf. *Time,* April 1, 1940, p. 48.

48. *Time,* June 2, 1941, p. 67.

49. As another example of Catholic collaboration with the "new order" in Europe, *Christianity and Crisis* quotes a "leading Catholic Czech newspaper": "There is no Catholic in Europe who should shed a tear to see the collapse of democratic political disorder and who, furthermore, would not welcome the fall of economic liberalism, which has been denonunced by the Pope's leading Catholic ideologists because it misuses working people in favor of a few capitalistic speculators.

"Czech Catholics see a clear line of duty, namely to contribute with all their strength to the consolidation of the new order in Bohemia and Moravia. Like the entire Czech nation, Czech Catholics stand united behind the Czech President, Dr. Hacha" (Feb. 24, 1941).

50. One might add that it also begins to look as though Soviet Russia is going to have to live with religious sentiments and powers, and is beginning to accommodate herself to them. The Kremlin has now recognized the Orthodox Church. Whether this is a temporary expedient or an example of the tenacity of religious belief remains to be seen.

51. *The U. S. Looks at Its Churches,* p. 2. B. Y. Landis, in the *Yearbook of American Churches,* 1943, estimates a church membership of 67,327,719, for the years 1941-1942.

52. For estimates, cf. Hopkins, *op. cit.,* pp. 79-85; Lynd and Lynd, *Middletown,* pp. 530-531; H. P. Douglass, *The Springfield Church Survey,* pp. 41-42. Douglass found that in Springfield, Massachusetts, almost twice as many Protestant church members lived in the best sections of town as their proportion of the population would indicate; while only half as many lived in the poorest sections. None of these studies, however, is widely generalizable or carefully controlled. Hadley Cantril, in an analysis of a sample of fourteen thousand cases, taken by the American Institute of Public Opinion and the Office of Public Opinion Research, 1939-1940, concluded: "The number of church members in a population increases with both the economic and the educational status of the members of the population. Or, conversely, the number of those without church membership increases as the income or educational levels are descended" (*American Journal of Sociology,* LVIII, March, 1943, 579).

53. See the 1926 and 1936 *Census of Religious Bodies.*

54. *Religion Today,* p. 117.

55. Cf, Jerome Davis (ed.), *Labor Speaks for Itself on Religion.*

56. April 3, 1939, p. 24.

57. *Time,* Sept. 23, 1935, p. 36; italics mine.

58. Their sampling technique is not sufficiently clarified to allow us to judge to what degree the sample is representative. In the judgment of the present writer, the sample probably overestimates liberal opinion in the churches, for it has been his experience that those interested in social and economic questions are more likely to respond to questionnaires than those who think such matters are not within the province of religion.

59. Trott and Sanderson, *op. cit.,* p. 20.

60. Socialism had been defined as democratic socialism. Note also that this study is not a representative sample of the opinions of the clergymen on those two subjects. We are simply illustrating here the discrepancy that exists between agreeing with an abstract statement and acceptance of the concrete steps necessary to its realization.

61. Trott and Sanderson, *op. cit.,* pp. 25-26.

62. *Ibid.,* p. 42.

63. Joseph Van Vleck, *Our Changing Churches,* p. 69.

64. *New Frontiers of Religion,* pp. 113-114. By permission of the Macmillan Company, publishers.

65. *Time,* Jan. 30, 1939, p. 33.

66. *Op. cit.,* p. 42.

67. "A Study of Protestant Church Boards of Control," *American Journal of Sociology,* XXXVIII, 418.

68. Cf., for instance, Harry P. Ward, *Our Economic Morality and the Ethic of Jesus,* pp. 309-310; Reinhold Niebuhr, *Reflections on the End of an Era,* p. 135; Maritain, *op. cit.;* Rauschenbusch, *op. cit.;* etc.

69. *Christianity and Economics,* p. 170.

70. *Ibid.,* p. 168.

71. For an error of this kind, see *ibid.,* pp. 181-189.

72. *New Frontiers of Religion,* p. 113.

73. *Ibid.,* p. 114.

74. Cf. *Information Service* of the Federal Council of Churches, May 31, 1941.

75. *Christianity and Crisis,* June 30, 1941, p. 1.

76. *Ibid.*

77. *Information Service* of the Federal Council of Churches, May 31, 1941, p. 3.

78. *Ibid.,* p. 2.

79. *Ibid.,* pp. 2-3. From "Propositions Accepted" and "Recommendations" of the Malvern report.

80. *Ibid.,* p. 5.

81. *Ibid.,* p. 2; italics mine.

82. Cf. *Time,* June 16, 1941, pp. 52-54, and *Christianity and Crisis,* June 30, 1941, p. 8.

83. June 16, 1941, p. 52.

84. The lectures have been published under the title *A Basis for the Peace to Come.* Several of the men have written extensively on the role of the churches in the present crisis. See, for instance, McConnell, *Christianity and Coercion;* Paton, *World Community* and *Church and the New World Order;* Hambro, *How to Win the Peace;* Dulles, *War, Peace and Change.*

85. Federal Council of Churches, *A Message from the National Study Conference on the Churches and a Just and Durable Peace,* p. 21.

86. *Ibid.,* p. 19. Cf. also *Christian Century,* March 25, 1942, pp. 342 ff., and *Time,* March 16, 1942, pp. 44-48.

87. *A Message from the National Study Conference,* p. 20.

88. Cf. *ibid.,* pp. 23-24. The Bretton Woods agreement may satisfy some of the intentions of this statement.

89. *Ibid.,* p. 20; italics mine. Note again that no attempt is made here to disparage the religious approach to an economic problem—the attempt to solve it by developing "Christian motivation." There is no denying its limitations, but the alternative—a radical challenge to the existing social structure—may be even less effective. We must not forget the dilemma of the churches.

90. *The Federal Council Bulletin,* April, 1943, pp. 11-12.

91. Cf. *Christian Century,* May 26, 1943, pp. 631-632.

92. *Ibid.,* April 8, 1942, p. 451.

93. Cf. *Information Service,* Oct. 9, 1943.

94. See the *New York Times,* Jan. 19, 1945.

95. This is in no way a cynical remark. There actually exists, of course, an objective difference in the ability of different economic systems to produce—under stated conditions—economic goods and services. In so far, therefore, as churchmen believe one system superior in this regard to another, and in so far as they consider economic goods—both in themselves and for associated benefits—desirable, they can be perfectly sincere in their discovery of "justice" in a system where they did not see it before. (For our purposes here, the objective validity of their analysis is unimportant.) One must note, however, that the institutional, traditional, and symbolic nature of religion makes

it unlikely that very many churchmen will proclaim the "justice" of an emerging economic system until long after those whose material interests are more immediately affected have made the proclamation.

96. Cf. Joseph Fletcher, "English Churches and the Peace," *The Protestant,* IV, 56-60.

97. It is interesting to note that the National Association of Manufacturers had a seated delegate at the Delaware Conference—the only nonchurch delegate, aside from consultants and men of the press, out of the 375 who were present. He was not reticent about offering his expert judgment to guide the church. Nor is the N. A. M. allowing the principles laid down by the conference to go uninterpreted to the wider public: it is sponsoring a group of meetings between its own representatives and clergymen to talk over the findings of the commission. In the one meeting upon which the present writer has direct report, there was a sharp split between the interpretation and support given by the clergymen and the interpretation and support given by representatives of the N. A. M.

Chapter VI

1. Cf. R. H. Bainton, "The Churches Shift on War," *Religion in Life,* XII (Summer, 1943), 323-335.

2. Cf. C. S. Ellsworth, "The American Churches and the Mexican War," *American Historical Review,* XLV, 301-326.

3. Cf. Curti, *Peace or War,* pp. 59-60, and the whole chapter on the Civil War, pp. 47-73.

4. Cf. *ibid.,* p. 210.

5. See esp. *Selected Quotations on Peace and War,* published by the Commission on Christian Education of the Federal Council of Churches, 1915.

6. The question we are raising here is: Was the idea that the war was a holy fight actually a cause of churchmen's supporting it, or simply a means of resolving a conflict between their religious beliefs and their political, social, and economic beliefs, the latter being the "real causes" of participation in the war? No simple answer can be given to this question. That religious beliefs made an abrupt change in 1914-1918 is logical evidence that they were simply bent in order to resolve the conflict in attitudes and hence were not the "original" causes. On the other hand, one can explain the change in church war-attitude by the fact that religious people were faced in 1914-1918 with a situation in which war was a reality: they chose war as less destructive of their beliefs than any other alternative. Both of these factors doubtless contributed to the support that churchmen gave to the war. It is the opinion of the present writer, however, based on this whole study of religious behavior, that the former was a more important influence on most people than the latter. That is, the loyalties that surround economic, patriotic, and prestige interests are for most individuals stronger than specifically religious loyalties; therefore, when there is a conflict, religious loyalties succumb or are restated in nonconflicting terms (generally the latter).

7. Cf. Abrams, *Preachers Present Arms,* pp. 15-30. We are very much indebted to this study in the next several pages.

8. Cf. *ibid.,* p. 26. We postpone until a later section the main interpretation of the sociological significance of this shift. Suffice it to say at this point that our comprehension of the church-type religious group, which we have developed at length in previous chapters, with its tendency to deal with the dilemma of the churches by compromise, with its secular as well as its purely religious significance, with its thoroughgoing attachment to the rest of society, would lead us to expect that the vast majority of churches would support the government in time of war.

9. We do not mean to suggest here that there are no atrocities in time of war. That is obviously not the case. In some instances the accounts of atrocities rank simply as news—at least so far as their accuracy is concerned. We shall use the phrase

"atrocity story" to refer, however, to incidents of viciousness that are widely publicized on the basis of insufficient or unreliable evidence, and which, therefore, are not properly classified as news. Such stories were prevalent in World War I, and are not entirely lacking today.

10. Newell Dwight Hillis, prominent clergyman, was among the most vehement. He wrote: "Society has organized itself against the rattlesnake and yellow fever. . . . The boards of health are planning to wipe out typhoid and the black plague. Not otherwise, lovers of their fellow men have finally become perfectly hopeless with reference to the German people. They have no more relation to the civilization of 1918 than an orang-outang, a gorilla, a Judas, a hyena, a thumbscrew, or a scalping knife in the hands of a savage. These brutes must be cast out of society" (quoted by Peter Odegard, *The American Public Mind,* p. 196). See also such works as *Religion and the War* (ed. E. H. Sneath) by members of the Faculty of the School of Religion, Yale University; Shailer Mathews, *Patriotism and Religion;* Basil Mathews (ed.), *Christ and the World at War;* W. Douglas MacKenzie, *Christian Ethics in the World at War.* These are, for the most part, moderate analyses; many more blatant attacks on Germany by the clergy could be listed. Cf. Granville Hicks, "The Parsons and the War," *American Mercury,* X, 129-142; cf. also the bibliography in Abrams, *op. cit.*

11. *Ibid.,* p. 115.

12. The meaning of the quotation marks around "plot" and "spies" is perhaps clear: there were, of course, plots and spies against which the country was seeking to protect itself. We are emphasizing here the extreme and not altogether wise zeal with which many clergymen participated in the efforts to expose them.

13. *Ibid.,* p. 128.

14. *Ibid.,* p. 126.

15. Cf. Norman Thomas, *The Conscientious Objector in America.*

16. Abrams, *op. cit.,* p. 134. This explanation is akin, of course, to the one given above to account for preacher participation in atrocity stories. Its truth is substantiated in part by the rapid postwar swing toward pacifism in the churches (see below).

17. Cf. the Federal Council's publication, *The Churches of Christ in Time of War* (1917).

18. Abrams, *op. cit.,* pp. 91-92.

19. In 1919 the Federal Council came out in favor of the release of conscientious objectors, although they had not been concerned with their welfare during the war. At that time, John Haynes Holmes, one of the few vigorous pacifist preachers, declared: ". . . I charge the men at the head of this body with cowardice and hypocrisy. They are guilty of the final indecency—that of doing late and in security, as though of their own accord, what they refused to do at some cost, when the honor and lives of men were hanging in the balance. . . . As a matter of fact the churches rivaled the security leagues and national defense councils in the fell business of fostering hate, sowing bitterness and persecuting non-conformity. There was not an atrocity against the soul of man, not a blasphemy against the Holy Spirit of God, of which they were not guilty. And, now, in a very few weeks, we shall behold these same churches, with their smug priests and laymen, coming forth in the security of a peaceful world, to talk again of tolerance, the free conscience, justice and love . . ." (quoted by Abrams, *op. cit.,* pp. 151-152).

20. Among nonmilitary matters the chief attention of the *Federal Council Bulletin* during the war was given to prohibition; the only factor which rivaled it for attention was the problems of the chaplain. Compared with the present crisis, in which, as we have seen, the churches are very much concerned with the problems of postwar reconstruction, even so liberal a body as the Federal Council was relatively unconcerned with war aims. They were, however, not completely disregarded. In March, 1918, the *Bulletin* stated (p. 20): ". . . the moral aims of the war . . . are conceived to be (1) to win the war against autocracy, (2) to make the world safe for democracy and democ-

racy safe for the world, (3) to secure for nations—small and great—safety, justice and equal economic opportunity and (4) to establish a League of Nations." This definition of moral aims was the statement of the National Committee on the Churches and the Moral Aims of the War, a committee under the auspices of the Church Peace Union and the League to Enforce Peace, "with the co-operation of the Commission on International Justice and Goodwill of the Federal Council of the Churches of Christ in America, and the World Alliance for International Friendship through the Churches." These were substantially the same as the minimum aims of President Wilson. To promote them the Council sponsored dozens of lectures. Cf. the *Federal Council Bulletin,* April, 1918, pp. 3-8.

21. Cf. Abrams, *op. cit.,* pp. 152-156.

22. Cf. *ibid.,* pp. 161-169. Isolationists in 1940-41 faced the same difficulty, of course.

23. Cf. *ibid.,* pp. 179-189, and Curti, *op. cit.,* pp. 228-261.

24. See Abrams, *op. cit.,* pp. 193-207.

25. *Ibid.,* p. 199. Holmes is still a pacifist.

26. This dilemma is peculiarly sharp in time of war, which contradicts so strongly the Christian ethic, but which for that very reason is the more in need of guidance if it is not to be motivated by sheer vengeance. There is very little chance of the churches avoiding the charge either of hypocrisy (which has been the frequent reaction to their behavior in World War I) or of obstructionism if not treason (which is the implication, for instance, of Stanley High's article in the *New Republic,* June 22, 1942). Abrams has the dilemma well in mind when he says of the behavior of the clergy in 1917: "Confronted with the necessity of every Sunday facing a congregation composed of Christians, spiritually troubled and anxious about not only the physical well-being but the spiritual aspects of the lives of their sons, ministers were under compulsion to re-enforce the hopes and faiths of the fathers and mothers, the brothers and sisters, wives and sweethearts. . . . To have remained silent or to have pointed out the spiritually devastating effect of warfare would have cost them their leadership and their jobs. The churches demanded ministers who gave comfort and dogmatic assurance, and they received it . . ." (*op. cit.,* p. 61).

27. In World War I American churches lost much of even this influence, because they permitted exceedingly few sectarian elements to remain among them. Because of a combination of circumstances, which we cannot analyze here, they were peculiarly unsophisticated in their reaction to the war. American religious groups did not maintain the balance between church and sect reactions, which, we have seen, maximizes their power. The Quakers were one of the outstanding exceptions. In the present war, however, as we shall see, the churches are much more effective. Years of crisis have stimulated able leadership.

28. The Versailles Treaty was the logical outcome of the mentality of the war. If the main weight of public opinion is different today from what it was in 1918 (as it seems perhaps to be) that fact will be reflected in a different kind of peace settlement after the present war.

29. Abrams, *op. cit.,* p. 235.

30. *Ibid.*

31. *Christian Century,* Jan. 31, 1924.

32. *World Tomorrow,* May, 1934.

33. This summary is drawn from Curti, *op. cit.,* pp. 262-300.

34. *Ibid.,* p. 275.

35. This is not to comment on the accuracy of the church hierarchy in judging the "merits of the case," even in terms of their own ethic, nor to imply that their apparently religious decision is not strongly modified by other than religious loyalties. That is doubtless almost always the case; but the matter is far too complex, of course, to explain in any such simple and unilateral terms as "sincere" or "hypocritical." Each situation must be judged on its merits.

36. June, 1938, p. 263.

37. Oct., 1938, p. 9.

38. Oct., 1939, p. 9.

39. Nov., 1939, p. 134.

40. *Ibid.,* p. 135.

41. *Ibid.,* p. 137. Some of these rules are that there be gross injustice on one side, that all other means of settlement have been tried and failed, that war be fought only for the holiest of motives.

42. *Catholic World,* May, 1940.

43. Many people interpreted this as another obvious sign of Catholic profascist leanings. This fails to take note of the great variety of Catholic opinions concerning fascism. Without denying that some Catholics, for example, Coughlin in the United States, are nursing an incipient fascism, we must also note the vigorous opposition both here and in Europe that the liberal wing has made to fascism.

44. *Christianity and Crisis,* July 14, 1941, p. 8.

45. Cf. Nathaniel Micklem, *National Socialism and the Roman Catholic Church* and the almost continual record of the conflict in the religious press, both Catholic and Protestant.

46. Cf. *Time,* Dec. 23, 1940, p. 38.

47. *Ibid.* Einstein is probably not referring specifically to the Catholic Church.

48. *America,* Nov. 22, 1941, p. 184.

49. *Ibid.,* Nov. 8, 1941, p. 128.

50. *Catholic World,* Sept., 1941, p. 651.

51. See *America,* Oct. 25, 1941, p. 71. Note that the statement of the questions was somewhat loaded. It is interesting also to note that the Catholic Laymen's Committee for Peace has sometimes been said to be associated with America First. But this has always been denied, and the poll must be judged statistically.

52. *Ibid.,* pp. 71-72.

53. *Time,* Dec. 22, 1941, p. 68.

54. *Christian Century,* Feb. 9, 1938, p. 168.

55. *Ibid.,* p. 169.

56. *Ibid.,* Nov. 9, 1938, p. 1358.

57. Cf. *ibid.* and the Aug. 23, 1939, issue, as well as references in Chapter V.

58. *Ibid.,* Nov. 22, 1939, p. 1431.

59. *Ibid.,* July 24, 1940, p. 920.

60. From a bulletin issued by the General Conference Commission on World Peace of the Methodist Church.

61. *Ibid.* See also the *Discipline* of the Methodist Church (1939), "The Social Creed."

62. *New York Times,* Oct. 7, 1940, p. 12.

63. *Ibid.,* Oct. 14, 1940, p. 22.

64. *Time,* June 23, 1941, p. 64.

65. Fosdick, Sockman, Buttrick, Muste, Reager, Latourette, Luccock, Georgia Harkness, Tittle, Bishop Kern (Methodist), Bishop Mitchell (Episcopal), *et al.*

66. Cf. *Christian Century,* Aug. 13, 1941, p. 1009.

67. The ministers came from Massachusetts, Michigan, and Wisconsin. Men from rural churches and small towns were about equally represented with those from larger cities. Salary and age distributions were fairly normal. The chief factors likely to bias the results were an overrepresentation of seminary-trained ministers (69 per cent), and an inadequate denominational distribution: 60 per cent were Methodist, 14 per cent Episcopal, 9 per cent Congregational, 7 per cent Baptist, and the remaining 10 per cent were divided among six other denominations. No Catholics were included.

68. Cf. *Time,* May 26, 1941, pp. 63-64.

69. *Ibid.,* Aug. 18, 1941, p. 53.

70. *Christian Century,* Sept. 10, 1941, p. 1099.
71. *New York Times,* July 1, 1940, p. 15.
72. *Ibid.,* Sept. 30, 1940, p. 20.
73. *Ibid.,* Oct. 21, 1940, p. 12.
74. The sponsors were: John C. Bennett, William A. Brown, William F. Cochran, Henry S. Coffin, J. Harry Cotton, Harold W. Dodds, Sherwood Eddy, Frank P. Graham, Henry W. Hobson, Ivan Lee Holt, Douglas Horton, Lynn Harold Hough, W. P. Ladd, Francis J. McConnell, Elizabeth C. Morrow, John R. Mott, William A. Neilson, Justin W. Nixon, Howard C. Robbins, William Scarlett, Henry K. Sherrill, Robert E. Speer, Charles P. Taft, Henry St. George Tucker, Charles T. White.
75. Cf. *Christianity and Crisis,* May 5, 1941, and June 16, 1941.
76. *Time,* June 9, 1941, p. 73.
77. *Ibid.*
78. Cf. *ibid.*
79. *Ibid.,* Dec. 22, 1941, p. 67.
80. Abrams writes, in reference to World War I: ". . . there is really nothing very surprising about the attitudes and activities of the religious groups and the ministers during the war. . . . The social behavior manifested by the church people and all other groups was not an accident but the result of a perfectly natural process. . . . The churches in such a crisis cannot disentangle themselves from the very fabric of society of which they are a part any more than they can do so in ordinary times when the whole economic and imperialistic system and the will of the vested interests receives their benediction" (*op. cit.,* pp. 243-245).
81. *Christian Century,* Dec. 17, 1941, p. 1565.
82. *Ibid.*
83. Cf. *Time,* Dec. 22, 1941, p. 68. In late 1941 the *Christian Century Pulpit* polled its readers to find their choice of the six most outstanding Protestant ministers. Every one of the six men chosen was, and is, a pacifist. Cf. the *Pulpit* for Jan., 1942.
84. Cf. *Christianity and Crisis,* July 13, 1942, p. 8.
85. Cf. Stanley High, "The Church Unmilitant," *New Republic,* CVI, 850-852. In this article, however, High is very much unaware of certain important facts in the case and insufficiently aware of the dilemma of the churches.
86. Through 1944 the three "peace-churches" had spent over five million dollars on maintenance and administration of C. P. S. camps. The government had spent less than three million dollars. Had the men received basic Army pay, the cost would have been over ten million dollars more.
87. See *The Reporter,* organ of the National Service Board for Religious Objectors, Oct. 1, 1943.
88. For example, a rider on a 1944 appropriation bill prevented the use of conscientious objectors in foreign service work. This required that a group of hospital workers on their way to China be returned to the United States.
89. See *Conscience and the War,* a report issued by the American Civil Liberties Union dealing with the treatment of conscientious objectors during the present war, and *The Experience of the American Friends Service Committee in Civilian Public Service.*
90. See *The Reporter,* Oct. 1, 1943.
91. Cf. *Christianity and Crisis,* Dec. 1, 1941, p. 8.
92. Although we have used the terms "conscientious objection" and "pacifism" as relatively synonymous, they are, strictly speaking, somewhat different. There can be conscientious objection to a particular war without pacifism; there can also be conscientious objection on nonreligious grounds.
93. "Vocational Christian Pacifism," *Christianity and Crisis,* Nov. 3, 1941, pp. 2-5.
94. *Ibid.,* Oct. 20, 1941, p. 2. Cf. the series of ten articles, five by pacifists, five by nonpacifists, in the *Christian Century,* Dec. 4, 1940-Feb. 5, 1941.

95. *Christianity and Crisis,* Jan. 12, 1942, pp. 1-2.
96. *Christian Century,* Jan. 14, 1942, p. 60.
97. *Christianity and Power Politics,* p. 42.
98. *Ibid.,* p. 4.
99. *Ibid.,* p. 5.
100. *Ibid.,* pp. 24-25.
101. Niebuhr, *Reflections on the End of an Era,* p. 139.
102. *Christianity and Power Politics,* p. 23.
103. One's reaction to this will depend upon how closely his values correspond to those of Christianity. We are attempting here simply to discover the power of religion.
104. Note again that that power, even at a maximum, may not be large, and that a majority of churchmen have probably not achieved this balance. Moreover, what is true in the midst of battle may not be true after a prolonged and bitter war.

Chapter VII

1. For a number of reasons the sectarian element is seldom complete, even in the religions of the poor. It expresses itself most often in otherworldliness.
2. Note that the term "qualified support" does not mean incomplete support. It is a qualitative rather than a quantitative modification and refers, in large measure, to the demands of the ablest churchmen that the war be an instrument of justice and not simply of vengeance.
3. *Reflections on the End of an Era,* p. 140.
4. See esp. Weber, *Wirtschaft und Gesellschaft,* pp. 250 ff., where Weber holds that the Oriental religions are weak in the development of "ethical prophecy," which is innovating, but conducive to "exemplary prophecy," which encourages living in harmony with the universal principles of order. Christianity, however, is conducive to ethical prophecy. One wonders how much this difference is due to the actual existence of social changes—independent of any religious influence—in the Christian environment, and their relative absence in, for instance, the Confucian environment. This proposition may be tested by discovering whether or not a religion achieves a greater capacity for ethical prophecy in a changing environment, e.g., China today.
5. Niebuhr, *op. cit.,* pp. 183-184.
6. Reinhold Niebuhr, in *Moral Man and Immoral Society,* has stressed the need for distinguishing between the power of religion over individual behavior in personal relations and its control over the complex problems of group life. "There are constitutional limitations in the genius of religion which will always make it more fruitful in purifying individual life, and adding wholesomeness to the more intimate social relations, such as the family, than in the problems of the more complex and political relations of modern society" (*Moral Man and Immoral Society,* p. 63). "All men cannot be expected to become spiritual any more than they can be expected to become rational. Those who achieve either excellence will always be a leavening influence in social life; but the political structure of society cannot be built upon their achievement" (*ibid.,* p. 73). Niebuhr suggests that despite these limitations, religion may be a powerful moral instrument, particularly by the aid it gives to the recognition of selfishness—that is, to the recognition that one's perspective may be relative and partial. "The absolute reference of religion eliminates these partial perspectives and premature justifications. There is no guarantee against the interpretation of the absolute in terms of faulty moral insights; and human vice and error may thus be clothed by religion in garments of divine magnificence and given the prestige of the absolute. Yet there is a general development in the high religions toward an interpretation of the divine as benevolent will, and a consequent increase of condemnation upon all selfish actions and desires" (*ibid.,* p. 52).

BIBLIOGRAPHY

Note: This bibliography is in no way an exhaustive list of titles relevant to the sociology of religion. The preparation of such a bibliography would itself be a very large undertaking. The studies listed here are only those to which I have referred in the course of my researches. I have not included complete references to the news notes and brief unsigned editorials in contemporary journals that I have cited. For those references, see the notes.

Abel, Theodore. *Systematic Sociology in Germany.* New York: Columbia University Press, 1929.

Abrams, Ray H. *Preachers Present Arms.* Philadelphia: Round Table Press, Inc., 1933.

American Civil Liberties Union. *Conscience and the War.* A Report on the Treatment of Conscientious Objectors in World War II. New York: American Civil Liberties Union, 1943.

American Friends Service Committee. *The Experience of the American Friends Service Committee in Civilian Public Service,* 1945.

Bainton, Roland H. "The Churches Shift on War," *Religion in Life,* XII (Summer, 1943), 323-335.

Barnes, Harry Elmer. *The Twilight of Christianity.* New York: Richard R. Smith, Inc., 1931.

——, and Becker, Howard. *Social Thought from Lore to Science.* 2 vols. Boston: D. C. Heath & Co., 1938.

——, Becker, Howard, and Becker, Frances B. (eds.). *Contemporary Social Theory.* New York: D. Appleton-Century Co., 1940.

Bates, Ernest Sutherland. *American Faith.* New York: W. W. Norton & Co., 1940.

Baxter, Richard. *Practical Works.* 23 vols. Edited by William Orme. London: James Duncan, 1830.

Beaven, Albert W. "The Meaning for Religions of the Trend Toward Nationalism," *Annals of the American Academy of Political and Social Science,* CLXXIV (July, 1934), 65-75.

Becker, Howard. "Sargasso Iceberg: A Study in Cultural Lag and

Institutional Disintegration," *American Journal of Sociology,* XXXIV (Nov., 1928), 492-506.

———. "Supreme Values and the Sociologists," *American Sociological Review,* VI (April, 1941), 155-172.

———. *Systematic Sociology,* on the basis of the *Beziehungslehre* and *Gebildelehre* of Leopold von Wiese (*see also* Wiese). New York: John Wiley & Sons, Inc., 1932.

Bennion, L. L. *Max Weber's Methodology.* Paris: Les Presses Modernes, 1933.

Bernard, L. L. "The Sociological Interpretation of Religion," *Journal of Religion,* XVIII (Jan., 1938), 1-18.

Brodrick, James. *The Economic Morals of the Jesuits.* London: Oxford University Press, 1934.

Calvin, John. *Institutes of the Christian Religion.* 2 vols. Translated by John Allen. Sixth American Edition. Philadelphia: The Westminster Press, 1921.

Cambridge Medieval History. Edited by J. R. Tanner, C. W. Previte-Ortan, Z. N. Brooke. Volume V, *Contest of Empire and Papacy.* Cambridge: University Press, 1926.

Cantril, Hadley. "Educational and Economic Composition of Religious Groups: An Analysis of Poll Data." *American Journal of Sociology,* XLVIII (March, 1943), 574-579.

Cavert, Samuel McCrea. "Rethinking the Social Function of the Church," *Religion in Life,* XII (Summer, 1943), 344-355.

Clark, Elmer T. *The Small Sects in America.* Nashville: Cokesbury Press, 1937.

Coulton, G. G. *Five Centuries of Religion.* 4 vols. Cambridge: University Press, 1923-1936.

Cunningham, W. *Christianity and Economic Science.* London: John Murray, 1914.

Curti, Merle. *Peace or War: The American Struggle, 1636-1936.* New York: W. W. Norton & Co., 1936.

Curtiss, John S. *Church and State in Russia: The Last Years of the Empire, 1900-1917.* New York: Columbia University Press, 1940.

Davis, Jerome. *Capitalism and Its Culture.* New York: Farrar & Rinehart, 1935.

——— (ed.). *Labor Speaks for Itself on Religion.* New York: Macmillan Co., 1929.

———. "The Social Action Pattern of the Protestant Religious Leader," *American Sociological Review,* I (Feb., 1936), 105-114.

——. "A Study of Protestant Church Boards of Control," *American Journal of Sociology,* XXXVIII (Nov., 1932), 418-431.

DEWEY, JOHN, and TUFTS, JAMES H. *Ethics.* New York: Henry Holt & Co., 1908.

DEWEY, JOHN. *Intelligence in the Modern World.* Edited by Joseph Ratner. New York: Modern Library, 1939.

DOUGLASS, H. PAUL. *The Springfield Church Survey.* New York: George H. Doran Co., 1926.

DUNNING, W. A. *A History of Political Theories.* 2 vols. New York: Macmillan Co., 1902.

DURKHEIM, ÉMILE. *The Elementary Forms of the Religious Life.* Translated by J. W. Swain. London: George Allen & Unwin, 1915.

ELLSWORTH, C. S. "The American Churches and the Mexican War," *American Historical Review,* XLV (Jan., 1940), 301-326.

FANFANI, AMINTORE. *Catholicism, Protestantism, and Capitalism.* London: Sheed & Ward, 1935.

FEDERAL COUNCIL OF CHURCHES OF CHRIST IN AMERICA. "The Malvern Conference Report, Official Version," *Information Service,* May 31, 1941.

——. *A Message from the National Study Conference on the Churches and a Just and Durable Peace,* March 3-5, 1942.

——. *Report of the Commission on the Church and Social Service,* 1912.

——. *Report of the First Meeting* (Philadelphia, 1908). New York: Revell Press, 1909.

FEDERAL COUNCIL OF CHURCHES OF CHRIST IN AMERICA, COMMISSION ON CHRISTIAN EDUCATION. *Selected Quotations on Peace and War.* New York, 1915.

FRY, C. LUTHER. "The Religious Affiliations of American Leaders," *Scientific Monthly,* XXXVI (March, 1933), 241-249.

——. *The U. S. Looks at Its Churches.* New York: Institute of Social and Religious Research, 1930.

GIORDANI, IGINO. *The Social Message of Jesus.* Translated by A. I. Zizzamia. Paterson, New Jersey: St. Anthony Guild Press, 1943.

GLADDEN, WASHINGTON. *Applied Christianity.* Sixth Edition. Boston: Houghton Mifflin & Co., 1886.

GLOYN, CYRIL K. *The Church in the Social Order.* Forest Grove, Ore.: Pacific University, 1942.

GOOCH, G. P. *English Democratic Ideas in the Seventeenth Century.*

Second Edition. With supplementary notes and appendices by H. J. Laski. Cambridge: University Press, 1927.

GORDON-WALKER, P. C. "Capitalism and the Reformation," *Economic History Review,* VIII (Nov., 1937).

HALÉVY, ÉLIE. *A History of the English People in 1815.* London, 1924.

HALL, THOMAS C. *The Religious Background of American Culture.* Boston: Little, Brown & Co., 1930.

HALLER, WILLIAM. *The Rise of Puritanism.* New York: Columbia University Press, 1938.

HAMMOND, J. L., and HAMMOND, BARBARA. *The Town Labourer, 1760-1832.* New impression of 1925 edition. New York: Longmans, Green & Co., 1928.

HICKS, GRANVILLE. "The Parsons and the War," *American Mercury,* X (Feb., 1927), 129-142.

HIGH, STANLEY. "The Church Unmilitant," *New Republic,* CVI (June 22, 1942), 850-852.

HOBSON, J. A. *God and Mammon.* New York: Macmillan Co., 1931.

HOLT, ARTHUR E. "Organized Religion as a Pressure Group," *Annals of the American Academy of Political and Social Science,* CLXXIX (May, 1935), 42-49.

HOOFT, W. A. VISSER 'T, and OLDHAM, J. H. *The Church and Its Function in Society.* Chicago: Willett, Clark & Co., 1937.

HOOK, SIDNEY. "The New Failure of Nerve," *Partisan Review,* X (Jan.-Feb., 1943), 2-23.

———. *Reason, Social Myths, and Democracy.* New York: John Day Co., 1940.

HOPKINS, CHARLES H. *The Rise of the Social Gospel in American Protestantism, 1865-1915.* New Haven: Yale University Press, 1940.

JAMES, EARLE K. "Church and State in Mexico," *Annals of the American Academy of Political and Social Science,* CCVIII (March, 1940), 112-120.

JAMES, WILLIAM. *The Varieties of Religious Experience.* New York: Longmans, Green & Co., 1902.

JOHNSON, E. A. J. *American Economic Thought in the Seventeenth Century.* London: P. S. King & Son, 1932.

JOHNSON, HEWLITT, DEAN OF CANTERBURY. *The Soviet Power.* New York: International Publishers, 1940.

KIRKPATRICK, CLIFFORD. *Religion in Human Affairs.* New York: John Wiley & Sons, 1929.

LASSWELL, HAROLD D. *Propaganda Technique in the World War.* New York: Alfred A. Knopf, 1927.

LEIPER, HENRY S. "Religion Confronts Caesarism," *Annals of the American Academy of Political and Social Science,* CLXXX (July, 1935), 176-182.

LENIN, V. I. *Religion.* New York: International Publishers, 1933.

LEO XIII, POPE. *The Great Encyclical Letters of Pope Leo XIII.* Second Edition. New York: Benziger Bros., 1903.

LEUBA, J. H. *The Belief in God and Immortality.* Second Edition. Chicago: Open Court Publishing Co., 1921.

LEWIS, JOHN, POLAYNI, KARL, and KITCHIN, DONALD K. (eds.). *Christianity and the Social Revolution.* London: Victor Gollancz, 1935.

LINDSAY, THOMAS M. *A History of the Reformation.* 2 vols. New York: Charles Scribner's Sons, 1928.

LIPPMANN, WALTER. *A Preface to Morals.* New York: Macmillan Co., 1929.

LIPSON, E. *An Introduction to the Economic History of England.* Volume I, *The Middle Ages.* London: A. & C. Black, 1920.

LOWIE, R. H. *Primitive Religion.* New York: Boni & Liveright, 1924.

LUTHER, MARTIN. *Luther's Primary Works.* Edited by Henry Wace and C. A. Buckheim. London, 1896.

LYND, ROBERT S., and LYND, HELEN M. *Middletown.* New York: Harcourt Brace & Co., 1929.

MACARTHUR, KATHLEEN W. *The Economic Ethics of John Wesley.* New York: Abingdon Press, 1936.

MACFARLAND, CHARLES STEDMAN. *Chaos in Mexico: The Conflict of Church and State.* New York: Harper & Bros., 1935.

——— (ed.). *The Churches of Christ in Time of War.* New York: The Federal Council of Churches (per the Missionary Education Movement), 1917.

———. *The New Church and the New Germany.* New York: Macmillan Co., 1934.

MACIVER, ROBERT M. *Social Causation.* Boston: Ginn & Co., 1942.

———. *Society: Its Structure and Changes.* New York: Farrar & Rinehart, 1931.

MACKINSON, JAMES. *Calvin and the Reformation.* London: Longmans, Green & Co., 1936.

MACMURRAY, JOHN. *The Clue to History.* London: Student Christian Movement Press, 1938.

———. *Creative Society. A Study of the Relation of Christianity to Communism.* New York: Association Press, 1936.

MARITAIN, JACQUES. *True Humanism.* Translated by M. R. Adamson. London: Geoffrey Bles, the Centenary Press, 1938.

MARX, KARL. *A Contribution to the Critique of Political Economy.* Translated from the second German edition by N. I. Stone. Chicago: Charles H. Kerr & Co., 1904.

MARX, KARL, and ENGELS, FREDERICK. *Communist Manifesto.* Chicago: Charles H. Kerr & Co.

MAURER, HEINRICH H. "Studies in the Sociology of Religion," *American Journal of Sociology.* I. "The Sociology of Protestantism," XXX (Nov., 1924), 257-286. II. "Religion and American Sectionalism. The Pennsylvania German," XXX (Jan., 1925), 408-438. III. "The Problems of a National Church Before 1860," XXX (March, 1925), 534-550. IV. "The Problems of Group-Consensus; Founding the Missouri Synod," XXX (May, 1925), 665-682. V. "The Fellowship Law of a Fundamentalist Group. The Missouri Synod," XXXI (July, 1925), 39-57. VI. "The Consciousness of Kind of a Fundamentalist Group," XXXI (Jan., 1926), 485-506.

MAYER, CARL. "The Problem of a Sociology of Religion," *Social Research,* III (Aug., 1936), 337-347.

MCGIFFERT, ARTHUR C. *Martin Luther. The Man and His Work.* New York: Century Co., 1910.

———. *Protestant Thought Before Kant.* New York: Charles Scribner's Sons, 1913.

MEANS, PAUL B. *Things That Are Caesar's: The Genesis of the German Church Conflict.* New York: Round Table Press, 1935.

MECKLIN, JOHN MOFFATT. *The Story of American Dissent.* New York: Harcourt, Brace & Co., 1934.

MICKLEM, NATHANIEL. *National Socialism and the Roman Catholic Church.* London: Oxford University Press, 1939.

MOSCA, GAETANO. *The Ruling Class.* New York: McGraw-Hill Book Co., 1939.

NEEDHAM, JOSEPH (ed.). *Science Religion and Reality.* New York: Macmillan Co., 1925.

NIEBUHR, H. RICHARD. *The Social Sources of Denominationalism.* New York: Henry Holt & Co., 1929.

NIEBUHR, REINHOLD. *Christianity and Power Politics.* New York: Charles Scribner's Sons, 1940.

———. *Moral Man and Immoral Society.* New York: Charles Scribner's Sons, 1932.

———. *Reflections on the End of an Era.* New York: Charles Scribner's Sons, 1934.

———. *Why the Christian Church Is Not Pacifist.* London: Student Christian Movement Press, 1940.

Nottingham, Elizabeth K. *Methodism and the Frontier. Indiana Proving Ground.* New York: Columbia University Press, 1941.

Odegard, Peter. *The American Public Mind.* New York: Columbia University Press, 1930.

Otto, Rudolf. *The Idea of the Holy.* Revised Edition. Translated by John W. Harvey. London: Oxford University Press, 1923.

Parsons, Talcott. "H. M. Robertson on Max Weber and His School," *Journal of Political Economy,* XLIII (Oct., 1935), 688-696.

———. *Structure of Social Action.* New York: McGraw-Hill Book Co., 1937.

The Persecution of the Catholic Church in the Third Reich. "Facts and Documents" translated from the German. London: Burns Oates, 1940.

Petegorsky, David W. *Left-Wing Democracy in the English Civil War.* London: Victor Gollancz, 1940.

Pirenne, Henri. *Medieval Cities: Their Origins and the Revival of Trade.* Translated by F. D. Halsey. Princeton: Princeton University Press, 1925.

Radin, Paul. *Primitive Religion: Its Nature and Origin.* New York: Viking Press, 1937.

Rauschenbusch, Walter. *Christianity and the Social Crisis.* New York: Macmillan Co., 1907.

———. *Christianizing the Social Order.* New York: Macmillan Co., 1912.

Robertson, H. M. *Aspects of the Rise of Economic Individualism: A Criticism of Max Weber and His School.* Cambridge: University Press, 1933.

Roll, Erich. *A History of Economic Thought.* New York: Prentice-Hall, Inc., 1940.

Ryan, John A. and Husslein, Joseph (eds.). *The Church and Labor.* New York: Macmillan Co., 1924.

Salomon, Albert. "Max Weber's Sociology," *Social Research,* II (1935), 60-73.

Schlatter, Richard B. "The Problem of Historical Causation in Some Recent Studies of the English Revolution," *Journal of the History of Ideas,* IV (June, 1943), 349-367.

———. *The Social Ideas of Religious Leaders, 1660-1688.* London: Humphrey Milford, 1940.

SCHWER, WILHELM. *Catholic Social Theory.* Translated by Bartholemew Landheer. Preface by Franz Mueller. St. Louis: B. Herder Book Co., 1940.

SEARS, LARRY. "Dualisms and Social Responsibility," *Ethics,* L (April, 1940), 314-328.

SÉE, HENRI. *Modern Capitalism.* Translated by H. B. Vanderblue and G. F. Doriot. New York: Adelphi Co., 1928.

SELBIE, W. B. *Religion and Life.* Cambridge: Harvard University Press, 1930.

SELDES, GILBERT. *The Stammering Century.* New York: John Day Co., 1928.

SHOTWELL, JAMES T. *The Religious Revolution of Today.* Boston: Houghton Mifflin Co., 1913.

SIMMEL, GEORG. "A Contribution to the Sociology of Religion" (trans. W. W. Elwang), *American Journal of Sociology,* XI (Nov., 1905), 359-376.

SMITH, PRESERVED. *The Age of the Reformation.* New York: Henry Holt & Co., 1920.

SOMBART, WERNER. *The Jews and Modern Capitalism.* Translated, with notes, by M. Epstein. London: F. Fisher Unwin, 1913.

———. *The Quintessence of Capitalism.* Translated and edited by M. Epstein. London: F. Fisher Unwin, 1915.

STAMP, LORD. *Christianity and Economics.* London: Macmillan Co., 1939.

STELZLE, CHARLES. *The Church and Labor.* Boston: Houghton Mifflin Co., 1910.

SWEET, WILLIAM W. *The Story of Religion in America.* Revised Edition. New York: Harper & Bros., 1939.

SWIFT, ARTHUR L., JR. *New Frontiers of Religion.* New York: Macmillan Co., 1938.

——— (ed.). *Religion Today: A Challenging Enigma.* New York: McGraw-Hill Book Co., 1933.

TAWNEY, R. H. *The Agrarian Problem in the Sixteenth Century.* London: Longmans, Green & Co., 1912.

———. *Religion and the Rise of Capitalism.* New York: Harcourt, Brace & Co., 1926.

———. "Religious Thought on Social and Economic Questions in the Sixteenth and Seventeenth Centuries," *Journal of Political Economy.* I. "The Medieval Background," XXXI (Aug., 1923),

461-493. II. "The Collision of Standards," XXXI (Oct., 1923), 637-674. III. "The Social Ethics of Puritanism," XXXI (Dec., 1923), 804-825.

THOMAS, NORMAN. *The Conscientious Objector in America.* New York: B. W. Huebsch, 1923.

TILLICH, PAUL. *The Interpretation of History.* Translated by N. A. Rasetzki and E. L. Talmey. New York: Charles Scribner's Sons, 1936.

———. "Protestantism in the Present World Situation," *American Journal of Sociology,* XLIII (Sept., 1937), 236-248.

———. "The Social Functions of the Churches in Europe and America," *Social Research,* III (1936), 90-104.

———. "The Totalitarian State and the Claims of the Church," *Social Research,* I (1934), 405-433.

TOYNBEE, ARNOLD J. *A Study of History.* 6 vols. London: Oxford University Press, 1939.

TROELTSCH, ERNST. *Gesammelte Schriften.* Zweiter Band, *Zur religiösen Lage, Religionsphilosophie und Ethik* (1922). Vierter Band, *Aufsätze zur Geistesgeschichte und Religionssoziologie* (1925). Tubingen: J. C. B. Mohr (Paul Siebeck).

———. *Protestantism and Progress.* Translated by W. Montgomery. New York: G. P. Putnam's Sons, 1912.

———. *The Social Teaching of the Christian Churches.* 2 vols. Translated by Olive Wyon. New York: Macmillan Co., 1931.

TROTT, NORMAN L., and SANDERSON, ROSS W. *What Church People Think About Social and Economic Issues.* New York: Association Press, 1938.

TRUEBLOOD, ELTON. "Vocational Christian Pacifism," *Christianity and Crisis,* I (Nov. 3, 1941), 2-5.

UNITED STATES DEPARTMENT OF COMMERCE, BUREAU OF THE CENSUS. *Census of Religious Bodies,* 1926 and 1936. Washington: Government Printing Office.

VAN VLECK, JOSEPH, JR. *Our Changing Churches: A Study of Church Leadership.* New York: Association Press, 1937.

WAGNER, DONALD O. *The Church of England and Social Reform Since 1854.* New York: Columbia University Press, 1930.

WALKER, WILLISTON. *A History of the Christian Church.* New York: Charles Scribner's Sons, 1920.

WALLIS, W. D. *Religion in Primitive Society.* New York: F. S. Crofts & Co., 1939.

WALSH, JAMES J. *The Thirteenth, Greatest of Centuries.* New York: Catholic Summer School Press, 1924.

WARD, HARRY F. *Democracy and Social Change.* New York: Modern Age Books, 1940.

———. *Our Economic Morality and the Ethic of Jesus.* New York: Macmillan Co., 1929.

———. *Which Way Religion?* New York: Macmillan Co., 1931.

WARNER, WELLMAN J. *The Wesleyan Movement in the Industrial Revolution.* London: Longmans, Green & Co., 1930.

WEARMOUTH, ROBERT F. *Methodism and the Working-Class Movements of England, 1800-1850.* London: Epworth Press, 1937.

WEBER, MAX. *General Economic History.* Translated by Frank Knight. New York: Greenberg, Publisher, 1927.

———. *Gesammelte Aufsätze zur Religionssoziologie.* 3 vols. Tubingen: J. C. B. Mohr (Paul Siebeck), 1922-1923.

———. *The Protestant Ethic and the Spirit of Capitalism.* Translated by Talcott Parsons. London: George Allen & Unwin, 1930.

———. *Wirtschaft und Gesellschaft.* Tubingen: J. C. B. Mohr (Paul Siebeck), 1922.

WESLEY, JOHN. *Sermons.* New York, 1868.

WHITE, ANDREW D. *A History of the Warfare of Science with Theology in Christendom.* 2 vols. New York: D. Appleton & Co., 1896.

WIESE, LEOPOLD VON. *Systematic Sociology.* On the basis of the *Beziehungslehre* and *Gebildelehre* (adapted and amplified by Howard Becker). New York: John Wiley & Sons, 1932.

WOODHOUSE, A. S. P. *Puritanism and Liberty.* London: J. M. Dent & Sons, 1938.

WORKMAN, HERBERT B. *The Dawn of the Reformation.* 2 vols. London: Epworth Press, 1901.

ZNANIECKI, FLORIAN. *Social Actions.* New York: Farrar & Rinehart, 1936.

INDEX

(The letter "q" after a page reference is used to identify the authorship of a quotation where such identification has not been made in the text.)